Shadow Networks
Border Economies, Informal Markets and Organized Crime in the Russian Far East

The breakdown of the Soviet Union led to fundamental changes in Russia. In the course of post-Soviet transformations the state partially lost its monopoly on violence and taxation, while new informal structures found fertile ground in a political and economic environment where trust was scarce and fragile. Personal ties, such as long-term friendships between individual actors, played an important role as the foundations of stable informal networks. Holzlehner shows that the capacity of these networks to adapt efficiently to rapid social and economic change and the ability to engage in symbiotic relationships with state actors and institutions are key to understanding their success. Exploring economic activities in the Russian Far East (Primorsky Krai) at street markets and border crossings, his central questions are: what are shadow networks? how are they structured? how is their social reality best described?

Both in terms of methodology and presentation, this book merges several genres. Ethnography, urban geography, investigative journalism, travelogue, and anthropological analysis each contribute to a reading of the urban space of post-Soviet Russia. The non-formal has its own peculiar structures. Similar to their legal and state-controlled counterparts, informality and illegality form networks of mutual aid and cooperation. The informal economic networks show highly dynamic features and have gone through rapid changes in recent years. Tracing their paths of emergence and documenting how they evolved, Holzlehner grapples with the more general issues of social and economic response mechanisms to rapid cultural change.

The Russian Far East is a borderland in multiple ways. The geographic vicinity to China, Korea, and Japan exposes the region to a variety of influences, commodities, and people. Labour migration from the successor states of the Soviet Union (especially from Central Asia) and the porous border to China have accentuated the multi-ethnic mosaic of the region's urban centres, especially Vladivostok. Drawing on strands of economic anthropology that engage with border space and locality, Holzlehner describes and develops the ideas of bazaar ecology, ethno-economic niches, borderland economy, and the geography of informal networks. The fast-changing social and economic environment of post-Soviet Russia demands a processual view of social phenomena. A special focus is therefore placed on the intrinsic dynamics of the observed informal networks. The dynamics, flexibilities, and adaptabilities of shadow networks are addressed diachronically in order to show the creativity of social and economic ties.

Halle Studies in the Anthropology of Eurasia

General Editors:

Christoph Brumann, Kirsten Endres, Chris Hann, Thomas Hauschild,
Burkhard Schnepel, Dittmar Schorkowitz, Lale Yalçın-Heckmann

Volume 30

LIT

Tobias Holzlehner

Shadow Networks
Border Economies,
Informal Markets and Organized Crime
in the Russian Far East

Cover Photo:
Sportivnaya Market, Vladivostok (Photo: Tobias Holzlehner, 2010).

Bibliographic information published by the Deutsche Nationalbibliothek
The Deutsche Nationalbibliothek lists this publication in the Deutsche Nationalbibliografie; detailed bibliographic data are available in the Internet at http://dnb.d-nb.de.

ISBN 978-3-643-90651-9

A catalogue record for this book is available from the British Library

©LIT VERLAG Dr. W. Hopf
Berlin 2014
Fresnostr. 2
D-48159 Münster
Tel. +49 (0) 2 51-62 03 20
Fax +49 (0) 2 51-23 19 72
E-Mail: lit@lit-verlag.de
http://www.lit-verlag.de

LIT VERLAG GmbH & Co. KG Wien,
Zweigniederlassung Zürich 2014
Klosbachstr. 107
CH-8032 Zürich
Tel. +41 (0) 44-251 75 05
Fax +41 (0) 44-251 75 06
E-Mail: zuerich@lit-verlag.ch
http://www.lit-verlag.ch

Distribution:
In the UK: Global Book Marketing, e-mail: mo@centralbooks.com
In North America: International Specialized Book Services, e-mail: orders@isbs.com
In Germany: LIT Verlag Fresnostr. 2, D-48159 Münster
Tel. +49 (0) 2 51-620 32 22, Fax +49 (0) 2 51-922 60 99, E-mail: vertrieb@lit-verlag.de

In Austria: Medienlogistik Pichler-ÖBZ, e-mail: mlo@medien-logistik.at
e books are available at www.litwebshop.de

Contents

	List of Illustrations	vii
	Acknowledgements	ix
	Note on Transliteration	xi
	Glossary	xiii
1	**Introduction: Reading Informal Space**	**1**
	Overview	4
	Understanding the Shadow	7
	Cityscapes and the Organization of the Shadow	11
	The Narrative	13
	Field and Methods	15
2	**Tiger and Bear: A Particular History of the Russian Far East**	**19**
	Coast	22
	Taiga	26
	City	38
3	**Urban Informality: Open-Air Markets and Ethnic Entrepreneurs in Vladivostok**	**45**
	Chinese Markets	49
	Bazaar Ecology	51
	Open-Air Markets in the Former Soviet Union	61
	Labour Migration into the Russian Far East	67
	Ethnic Entrepreneurs – An Uzbek Case	73
4	**Eastern Porosity: Cross-Border Trade in the Russian Far East**	**87**
	Chelnoki – Weaving Shuttles	91
	Informal Cross-Border Trade	100
	Poaching Economies	105
	Small Business, Big Business	114
	The Anti-Programme	122

5	**'The Harder the Rain the Tighter the Roof':** **Organized Crime Networks in the Russian Far East**	**129**
	The Thieves Professing the Code	136
	Violent Entrepreneurs	144
	Testimonies	148
	Organized Crime in Vladivostok and Primorsky Krai	158
	Russian Organized Crime in Perspective	169
	Organized Crime as a Multifunctional Entity	173
	Organized Crime as an Interpenetrative Network	175
6	**The Social Organization of the Shadow:** **A Conclusion**	**179**
	Chinese Guilds	181
	Ethnic Entrepreneurs	181
	Informal Cross-Border Traders	182
	Organized Crime	183
	Appendix	191
	Bibliography	199
	Index	215

List of Illustrations

Figures

1	Organization of Chinese trading guilds and commodity flows during the nineteenth century, Primorye Region	36
2	Balyaeva Market	191
3	Sportivnaya Market	192
4	Vtoraya Rechka Market	193
5	Spatial transformation of the Lugovaya Market (before 2003; 2003; August 2004; November 2004)	194
6	Affiliation among ethnic and non-ethnic traders in Vladivostok's open-air markets	83
7	Cross-border trade circuits	126
8	Social organization inside the prison camps	140
9	Evolution of criminal organizations in Vladivostok	195
10	Baul's shadow franchise (1990-2003)	196

(all figures by the author)

Maps

1	Vladimir Arsenyev's Sikhote-Alin Expedition in 1906 (map adapted from Arsenyev 1906)	23
2	Amur and Primorye Regions in the nineteenth century	26
3	Chinese markets in Vladivostok	51
4	International border crossings in Primorsky Krai	93
5	Illegal cross-border flows in and out of Primorsky Krai	107

(all maps by the author unless noted otherwise)

Plates

1	Svetlanskaya Street, Vladivostok 2009	2
2	Sikhote-Alin Mountains, Primorsky Krai 2012	21
3	Sea cucumber (*trepang*), wild ginseng (*zhen'shen'*), and antler velvet (*panty*), clockwise from top (in Arsenyev 1926: 120)	32
4	Russian game wardens destroying huts of Chinese poachers (in Arsenyev 1926: 98)	34
5	Inside the maze of Sportivnaya Market, 2012	47

6	Rows of container kiosks, Lugovaya Market, 2009	58
7	The author with an Uzbek spice trader, Sportivnaya Market, Vladivostok 2004	77
8	Last bus station before the Chinese border, Pogranichnyy, 2004	89
9	Pre-packed packages ready for shuttle transport, Suifenhe, China 2004	94
10	Russian 'tourists' in Suifenhe, China 2012	99
11	Custom control zone, Vladivostok harbour 2004	104
12	Wild ginseng from Primorsky Krai for sale in Heilongjiang Province, China, 2012	112
13	Green Corner used car market, Vladivostok 2012	115
14	Dzhem's grave, Komsomolsk-na-Amure 2004	130
15	Koval's grave, Vladivostok 2004	153
16	Graffiti on an apartment block in Vladivostok, 2004	169

(all photographs by the author, 2004-2012)

Tables

1	Spatial order of a Chinese market	56
2	Main bio resource exports of the Russian Far East	197
3	Average prices for poached animals and plants paid by Chinese wholesale buyers to Russian sellers in Roshchino, Primorsky Krai	111
4	A diachronic summary of shadow networks and their underlying relational ties	180
5	Shadow networks and their relationship to the state	186

Acknowledgements

This book stands at the end of a long journey that started in Fairbanks, Alaska, took me to Vladivostok and the Russian Far East, to Berkeley in California, back to Fairbanks, and finally to Halle (Saale) in Germany. In the course of this passage, I owe a great deal to many people, without their indispensable help this book would have been impossible to envision and craft.

The journey started as a dissertation project at the Department of Anthropology at the University of Alaska Fairbanks. I am greatly indebted to my main adviser and friend Peter Schweitzer, who supported and mentored me vigorously in this endeavour. I also greatly appreciated the valuable help and advice of Patty Gray, David Koester, and Phyllis Morrow. Throughout the years, many people supported me in Fairbanks and made life and study at the arctic frontier a truly inspiring and memorable experience. I especially would like to mention and thank Sveta and Igor Yamin-Pasternak, Mike Koskey, Sarah Deutschmann, Patrick Plattet, Josh Wisnewski, Takashi Sakurai, Patrick Hall, Jason Tinsley, Mark Winterstein, Matthias Erickson, and Alice Orlich.

The research for this book would not have been possible without the generous support of several funding agencies. The first period of fieldwork in 2002 was supported by the Otto Geist Fund of the Museum of the North at the University of Alaska Fairbanks. The long-term fieldwork in Vladivostok and Primorsky Krai in 2004 was financed by a Dissertation Fieldwork Grant from the Wenner-Gren Foundation (Dissertation research grant No. 7095, Cosmopolitan Xenophobia: Cultural Dynamics of Consumption and Ethnic Interaction in Vladivostok, Russia). A subsequent three months research in 2012 was supported by the National Science Foundation, Arctic Social Science (Grant No. 1124615, Far Eastern Borderlands: Informal Networks and Space at the Margins of the Russian State). The Graduate School of the University of Alaska Fairbanks provided me with a Thesis Completion Fellowship.

The various research trips to Vladivostok and Primorsky Krai were greatly supported by Nikolay Kradin of the Far Eastern Federal University in Vladivostok, whose scholarly advice and facilitating skills were invaluable for the success of my research. I would also like to acknowledge the generous support and hospitality of the researchers and staff at the Department of Social Anthropology at the Far Eastern National Technical University and at the Institute of History, Archaeology, and Ethnology, Far East Branch of the Russian Academy of Sciences in Vladivostok. I am particularly grateful for the help of student researchers Aleksandr Polyakov, Julia Girnika, and Nina Tsarevoy. During my stays in the Russian Far East, I was supported by numerous persons who shared their lives and company with me. For reasons of confidentiality, I cannot use their real names here or in the rest of the book. Yet, their kindness, willingness to share their stories, and their unconditional friendship were pivotal in my research and are unforgettable. Their names appear in pseudonyms throughout the book.

I would like to give special recognition to Yuri Slezkine and Ned Walker of the Berkeley Program in Soviet and Post-Soviet Studies, University of California, Berkeley, who supported me with a yearlong Mellon-Sawyer Postdoctoral Fellowship in 2007 and whose critical advice provided valuable assistance. The recognition extends to the group of the research seminar 'Private Wealth and Public Power: Oligarchs, Tycoons and Magnates in Comparative Perspective' at the Berkeley Program in Soviet and Post-Soviet Studies, who gave valuable input and critique at an early stage of the project.

I am especially indebted to Thomas Hauschild, who triggered the decision to finally work on the manuscript and whose long-term mentorship provided indispensable backing. Chris Hann offered me the opportunity to publish the book and I am extremely grateful for his patience during some difficult times. Without his support this book would not have been possible. I also owe a special debt to Lale Yalçın-Heckmann, who read and commented on early drafts of the manuscript. Jennifer Cash meticulously edited the manuscript and I would like to give her my special thanks. I would also like to thank Berit Westwood for her help during the final stages of the book production. I have tried to incorporate most of their valuable critique and comments, and all shortcomings rest on my shoulders.

Parts of the book were previously published in different forms. Chapter 5 is based on a journal article, 'The Harder the Rain, the Tighter the Roof: Evolution of Organized Crime Networks in the Russian Far East', *Sibirica*, 6 (2), 2007, pp. 51-86. Parts of chapter 4 were published in 'Trading against the State: Il/legal Cross-Border Networks in the Russian Far East', *Ethnofoor*, Borders, 26 (1), 2014, pp. 13-38.

Note on Transliteration

Russian usage follows the BGN/PCGN (British Standard) romanization system. For some geographic terms, I opted for a more widely accepted standard spelling to increase readability (e.g. *Primorye* instead of *Primor'ye* or *Primorsky Krai* instead of *Primorskiy Kray*). For Chinese terms that appear in Russian language sources, I analogously used the BGN/PCGN transliteration system (e.g. *fansy*, *zaitun*, *trepang*, *panty*, etc.).

Glossary

avtoritet (authority)
bratva (brotherly comrades)
brigada (criminal 'brigade')
brigadir (brigade leader)
byki (bulls)
chelnoki (lit. shuttle, i.e. tourist) traders
        naemnye chelnoki (hired shuttle traders)
        svobodnye chelnoki (independent shuttle traders)
chushki (piglets)
da-je (village elders)
fansa (Chinese farm building)
firmy-posredniki (broker companies)
fraer (guys)
gruppirovka (criminal group)
kachki (lit. iron pumpers)
kasty (prison 'castes')
khosyain (proprietor)
khunkhusy (lit. red beards)
kitayskie rynki (Chinese markets)
klichka (nickname)
komsomoltsy (members of the communist youth organization)
kontrafakty (counterfeits)
koronatsiya (coronation)
kreshchenie (baptism)
krestniy otets (godfather)
krestnaya mat' (godmother)
krysha (lit. roof, i.e. protection arrangement)
        banditskaya krysha (bandit roof)
        krasnaya krysha (protection arrangement facilitated through state security agencies)
lotki (tents)
maloletki (aspiring future criminals)
muzhiki (men)
obshchak (communal monetary fund)
optovaya baza (wholesale centre)
optovik (wholesale dealer)
panty (blood-rich antlers-in-velvet)
pao-tou (hunters' federation)
polozhentsy (regional appointees)
pomogaika (helper)

propusk (entry permit)
razborka (violent confrontation between gangs)
semichki (sun flower seeds)
sinie (lit. blue ones)
skhody (criminal 'conferences')
sportsmeny (sportsmen)
suki (bitches)
tabor (traditional gypsy encampment)
torgovyy tsentr (shopping centre / mall)
trepang (sea cucumber)
ugolovniki (convicts)
yaponomarki (Japanese makes)
vodichnyy bizness (vodka trade)
vor v zakone (a thief professing the code)
vorovskoi sud chesti (thieves' honour court)
vorovskoy zakon (thieves' law)
zaitun (landlord)
zakonniki (honourable thieves)
zemlyaki (fellow countrymen)
zheltaya opasnost' (yellow peril)

To my parents

Chapter 1
Introduction: Reading Informal Space

From the window of my apartment you can see the end of the port of the Golden Horn Bay where freight cranes rake their skeletal arms into the sky and old trawlers are moored at rusty quays. This part of the harbour remains in unnatural immobility. In 2004, the formerly prospering wharf Dalzavod employs only a fraction of its previous workforce. The fires in the forges died years ago and the impressive brick smokestacks, which mark the end of the bay like lighthouses, have long since cooled. A ship heaved in dry dock has been lying there for months with no observable changes on its battered hull. The steel barriers of the dock enclose the ship like coffin walls.

The calmness of the harbour stands in contrast to the buzzing of the street. Svetlanskaya Street is the central artery of Vladivostok. An endless stream of vehicles presses every day through the narrow space between the bay and the steep hillsides. The geographic proximity to the Japanese used car market has tumbled the city into transportation chaos. Too many Japanese vehicles roam the small roads which were built for times when it was a privilege to have a car. During rush hour, in the morning and early evening, the two-lane road is jammed with traffic and the old streetcars laboriously work through the turmoil. The streetcars' heavy pounding over the asphalt regularly triggers the alarms of the parked cars. The rhythmic thumping of streetcars, the whining of car engines, and the buzzing of alarms merges into a roaring sound carpet. Against this background, the old Soviet streetcars look like sleepwalking behemoths, lost in the undertow of modern mobility. Their drivers are almost exclusively women. On Sundays they wear heavy lipstick, pearl necklaces, and extravagant hats. Through the dirty windshields of the streetcars, the drivers seem like apparitions from a different time.

Unimpressed by the humming of the traffic artery, an old woman attends the flowers in a small bed between my house and the street. She cares affectionately for the awakening green every day, watering the plants with the help of an old Coca-Cola bottle. Her back is crooked, her love of flowers unbroken. Time has engraved itself in the faces of the city's old dwellers. Sometimes an old woman tries to cross the heavily frequented street. Her face and eyes show a mixture of bewilderment and repulsion. The bodies and faces are bearers of history, unlike the housing facades along the streets that are subject to constant change. Only a week ago, a sign was still hanging above the little Soviet-era grocery shop around the corner from my apartment. *Moloko* (milk), advertised the blue neon letters. Since then, Chinese construction workers stripped and whitewashed the interior and the shop now stands empty. A red-and-white tent in front of the shop serves as a provisional sales booth. Coca-Cola is written in big letters on the side. At the corner, close to the bus stop, pensioners sell pickles, berries, and potted plants. At night, street hookers take over.

I step into one of the buses. The city's public transportation buses are made in South Korea. The interiors are covered with Korean billboards. Comic strips explain the benefits of clean shirts in the sweaty world of commuters. Russian pop fills the inside with ingenuous melodies as the bus drivers skilfully avoid the large potholes in the road's surface and slowly advance with jerky movements through the dense traffic. Sometimes it is faster to walk along Svetlanskaya. It is hot and sultry inside the buses. The passengers are huddled close together. Often, there is an old man sinking into his seat under the weight of alcohol, and empty beer bottles roll under the seats, seemingly unnoticed by passengers.

Plate 1. Svetlanskaya Street, Vladivostok 2009.

Art nouveau buildings line the street, one after the other. A sign of modernity, engraved in the facades at the beginning of the last century, a modern dream in pastel colours. Vladivostok's turn-of-the-century architecture is a wild mélange of different styles: classic Ionian columns mix with curved Asiatic gable and window forms, house fronts are crowned with little gothic towers, and exterior brick walls are ornamented with baroque baubles.

First, the Russian Central Bank and then the headquarters of the Pacific Border Guard glide by the bus window. Young recruits on duty are busy maintaining the flowerbeds in front of the entrance. On the other side of the road, a monument to the Far Eastern Merchant Marine rises out of a small park. The merchant fleet suffered many casualties from submarine attacks during the Second World War. An eternal flame burns in front of the bronze sculpture for the ones lost at sea. Their names are engraved in brass plates. Gravestones remember each of the sunken ships, 24 in total. During military holidays, carnations are placed on the plates, always in even numbers.

Young students board at the bus stop 'Universitet'. The open door lets fresh air into the congested space of the bus, and the driver turns up the volume of the music. His hands are blackened from the coins that pass daily through his hands. He swings the bus back into the traffic. Inside, it is stuffy again.

Svetlanskaya Street has changed tremendously over the course of the last years, almost like it attained a new face. Perfumeries, barber shops, jewellers, travel agencies, apparel stores, European fashion, kitchen furniture, supermarkets, banks, internet cafés, restaurants, and night clubs – Svetlanskaya Street is the pulsating economic nerve centre of Vladivostok. Freshly renovated facades gleam in bright pastel colours above the streaming mass of people strolling on the sidewalks. Only a year ago, in 2003, construction teams from North Korea cobbled the sidewalks. Back then, high heels punctured the sand; a year later, they glide effortlessly over the new surface. Colourful signs and billboards hang above the new shop windows. Slightly reflective, the shop windows have a peculiar quality: they focus the view on the commodities on display and at the same time allow the passerby to see his or her own image mirrored in the glass. Bodies stage themselves on the city's reflecting surfaces and fashion mirrors itself in the display cases. Svetlanskaya Street is theatre stage and consumer space at the same time.

However not everybody keeps up with the new pace of the urban beat. There are the bodies left behind: war veterans, pensioners, the unemployed, and the homeless. From time to time, their shadows break into the bright mirror world of consumption. A beggar lies sunken down on the boardwalk. Blood flows out of his nose. Without stopping to help, the passersby evade him. An old woman crouches on the concrete flight of steps of an underpass. Her small hands are folded in prayer above a wooden icon on her lap. Her gaze is lowered, and all she sees are the legs of the hustling passersby, one after the other, in endless repetition.

Overview

The breakdown of the Soviet Union led to fundamental changes in Russia. New cultural and economic practices emerged out of the fragments of the collapsed state. Formerly state-controlled sectors of the economy faded into the shadows of a new, post-Soviet economy. Powerful and wealthy individuals, business associations, and their political partners took control of banking institutions, large industries and natural resource extraction. For Russia, the decade of the 1990s was characterized by large-scale informal and illegal marketeering at all levels of society. During these years, the Russian state partially lost its monopoly on violence and taxation. Complex networks evolved in the grey zone of monopolization, asset stripping, shady export schemes, political patronage, and organized crime. This process ran vertically through the country's political and economic life. Spheres of informality grew and expanded in the Russian Federation on all levels: from high finance in Moscow to the backstreet vendors in Vladivostok. Privatization of the economy and the rearrangement of state power produced pragmatic adaptations to new local realities. The transition period has evoked creative economic and social answers to commodity shortages, new forms of labour migration, and institutional weaknesses in the post-Soviet political system.

The research on which this book is based examines these informal economic practices and non-regulated commercial organizations and networks. Exploring economic activities in the Russian Far East at open-air markets and border crossings, I seek to understand the emerging roles of entrepreneurs, organized crime, and the state in post-Soviet Russia. The questions at the centre of my inquiry are: what are shadow networks, how are they structured, and how is their social reality to be described?

This book constitutes a metaphoric walk through the new landscape, or – to be precise – three strolls and a historic stride. It is organized around these walks, which in the form of vignettes open up the central chapters. Together, these vignettes introduce a narrative of state erosion, border porosity, and criminal penetration. In the course of this work, different shadow economies are revealed. Stages of my inquiry into the shadow are spatial nodes, where space, people, and commodities condense – at open-air markets, border crossings, and a graveyard. My research is an attempt to shine some light into the shadow that engulfed the economic sphere of post-Soviet Russia by focusing on parallel structures in a time of political and economic transition.

Both in terms of methodology and presentation, this book merges several genres. Ethnography, urban geography, investigative journalism, travelogue, and anthropological analysis each contribute to a reading of the urban space of post-Soviet Russia. To convey a sense of the urban experience I introduce each chapter with a vignette. The vignettes are not mere narrative ploys. Besides conveying the appearance, smells, and sounds of the ethnographer's fieldsite, they convey key aspects of the informal networks under discussion. In this approach, I am guided by Walter Benjamin's (1979) explorations of the urban experience with the help of *Denkbilder* (thought-images). Benjamin's cityscapes and urban pen-pictures carry the decisive mark of journalistic reportage. His urban writings are inhabited by marginal city dwellers and characters from the darker side of city life. Benjamin's language is the language of experience and reflects an extensive exposure to urban life. Categories of modern experience, like 'porosity', 'threshold', and 'shock', appear repeatedly in Benjamin's writings. His style reflects these experiences and has them fundamentally embedded. With his exploration of the modern cityscape he tries to uncover the relationships between architecture, commodities, and experience. Inspired by him, I similarly explore the relationships between space, commodities, and informal social networks in the Russian Far East.

How and why did informal networks partially replace their state regulated counterparts in the former Soviet Union (Ledeneva 1998, 2006, 2013)? Why have they been relatively successful, abundant, and profitable? The non-formal has its own peculiar structures. Similar to its legal and state-controlled counterparts, informality and illegality form networks of mutual aid and cooperation. The informal economic networks show highly dynamic features and have gone through rapid changes in the last years. Tracing their paths of emergence, documenting how they evolved and subsequently changed, addresses the very nature of social and economic response mechanisms to rapid cultural change.

What factors shaped those networks? Economic explanations tend to see informal structures as a direct result of economic transition. After the breakdown of the Soviet Union's formal structures, informal structures emerged to fill the void before new formal structures were erected. In this book, I question how locality may have played a role in forming the specific structures of informal networks. Or framed in a slightly different way: What roles do (urban) space and (border) locality play in the formation of shadow networks? The city's geographic location close to the Russian-Chinese border, and within the borderland formed by it, is of crucial importance, as is the fact that Vladivostok itself harbours an international port. My argument is that the spatial proximity to the Chinese border had a formative influence on the emergence of informal networks after the collapse of the Soviet Union.

Post-Soviet labour migration and border porosity have created new informal networks. The Russian Far East is a borderland in multiple ways. The geographic vicinity to China, Korea, and Japan exposes the region to a variety of influences, commodities, and people. Labour migration from the successor states of the Soviet Union, especially from Central Asia, and the porous border to China added in the last years to the multi-ethnic mosaic of the region's urban centres. To gauge these influences on the formation of informal networks, I want to address and explore the peculiar geographic exposure of this borderland and the role locality played in giving those networks their unique characteristics.

Shadow networks have a specific history and geography that ties them to a physical space, and shadow networks strategically use urban space to their economic advantage. In exploring these relations, I draw on strands of economic anthropology that are conscious of the role of border space and locality. I describe and develop the ideas of bazaar ecology, ethno-economic niches, borderland economy, and the geography of informal networks. The fast-changing social and economic environment of post-Soviet Russia demands a processual view of social phenomena. Therefore, a special focus will be placed on the intrinsic dynamics of the observed informal networks. A diachronic view is necessary to address the dynamics, flexibilities, and adaptabilities of shadow networks to show how flexible social and economic ties are able to react efficiently to rapid cultural change.

To answer these questions in an adequate and thorough way, I develop a detailed and bottom-up perspective to analyze four different shadow economies. My first example is a historical analysis of Chinese trading networks that operated in the city and especially in the backcountry of Vladivostok at the beginning of the twentieth century. The second and third examples, based primarily in the port city of Vladivostok, are drawn from my ethnographic research on large open-air markets and small-scale cross-border trading in the early 2000s. Most of this trade was conducted by ethnic Russians who cross the Russian-Chinese border on a regular basis to import cheap goods for local markets. The fourth and final example is that of organized crime groups which evolved during the 1990s.

To explore and to cast some light into the shadows I have chosen three different, yet compatible approaches. The first is essentially a social network approach that looks at the different qualities of relationship ties, which underscore the specific networks. In order to see the different shades of grey, and to differentiate various informal networks not only according to their economic specifications, I concentrate on the specific qualities of the social ties interconnecting the individual actors. This is at the same time a search for the social glue and lubricant of informal relationships. The second approach concentrates on the economy of informal networks, by analyzing the economic base and the formative role economic incentives played in shaping its structures. Yet these networks are not mere reactions to new economic realities. While being influenced by new circumstances, they also contribute simultaneously to the shaping and organization of their economic base; informal networks are effect and cause at once. With the third approach, I try to grasp the spatial dimension of informality by examining how space and locality influence the formation and operation of networks. Together, these approaches constitute an anthropology of economic spaces.

Understanding the Shadow

Central to my inquiry are the notions of the 'shadow', 'grey', or 'informal' economy. While normally used as interchangeable terms, all denoting economic practices that are not part of the formal economy and therefore not subject to the same degree of control and monitoring by the state, I use the terms slightly differently. As with every physical shadow, a shadow economy is created by light falling on an object. I see therefore informal economic practices as social and economic structures in the shadow of formal economic and political institutions. These formal economic institutions are the objects which cast the shadows. The shadow fills the gaps between formal institutions and diverse angles of light produce various lengths and intensities of the shadow, which further result in different shades of grey.

My central argument builds on Carolyn Nordstrom's concept of shadow networks. Her efforts to render the shadows of political institutions visible in the context of post-war West Africa initially inspired my study of the Russian Far East. Nordstrom applies the term 'shadow' to a range of networks that she describes in the context of her fieldwork in West African war zones (Nordstrom 2004). The underlying qualities of these networks usually defy a simple black and white categorization, and it is for this reason that Nordstrom prefers the term 'shadow' to the more frequent alternatives of 'criminal' or 'illegal': 'the transactions defining these networks are not confined solely to criminal, illicit or illegal activities – but they do take place outside formal state institutions' (Nordstrom 2000: 35). In a similar manner,

I use 'shadow' to refer to the informal economic practices outside of state control that defy simple categorization as legal or illegal.

Nordstrom's approach is, of course, not the only one. Different theoretical models have tried to describe the contours of shadow economies from various perspectives. Ideological, legal, and economic definitions are attempts at separation and compartmentalization. In these models, clear categories divide the legal from the illegal, and subcategories of illegality define the different compartments of informal economies. The question that lies beyond overturning the legal/ illegal dichotomy is – how do shadow economies differ?

In the following chapters I untangle the complex relationships between commodity flows, individual actors, and social and economic networks. The physical locality of networks in a borderland plays an important role. Commodities and people are intertwined in complex social networks that are organized by various principles. These networks, which cross borders and involve a range of actors, are difficult to categorize, partially due to their elusive nature. The shadow networks not only cross national borders, they also transcend categorical boundaries. The examples show how blurred the boundary between legality and illegality actually can be. Shadow economies can run through all levels of society, integrating small-scale entrepreneurs in open-air markets, as well as businessmen who are part of the political elite.

Since Keith Hart (1973) distinguished between formal and informal economic sectors with data based on wage-earning and self-employment in Ghana, informal economies have been labelled as grey, underground, coloured, shadow, or second economies, depending on the definitional criteria used to separate them from a formal economy. The diversity of labels reflects not only different theoretical approaches, but also testifies to the heterogeneity of informal economies. 'Informal' economic activities range from unreported income among the self-employed to clandestine trade in illegal commodities. Economic, juridical, and disciplinary definitions of informal economies have to be distinguished. For instance, a generally accepted definition of the shadow economy in the field of economics is: 'All economic activities that contribute to the officially calculated (or observed) gross national product but are currently unregistered' (Schneider and Enste 2000: 78). Shadow economies have been studied worldwide, but it is sufficient to review the literature on the informal economy in Russia to demonstrate the range of issues that can and must be addressed through the concept.

In the Soviet context, the informal economy was often referred to as the 'second economy'. Gregory Grossman's prominent definition stresses a legal framework: 'the second economy comprises all production and exchange activities that fulfil at least one of the following tests: (a) being directly for private gain; (b) being in some significant respect in knowing contravention of existing law' (1977: 25). Other authors, for instance Maria Los, have adapted a more ideological definition arguing that, 'the second economy includes all areas of economic activity which are officially viewed as being inconsistent with the ideologically sanctioned dominant mode of economic organization' (1990: 2).

In another approach, Louise Shelley (1990) distinguished between the legal second economy and the illegal second economy in the Soviet Union. The legal second economy included, for example, the sale of agricultural products raised on private plots or products for sale from private manufacturing. The illegal second economy was subdivided by Shelley into two realms, the internal and parallel sectors. Embezzlement and diversion within the consumer industry, illegal labour, and corruption were part of the internal illegal economy, and were closely tied to the state economy. Unlicensed production and sales (e.g. bootleggers and speculators) or black markets (for goods in short supplies, or illegal commodities like drugs and contraband) were part of the parallel illegal economy, separated from the structures of the state economy.

During Soviet times, alternative economic networks also sprang up to supplement an inefficient centrally planned economy. The resilience of the second economy was partially a result of its interwoven relationship with the official political and economic elite, as Louise Shelley pointed out, 'The web of associations between the official and the unofficial economy, as well as the state-directed economy's need for the second economy ensure[d] ... perpetuation even in the face of numerous party orchestrated campaigns [against it]' (Shelley 1990: 23). At the same time, the flexibility and adaptability of the second economy helped the formal Soviet economy to survive. As Grossmann noted, the second economy 'ke[pt] the wheels of production turning' (Grossman 1977: 40). Thus the second economy partially played the role of an economic booster for the Soviet system. Similarly, the shadow networks of the transition period acted as incubators for the new capitalism that has emerged in post-Soviet Russia.

Aron Katsenelinboigen went a step further in distinguishing the diverse economies of the Soviet Union by establishing a typology of 'colored markets' (Katsenelinboigen 1977). His colour-coded typology – red, pink, and white for legal markets, grey for semi-legal markets, and brown and black for illegal markets – distinguished different markets according to the degree of legality (legal, semi-legal, and illegal) that characterized the involved transactions – the nature of the sold commodity, the source of the commodity, and the method of sale. For instance, the grey market of privately rented apartments or dachas in the Soviet Union was both legal in terms of the offered commodity as well as the source. The only semi-legal aspect of that specific transaction was that the respective income for the tenant was not officially reported, thus tax-free. A brown market, according to Katsenelinboigen, was an informal market that thrived on the scarcity of a certain commodity. Although the commodity itself was legal, the source and the method of sale ranged from semi-legal to illegal. Black markets were similar to brown ones, but required the involvement of an illegal wholesale specialist in the transaction, the so-called speculator. This colour-coding of economic spheres according to different legal dimensions can be exercised on numerous levels and also be applied to the shadow economies of contemporary, post-Soviet Russia.

For instance, the open-air markets run by ethnic traders would fit into Katsenelinboigen's category of the grey economy. The traders offer legal commodities from a legal source, but the sale is semi-legal because it is made outside formal institutions and taxation. In contrast, the sale of poached animals and other bio-resources are clearly illegal in all aspects, from the source of the commodity to its sale, and thus can be categorized as constituting a black market. Cross-border shuttle trade presents a more complex case in terms of its classification. Although all the transactions are actually legal, shuttle trade is used on a large scale to evade import taxes, thus constituting an illegal act. In addition, shuttle trade can integrate legal (e.g. import of clothes) and illegal (e.g. smuggling of alcohol) conduct in one transportation channel.

Increasingly refined typologies, however, cannot deny that it is exactly the conceptual fuzziness and indistinct boundary between legal and illegal that so often characterizes shadow economies. Even early writers, like Grossman (1977), pointed to the blurred boundary between the legal and illegal economies of the Soviet Union. By his own acknowledgment, what Grossman called the 'second economy' covered a wide and diverse range of activities (including diverting goods from state factories and trade in illegal imports) that combined legality and illegality in multiple ways (1977: 25).

The blurring of legality and illegality must also be seen as a sign of the interdependence of formal and informal economies. Once again, analysts have been drawn to typologization to explain these relations. Ferdinand Feldbrugge, for example, proposed a five-point typology based on different degrees of interdependence between the first and second economies in the Soviet Union: (1) largely unconnected; (2) imbalanced competition; (3) balanced competition; (4) parasitic symbiosis; (5) cooperative symbiosis (Feldbrugge 1984: 531).

As the above review suggests, the point of observation becomes crucial in evaluating shadow economies. From a state perspective, shadow economies are subversive and essentially illegal. However, seen from 'below', from the perspective of the involved actors, things look different, especially in respect to the self-perception of their work. As Caroline Humphrey has pointed out, in Russia 'people who engage in activities defined by the state as illegal do not necessary define themselves as criminals' (Humphrey 1999: 199). In my own research, I found that shuttle traders and ethnic entrepreneurs also did not see their economic activities as necessarily illicit when trading in contraband or working illegal on a market. Itty Abraham and Willem van Schendel have addressed this problem by hinting at the distinctions between legal and licit, and illegal and illicit respectively: 'We build upon a distinction between what states consider to be legitimate ("legal") and what people involved in transnational networks consider to be legitimate ("licit"). Many transnational movements of people, commodities, and ideas are illegal because they defy the norms and rules of formal political authority, but they are quite acceptable, "licit", in the eyes of participants in these transactions and flows' (Abraham and van Schendel 2005: 4).

Taking the blurred borders between illegality and legality into consideration, I move beyond the legal/ illegal dichotomy in my analysis of informal economic networks. In the following chapters, I present a social perspective on shadow networks that will address more thoroughly the 'intimate economies' (Wilson 2004: 9) that intertwine commodity flows, people, social networks, and the state. My focus lies hereby on the social organization of informality.

Cityscapes and the Organization of the Shadow

Commodities flow in economic and social networks and economic exchange creates socially constructed value (Appadurai 1986: 3). Thus by analyzing commodity flows I attempt to explore the underlying forms of social organization. My emphasis on commodity flows has its counterpart in Walter Benjamin's increased awareness of the commodity and its pivotal role in modern urban life. I share here his interest in the minutiae and marginalia of the urban setting. As Graeme Gilloch has pointed out, Benjamin's main themes evolve around, 'the fragmentation, commodification, interiorization and marginalization of experience' (Gilloch 1996: 7). From the chaos of the Neapolitan street market to the department stores of Paris, Benjamin shows that the modern city is essentially a site of the commodity. Open-air markets and cross-border trade routes in the Russian Far East are equally commodified spaces that on first glance seem to be chaotic and marginalized economic spheres.

Architecture plays an important role in Benjamin's cityscapes. Buildings, streets, and other urban features exist as a stage for the urban actor. Details and characteristics of the architectural world are of central importance in Benjamin's urban phenomenology. In his essay 'Naples', part travel account, part sociological analysis, the peculiar architecture of Naples represents a key to understanding the lively world within it. The building material itself is a representation of the city's chthonic character: 'As porous as the stone is the architecture. Building and action interpenetrate in the courtyards, arcades and stairways. In everything they preserve the scope to become a theater of new, unforeseen constellations. The stamp of the definitive is avoided' (Benjamin 1996: 416).

Benjamin is not just describing a city. The city itself is an object of philosophical reflection. The transitory quality of the modern experience is incorporated in his reflections on the urban environment. Thus, in using Naples as a background for philosophical reflection, Benjamin expresses the transitory character in the spatio-temporal categories of 'porosity' and 'transitivity'. Naples' architecture expresses the temporal ambiguity between construction and ruin. The temporal transition is experienced in transitivity; spatial transition in porosity (Caygill 1998: 122). Porosity permeates the whole city and represents for Benjamin also a characteristic of the private life of Naples' citizens. The Camorra, Naples' domestic mafia, with its formless power dispersed over the city and suburbs, depicts the same 'spectral feature of porosity' (Benjamin 1996: 416).

In Naples, the interior opens itself on the street. Benjamin applies a dramaturgical perspective to analyze the city's bustling life. His approach is essentially an attempt at a microsociology of space. More than thirty years later, the sociologist Erving Goffman followed a related approach to focus on a similar sociological space (Goffman 1959; see also Dawe 1973: 246). Envisioning the city as a theatre, and society as a stage, Goffmann explored the microsociology of everyday communication among urban actors. Like Benjamin before him, he drew attention to the differences in dramaturgical performances according to actors' spatial position in the urban environment.

Benjamin's writing on cities also included early Soviet Moscow. 'Mobilization' was the vehicle for his reflections: 'The country is mobilized day and night, most of all, of course the party' (Benjamin 1979: 186). Benjamin described Moscow in 1927. It was then a city under the sway of the New Economic Policy (NEP) which from 1921-28 allowed for certain private economic initiatives to thwart the chronic food shortages that had been caused by the earlier policy of War Communism. Although street trading under the NEP was not legal, it was tolerated. Hence, 'all this goes on silently; calls like those of every trader in the South are unknown' (Benjamin 1979: 181). Again, Benjamin describes a city vibrating with public street life. Street vendors, racing automobiles, kiosks, and blinding streetlights pierce the wintry night to create the mosaic of a city in constant motion. Benjamin's urban experience is characterized by 'the complete interpenetration of technological and primitive modes of life' (Benjamin 1979: 190). He witnesses a fusion of modernity and primitivism, of communist future and peasant past.

As in Naples, private life dissolved in the city, but for different reasons. The architectural and social porosity in Moscow was imposed upon the city by the party-state (Caygill 1998: 125). The spectral feature of the Neapolitan mafia found its Soviet counterpart in the all-permeating presence of the party police. Addressing the unique character of the communist capital and its difference from other European cities, Benjamin concluded with a prophecy: 'Should the European correlation of power and money penetrate Russia, too, then, perhaps not the country, perhaps not even the Party, but Communism in Russia would be lost' (Benjamin 1979: 196).

My method to explore the post-Soviet urban space and its informal networks links directly to Benjamin's approaches. A focus on architecture, which includes topographic investigation of open-air markets, the spatial exploration of a border region, and the reading of a graveyard, incorporates the analysis of urban space, commodities, and social networks. Mobility and porosity are Benjamin's metaphors for urban life. Likewise I use these metaphors to address the transitory character of the Russian Far East after the breakdown of the Soviet Union. The porous character of economic life, penetrating formal and informal sectors and blurring the border between them, is not only visible in open-air markets, but is a defining feature of the Russian Far East as a historical and contemporary borderland. The opening of the border to China after the collapse of the Soviet Union created new holes and opportunities in a formerly closed space, and post-Soviet cross-border flows of migrants and commodities permeate the economic life of the Russian Far East to a formerly unknown degree.

The Narrative

The ground of my inquiry into the shadow networks of post-Soviet Russia is not a single site, but rather composed of multiple fields. This is a multi-sited ethnography that demonstrates George Marcus's remark that multi-sited ethnography is 'an exercise in mapping terrain' (Marcus 1995: 99). The following chapters are 'maps' of the terrain of the Russian Far East, which are at the same time a guide through the shadow of post-Soviet informal economic practices. Different locations – open-air markets, a border-crossing to China, and a graveyard – constitute this terrain.

These locations present the observer with shifting ground. James Clifford poignantly observed that 'ethnographies are now written on a moving earth' (Clifford 1988: 23). Others, stressing rootlessness and alienation, have described the predicaments of late capitalism as rhizomic or even schizophrenic (Deleuze and Guattari 1987). Arjun Appadurai distinguished different streams or flows along which cultural material may be seen to be moving across national boundaries (Appadurai 1996). All of these approaches try to grasp how cultural formations, people, and commodities overlap and move in an increasingly global and transnational culture. Flows of goods and people merge in the shadows of a formal economy; networks form and dissolve and intertwine with legal and illegal structures. Willem van Schendel and Itty Abraham addressed this fluid condition by encouraging researchers to look for the social embeddedness of these flows: 'We need to approach flows of goods and people as visible manifestations of power configurations that weave in and out of legality, in and out of states, and in and out of individuals' lives, as socially embedded, sometimes long-term processes of production, exchange, consumption, and representation' (Abraham and van Schendel 2005: 8).

Studying flows and networks nevertheless requires some effort to fix them, if even for a moment, for the purposes of description and analysis. I have used a method of situational analysis that isolates social phenomena by studying social events delimited in time and space (Rogers and Vertovec 1995). To capture the nodal points of social phenomena I specifically focus on social condensations in space. The methodological goal is therefore to grasp, that is to freeze in motion, flows of people and commodities to analyze their configurations. In the words of Clyde Mitchell, my approach consists of, 'the intellectual isolation of a set of events from the wider social context in which they occur in order to facilitate a logically coherent analysis of these events' (Mitchell 1983: 187). I focus therefore on events that represent condensed forms of social action; these are events where flows of goods and people surface in a visible form and social and economic networks materialize. For instance, open-air markets represent a condensed social space because the flow of commodities, buyers, sellers, and other actors temporarily surfaces, becoming visible to the anthropological observer.

Field and Methods

In my attempt to understand informal economic networks in contemporary Russia I draw from a variety of sources. I conducted fieldwork in Vladivostok, Komsomolsk-na-Amure, and in several other locations in Primorsky Krai (Maritime Province)[1], and the bordering Chinese province of Heilongjiang. The total field research amounted to seventeen months (one month in 2002, eleven in 2004, and five months spread across trips taken in 2009, 2010, and 2012). Observations in open-air markets and at border crossings set the stage for my inquiry. Interviews with market sellers and customers, participants of informal economies, and 'expert' informants filled the stage with characters and content. Sources acquired through archival research comprise the historic background. Research in newspaper archives supplements information on recent events and captures episodes that span the 1990s and early 2000s. Each case study draws on its own set of methodologies, outlined in more detail in the respective chapters.

Chapter 2, 'Tiger and Bear', is a historical introduction to the Russian Far East focused on relations between China and Russia and on the peculiar political and economic geography of Primorye Region (Maritime Region). This was a volatile frontier province carved out of the weakened Chinese Empire in the middle of the nineteenth century. The geopolitical move to annex this territory made the Russian Empire's long-harboured dream come true: an (almost) ice-free port on the Pacific coast. With the incorporation of Primorye, the city of Vladivostok became Russia's gate to the Pacific, but Chinese influence was still felt heavily in the region. Especially in the backcountry, in the valleys and taiga of the Sikhote-Alin mountain range, Chinese trading guilds that were hierarchically-organized into powerful brotherhoods constituted a state within the state until the consolidation of Soviet rule in the early 1920s. Throughout its history, Vladivostok was a trading hub for the Russian Far East and Siberia. Especially during the Russian Civil War (1917-22), the city was a multinational melting pot and a place of encounter between East and West. After the Second World War, the city of Vladivostok was closed to foreigners and foreign shipping. Since the breakdown of the Soviet Union, the port city has opened, ending Vladivostok's political, economic, and cultural isolation and the city is gradually becoming again an active player in the international Pacific community.

---

[1] Primorsky means 'against the sea', and is often translated into English as 'Maritime'. I use the term Primorsky Krai, which can be translated as Maritime Province, when I refer to the modern-day federal subject of the Russian Federation. I use the terms Primorye Region and Maritime Region, when I refer to the historic administrative unit that existed until the beginning of the twentieth century (see chapter 2).

Chapter 3, 'Urban Informality', introduces a peculiar economic form characteristic of many urban centres in the former Soviet Union, especially in the Russian Far East. Large-scale open-air markets offering consumer goods of mostly Chinese origin, the so-called Chinese markets, represent a direct answer to the ongoing severe economic shortages, brought about by the breakdown of the Soviet Union. New forms of labour migration and commodity flows emerged and created a space for private entrepreneurial initiatives. These outdoor markets represent heavily contested arenas of spatial interaction, subject to the constant (re)negotiation of economic public space. Systematic mapping and the recording of inventories of several major Chinese markets in Vladivostok present the spatial layout of these markets, often described as chaotic and anarchic by scholars and locals alike. In fact, the spatial groupings of foreign traders and their commodities reveal a highly structured and organized economic sphere, albeit one that is often on the brink of legality. Interviews with vendors, suppliers, market administrators, and clients complete the picture of a complex and condensed niche economy, where different ethnic groups occupy marked spatial positions and monopolize whole categories of consumer goods. Family relationships and ethnic ties play an important role in the transactions among ethnic entrepreneurs. These entrepreneurs rely heavily on each other and form enclosed groups according to their ethnicity, thus granting them an economic advantage over the comparatively unorganized Russian traders.

Chapter 4, 'Eastern Porosity', opens the view on larger networks of informal trade and trafficking. The breakdown of the Soviet Union fundamentally changed the border landscapes of Eurasia. On the one hand, new borders were suddenly drawn between the Russian Federation and the newly independent states in Eastern Europe, Central Asia, and the Caucasus. On the other hand, the old and strictly controlled border between China and Russia suddenly became porous and permeable for both Chinese and Russians citizens alike.

Focusing on the illegal export of bio-resources from Russia to China and on a peculiar form of shuttle trade between the two countries, this chapter analyzes different forms of border economies and explores the global interlinkages between local markets and larger economic systems. The export of bio-resources (timber, ginseng, deer antlers, tiger products, bear paws, frogs, and sea cucumbers) for the Chinese market constitutes a rising ecological problem for the Russian Far East. At the same time, poaching is often the sole opportunity for gaining a cash income that is available to backcountry residents. Chinese demand has created shadow joint ventures between Russian poachers and Chinese middlemen smuggling the contraband into Heilongjiang Province. Following Russian tourist traders (*chelnoki*) to China, this chapter also explores the inner workings of business networks disguised as tourism. The structural flexibility inherent in this system makes it extremely adaptable to change, and for individual actors it represents an opportunity for upward social and economic mobility.

Chapter 5, 'The Harder the Rain, the Tighter the Roof', introduces yet another parallel institution which forcefully established itself in the post-Soviet political and economic sphere. Organized crime is not a new phenomenon in Russia, its historical roots reach back to Stalinist times. Yet recent organized crime in Russia differs significantly, in quality as well as in quantity, from its predecessors. Using the Russian Far East, especially the city of Vladivostok, as a case study, I sketch the evolution of organized crime in Russia from the mid-1980s to the 2000s. In the course of this evolution the traditional underworld has been slowly but thoroughly replaced by a new generation of 'violent entrepreneurs' (Volkov 2002b). A network-centred approach, tracing interconnections and animosities between various criminal groups through time, shows that quick reactions to new market opportunities and ruthless annihilation of opponents are key for successful entrepreneurship. In addition, powerful political elites have emerged and monopolize whole sectors of the industry. Fishing and shipping have been especially lucrative industries for the new entrepreneurs.

The conclusion, under the title of 'The Social Organization of the Shadow', presents a theoretical synthesis of the three main chapters. Why – I ask – are shadow structures so prevalent and powerful in post-Soviet Russia? I have already presented some of the answers. Border porosity and the disintegration of the Soviet state apparatus led to fundamental changes in Vladivostok and the Russian Far East. Tourist traders, Chinese merchants, Central Asian entrepreneurs, and Russian politicians found small niches in the evolving market economy. Accumulated capital is now reinvested in larger businesses and joint ventures, especially with Chinese partners. Open-air markets and organized crime have fundamentally changed in the last years. The accumulation of capital and economic consolidation reveal their effect. Street kiosks have moved into newly-built shopping malls and former criminals turned into politicians and businessmen. Ethnic entrepreneurs as well as criminal groups tried to control the emerging market and are now transformed by that same market.

Yet economic approaches give only a partial answer. The political vacuum after the breakdown of the Soviet Union led to the privatization and compartmentalization of state powers, although cause and effect are blurred and reversible in this case. In the course of the post-Soviet transformations the state has partially lost its monopoly on violence and taxation, while new shadow structures found fertile ground in a political and economic environment where trust is scarce and fragile. To a certain degree, the shadow structures have replaced the state as a sole guarantor of law and order. Exploring the institutional framework of that environment helps to understand the reasons for the emergence of extra-state networks and coalitions. The analysis of their specific social and political foundations explains their persistence. Personal ties, such as long-term friendships between individual actors, play an important role as foundations of stable shadow networks. The capacity of these networks to adapt efficiently to rapid social and economic change and the ability to engage in symbiotic relationships with state actors and institutions are key to understanding their success. These propositions raise new questions on the fundamentals of social order.

Chapter 2
Tiger and Bear: A Particular History of the Russian Far East

Sikhote-Alin, July 1906, Olga Bay. The group had already been travelling since before sunrise, following the narrow horse trail through thick stands of reed onto a low ridgeline covered with alder trees. This late July afternoon brought a warm breeze from the adjacent sea. As in the days before, during the early afternoon anvil-shaped clouds had formed along the coast and rolling thunder was slightly audible from further inland where the densely wooded coastal mountain range rose abruptly above the tree line. Surrounded by stands of Mongolian oak, alder, and fern thickets, the small detachment with their pack horses seemed almost lost in the lush deciduous forest. Yet they were all well-seasoned travellers. Led by the tsarist officer Vladimir Klavdievich Arsenyev, their journey was one of the first systematic expeditions into the mountainous forest of the Russian Far East.[2] Arsenyev's official mission was to conduct scientific and historic research along the Sikhote-Alin mountain range, explore the headwaters of the Ussuri and Iman rivers, and chart the coast north of Olga Bay. Under the direct orders of the Priamur Governor-General Pavel Fedorovich Unterberg, Arsenyev equipped and commanded a small expeditionary force composed of 3 officers, 12 soldiers from the 24th Eastern Siberian Gunner Regiment, 6 Cossacks from the Ussuri-Cossacks Division, and 24 pack horses. The group started their journey at the western end of the mountain range in late May 1906. It was a rainy summer.

    In July, after almost a month of travel along the Ussuri River Valley, they had crossed the watershed and descended towards the Pacific in the direction of Olga Bay. St. Olga was a small Russian settlement and harbour founded in 1859 by the crew of a Russian cannon boat which had escaped

---

[2] This chapter's opening is based on Arsenyev's (1921) travelogue and account of his 1906 expedition.

British warships during the Crimean War by turning in to the fog-shrouded bay.

St. Olga had seen better days. Once a prospering outpost of the Russian Empire, St. Olga was in decay at the time of the group's arrival. The population had dropped visibly: abandoned houses lined the central road, their windows and doors barred, and the church yard had turned into an overgrown garden. The early settlers' dream of establishing a vital seaport with city status never materialized. Vladivostok was only 300 kilometres to the south, and in 1861 it was designated the principal harbour for the Siberian Military Flotilla.[3] The subsequent rise of Vladivostok as Russia's gate to the Pacific lured away many of St. Olga's early settlers and soon the settlement dwindled.

The former Chinese settlement at the east end of the bay showed similar signs of abandonment. Large Chinese warehouses still flanked the beach, reminding the travellers of the regional importance of the former trading post. *Chi-myn* (Stony Portal), as the Chinese had called this station, was a former trading hub for the wider region. For the Chinese, the natural harbour formed by the protected bay was a perfect place to access the rich backcountry of the Sikhote-Alin Mountains. Only a decade earlier, sable pelts, ginseng, and fresh deer antlers from the Ussuri taiga filled the wooden longhouses along the pebble beach, ready to be loaded on junks for export to a demanding Chinese market. In exchange, goods from mainland China made their way through this trading post to Chinese and native settlements in the remote and wooded valleys of the backcountry.

The Sikhote-Alin Mountains, also known as the Far Eastern Urals, divide the Maritime Province into two ecological zones that are shaped by the Asian monsoon system that blows from Siberia in the winter and from the Sea of Japan during the summer. Compared to the western slopes that face inland, the eastern maritime slopes are favoured with warmer winters and lush vegetation. Deep ravines and valleys drain eastwards from the Sikhote-Alin Mountains into the Pacific Ocean and westward into the Ussuri and Amur rivers. A deciduous forest covers the lower slopes of the mountains with oaks, cottonwoods, birches, alders, maple, and walnut trees. In higher altitudes, Korean cedar and Siberian conifers reach up to alpine tundra. The peculiar climate has created a habitat for rare species of flora and fauna. Ginseng grows wild in the forest and the Siberian tiger, the world's largest cat, lives in the remote parts of the mountains. In the summer, salmon run the rivers and a warm, seasonal summer current along

---

[3] The remnants of the Siberian Military Flotilla (or Siberian Fleet) were re-organized after the 1905 Russo-Japanese War to form the Pacific Fleet.

the coast allows for sea cucumbers, scallops, sea urchins, and a broad variety of fish.

Plate 2. Sikhote-Alin Mountains, Primorsky Krai 2012.

The trail that Arsenyev and his men took through the mountains followed a small ridgeline that demarcated the watershed between the Olga and Vladimirovka rivers before giving way to a recently-smoothed track. The track had been a narrow path used by Chinese hunters to commute between St. Olga and Vladimir Bay, but in 1906, the trail was broad enough to accommodate horse carts. Just a year earlier, during the 1905 Japanese-Russian War, the Russian cruiser *Izumrud* had beached in the shallow Vladimir Bay. The extraction of equipment from the abandoned wreck and its removal to the settlement in Olga Bay had resulted in the recent upgrading of the road. The mesmerizing sound of crickets filled the air while the group found its way through wind torn alders and willows to the sandy beach lined by granite boulders. Chinese reed thatched huts spread along the beach. These were seasonal camps of Chinese fishermen, who came here in the summer to harvest a variety of sea foods in the shallow waters of the bay. The remnants of fishing activities were easily visible. As Arsenyev's group passed along the beach, they encountered large middens of crab hulls and clam shells piled high next to the Chinese huts. Long strands of sea cabbage hung from wooden drying racks. It was not their first encounter with Chinese in the region. Throughout their journey, the group had occasionally come across abandoned camps of Chinese hunters, trappers, and ginseng collectors. In the fertile river valleys, they had encountered Chinese farmers who cultivated wheat and opium poppies.

Coast

> 'It was evident that, sooner or later, with or without the support, or even against the wish of the Russian government, both banks of this river [Amur], a desert now but rich with possibilities, as well as the immense unpopulated stretches of North Manchuria, would be invaded by Russian settlers, just as the shores of the Mississippi were colonized by the Canadian voyageurs'.
> – Peter Kropotkin, *Memoirs of a Revolutionary*

At the end of the nineteenth century, Russia was reinventing itself as a European nation with a civilizing agenda at its eastern border. Russian explorers of the Amur and Ussuri regions saw their efforts as part of a mission to civilize the indigenous populations and to free them from Chinese influence. Referring to the presence of Korean settlements in the region of the Ussuri River, the Russian explorer Nikolay Przhevalsky foresaw a cultural mission for Russian settlers to transform and regenerate 'the stubborn and immobile [...] peoples of the Asiatic East' (Bassin 1999: 193). The Russian Far East was frontier land, a newly and yet untamed acquisition of the Russian Empire.

Russia wanted to rule its Far East, but who was actually ruling it? To explore this question, I trail Vladimir K. Arsenyev, a Russian military officer and explorer who conducted extensive reconnaissance travels in the mountainous backcountry of Primorye Region at the beginning of the twentieth century. Arsenyev was born in St. Petersburg in 1872. After military schooling he served in Vladivostok's fortress from 1900 to 1906. From 1906 until 1919 he lived in Khabarovsk. In 1906, he embarked on his first expedition to the Sikhote-Alin Mountains, as partially described in the opening vignette (see also Figure 1). Two more expeditions, in 1908 and 1910, followed the first. Arsenyev published several detailed descriptions of his journeys, part narrative travelogue, and part ethnographic and geographic depiction. He became most famous for the account that portrayed his travels with Dersu Uzala, a native Udege hunter and Arsenyev's resourceful guide (Arsenyev 1923).[4] Arsenyev's mission mixed scientific discovery with military and civilizing agendas. Arsenyev was expected to map the mountain

---

[4] The Japanese filmmaker Akira Kurosawa directed and produced the movie *Dersu Uzala* in 1975, which is closely based on this travel account.

range and give a general account of the geography and local population, and to chart the terrain and count the resources of the newly acquired Maritime Region. Besides collecting this geographic information on his journeys, Arsenyev was also expected to survey the coast for potential landing points of an anticipated Japanese invasion, and to evaluate the region's prospects for future settlement by Russian colonists (Nesterenko and Kulesh 2002: 42).

Map 1. Vladimir Arsenyev's Sikhote-Alin Expedition in 1906 (map adapted from Arsenyev 1906).

Arsenyev and his group were among the first Russians to explore the remote and hardly accessible Sikhote-Alin Mountains. This territory, east of the Ussuri River and north of the Amur River, was incorporated into the Russian Empire only in 1886. During the mid-nineteenth century, Russian expansion into the Russian Far East commenced under Nikolay Muravyov-Amursky, the Governor-General of Eastern Siberia from 1847 to 1861. Shortly before, in 1821, Irkutsk had become the first capital of the Russian Far East. From this Siberian city at the southern end of Lake Baikal, the first waves of settlers moved to the East and established trading posts and small settlements along the lower Amur River as early as 1849.

In 1848, the Governor-Generalship of Eastern Siberia was divided to establish a Priamur Governor-Generalship. Beginning at the confluence of the Shilka and Argun rivers, the Priamur Governor-Generalship stretched to the shores of the Pacific with Khabarovsk as its capital. It was subdivided into two administrative regions: Amur Region (Amurskaya Oblast') with the capital of Blagoveshchensk and Primorye Region (Primorskaya Oblast') with the capital of Vladivostok. The Ussuri region remained an unofficial geographic designation without administrative status. Within post-Soviet Russia, the Priamur is further divided into the administrative units of Amurskaya Oblast', Evreiskaya Autonomous Oblast', Khabarovsky Krai, and Primorsky Krai. Of these, Primorsky Krai (Primorye or Maritime Province) remains the central focus of subsequent chapters.

Muravyov-Amursky used the pretext of the looming Crimean War to assert control of the Amur, which was technically governed by China (March 1996: 125). In 1854 and 1855, Muravyov-Amursky sent expeditionary forces down the Amur to support the settlements and ports around Kamchatka. The following years saw an increase of Russian settlements along the river. Strictly speaking, Muravyov-Amursky's settlement policy was illegal and the new Russian settlements along the Amur occupied an extra-legal situation as subjects of the Russian state within Chinese territory.

Fortunately for the Governor-General, the Chinese Empire was in a state of disarray. Weakened by the first (1842) and second (1857-58) Opium Wars, China was unable to defend its territorial integrity at its north-eastern border. Muravyov-Amursky gained the Amur peaceably: he piloted an armed steamboat to the entrance of the city of Aigun (Heihe), across the river from Blagoveshchensk, and pressed the Manchu Commander-in-Chief Yi Shan for concessions. Muravyov-Amursky's 'cannon boat politics' resulted in the Treaty of Aigun on 16 May 1858. The treaty demarcated clear territorial divisions and provided Russia with exclusive use rights of the territories that had been lost to Imperial China under the Treaty of Nerchinsk in 1689. The Treaty of Aigun set the backdrop for Chinese and Russian economic activities in the Amur Region for the years to come and clarified the citizen status of the local population. Due to the political and economic importance of the treaty, I cite it here in full:

1.
The left bank of the Amur River, starting from the Argun River to the estuary of the Amur River, shall be the property of the Russian State. The right bank, down to the Ussuri River, shall be the property of the Tai-jing State [China]. Places and lands from the Ussuri River to the sea, until the border between the two states is established,

shall be owned jointly by the Tai-jing and Russian States. Only ships owned by the Tai-jing and Russian States shall be allowed on the Amur, Sungari and Ussuri Rivers. Ships belonging to any other states are prohibited from taking these rivers. The Manchu people living on the left bank of the Amur River, from the Zeya River southwards to the village of Hormolzin, shall remain forever at their places of residence under the governance of the Manchu authorities and be protected from abuse by the Russian people.

2.

To foster mutual friendship between subjects of the two states those living along the Ussuri, Amur and Sungari Rivers shall be allowed to trade with each other while the governors on both banks shall encourage trade between the two states.

3.

What Muravyov-Amursky, Governor-General by appointment to the Russian State, and Yi Shan, Amur Commander-in-Chief by appointment to the Tai-jing State, have established by common sense shall be effected to the letter and be inviolable forever. Muravyov-Amursky, Governor-General of the Russian State has written [this document] in the Russian and Manchu languages and given it to Yi Shan, Commander-in-Chief of the Tai-jing State. Yi Shan, Commander-in-Chief of the Tai-jing State, has written it in the Manchu and Mongolian languages and given it to Muravyov-Amursky, Governor-General of the Russian State. What has been written here shall be made known to frontier people of the two states. The city of Aigun, 16 May 1858 (cited in Trovimov 1992: 20).

This document and the Treaty of Beijing, which followed two years later on 2 November 1860 and ratified the territorial expansion of Russia east of the Ussuri River, marked the end of a long dispute of Russia's role and expansion in the Far East (see Figure 2). Russia slowly consolidated its power in the Amur and Ussuri regions bordering the Chinese Empire. During the 1860s, an increasing number of Cossack groups and Russian settlers moved into the Amur and Primorye Regions and soon outnumbered the local indigenous population.

The opening of China after the Opium Wars, and Japan's opening to Western trade in the mid-nineteenth century, promised a bright commercial future for the Russian Far East, with the Amur River as its main artery and the town of Nikolaevsk, at the river's mouth, as its hub (Bassin 1999: 146). It was a time for dreamers and visionaries. For instance, having the successful colonization of the American West as a role model in mind, the late nineteenth century anarchist Peter Kropotkin compared the Cossacks in the Russian Far East with the Canadian voyageurs on the Mississippi (Kropotkin 1971: 205). Muravyov-Amursky himself referred to Nikolaevsk as the San Francisco of the Russian Far East, a claim Nikita Khrushchev would make again in 1954 in reference to Vladivostok (Bassin 1999: 170).

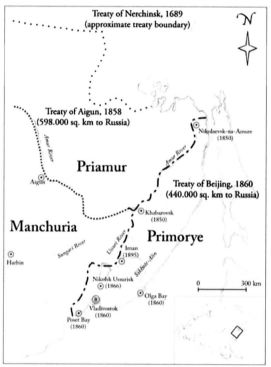

Map 2. Amur and Primorye Regions in the nineteenth century.

Taiga

'Between 1911 and 1917 no Russian village in the Ussuri and Priamur region existed without a Chinese trading post'.
 – Vladimir Arsenyev, *Russen und Chinesen in Ostsibirien*

Sikhote-Alin, November 1906, Valley of the Iman. Winter had approached swift and cold. The forest was barren and the ferns blackened by frost. Snow had fallen. Arsenyev and his group had boarded a small water craft to float the Iman, a fast flowing river which cuts snakelike through the western slopes of the Sikhote-Alin Mountains. The Iman drains into the Ussuri River at the settlement of Iman.[5] On their journey downriver, the expedition passed small settlements of native Udeges, abandoned fish camps, and occasionally Chinese outposts. After several days, growing ice on the river had trapped the group's boat and they had to continue their journey on land. After travelling through deep snow and low on supplies, the group finally reached the Chinese settlement of Sjanschichesa on 6 November. The Chinese were puzzled by the appearance of the small Russian expeditionary force, and after some initial confusion the group was finally hosted by a Chinese man named Litankui, the local *zaitun* (landlord) who controlled the fur trade with the native population in this part of the valley. Arsenyev felt uneasy with the boisterous demeanour of the landlord. Despite Litankui's attempts to soothe his concerns, Arsenyev stayed suspicious, and rightly so. 'I woke up during the night after somebody shook my shoulders: I quickly rose and saw Dersu standing next to me. He signalled me to be quiet and told me the following: Litankui had offered him money to convince me of another travel route. He did not want us to go to the Udege in Wagunbe and planned to give us special guides and porters, which should divert us around the natives' yurts' (Arsenyev 1924: 402).

The next day, the group continued travelling on their planned route. Steep mountains rose on both sides of the river. Several Chinese farms were spread on large patches of cleared forest along the river, and Arsenyev spotted well-armoured Chinese. According to plan, they soon arrived at the native settlement of Wagunbe. Immediately, a group of Udeges approached Arsenyev and his men, first with suspicion, and then asking him why he had spent the night in the Chinese landlord's house. After a short conversation, it became clear that the natives were not on good terms with the landlord. Arsenyev described it thus: 'A whole tragedy was taking its course. The Chinese Litankui was the *zaitun*, the most powerful man and landlord in the Iman Valley. He inhumanely exploited the natives and punished them cruelly if they did not bring in the required numbers of furs within the time limit assigned. He had ruined many families, raped the women, abducted children and sold them off for money owed to him' (Arsenyev 1924: 404).

The Chinese landlord had established a system of debt peonage in the valley and extracted fur tribute from the local native population. Some of the Udeges protested and had sent two emissaries to Khabarovsk to complain at the Governor's office. As a result of their action, they had been severely punished by the landlord who meanwhile had gotten word of their plea for

---

[5] On the first Russian maps of the region, the Iman River is called *Niman*, the Manchurian word for mountain goat. The Udege called the river 'Ima', the Chinese added the suffix – *che* (river) and called it 'Imache' (Arsenyev 1924: 386). Today, the Iman River is called Bolshaya Ussurka, and the settlement of Iman is Dal'nerechensk.

help from the Russian authorities. Arsenyev and his small group of Cossacks were helpless. After promising to arrange for a military detachment from the Russian settlement of Iman, Arsenyev's group continued its journey through the valley. Cedar trees contrasted in dark green with the snow covered hillsides. At the boundary between deciduous and mixed forest, the group reached the village of Kartun at the end of the day:

> The sun had just disappeared behind the horizon, the rays still playing in the clouds, casting a pale light on the landscape. Further away from the river Chinese houses [*fansa*] became visible. They were hidden among the spruce trees, as if to protect them from the eyes of the passing traveller [...] I have nowhere seen richer Chinese houses. They were situated along the right side of the River and in terms of their size looked more like factories then dwellings (Arsenyev 1924: 409-10).

Arsenyev counted 43 houses, 575 men, 3 women, and 9 children; Kartun was the largest Chinese settlement along the Iman River. At this point, Arsenyev and his group were met with outright suspicion by the Chinese settlers, and denied any form of hospitality. Words of his travel had spread through the valley. Despite travelling on Russian territory, Arsenyev could hardly exert any influence as an official representative. He described the backcountry as Chinese land, 'In 1906, Russian rule was limited to the Ussuri Valley and the coast up to St. Olga Bay. The rest of the country was under Chinese control' (Arsenyev 1926: 73).

At the end of the nineteenth century, the population of the Amur and Primorye Regions of the Russian Far East was a diverse ethnic mix. Russian settlers, Chinese merchants, Korean farmers, Japanese barbers, Manchurian brigands, and indigenous hunters lived side-by-side in the river valleys and forested mountains of Russia's maritime frontier. As in other cases during the colonization of Siberia and the Russian Far East, the first Russian settlers to arrive were bands of Cossacks who spearheaded the settlement along the Amur and Ussuri rivers. The first *kazachestvo* (Cossack collective) was founded in 1859 along the Amur River. Ten years later, in 1869, a second followed along the Ussuri River. Despite their military prowess, the agricultural success of Cossack settlements was rather meagre – Chinese and Koreans were frequently employed as fieldhands and many unsuccessful Cossack settlers turned to brigandage (Stephan 1994: 63).

The regular migration of Russian peasants came in three waves. The first one, between 1859 and 1882, focused on the Amur Region. Attracted by free land allocation approximately 14,000 peasant migrants arrived during that time in the Russian Far East (Stephan 1994: 64). Isolated from the Russian heartland and plagued by frequent attacks on their settlements by

Chinese marauders, the so-called *khunkhusy* (lit. red beards), Russian settlers had to defend the newly acquired territory while beginning to farm in an unfamiliar region. The second phase of settlers arrived between 1882 and 1907. This time, newly established transportation corridors allowed for greater numbers of settlers. In 1901, the Chinese Eastern Railroad was completed, and regular maritime transport from Odessa to Vladivostok (in 46 days) was becoming more popular. The new water route led to a high percentage (64 per cent) of Ukrainians among the 234,000 peasants who had migrated to the Far East by 1907 (Stephan 1994: 65). The last phase, from 1908 to 1917, brought another 300,000 settlers to the region. This influx of settlers created a vital economic environment. John Stephan argued that the Primorye Region 'was one of the most economically dynamic provinces of Imperial Russia during the last decade of tsarist rule' (Stephan 1994: 67). Russian peasants settled in the fertile floodplains north of Vladivostok and along the Ussuri and Amur rivers. An exception was the coastal settlement of St. Olga, which although it was among the earliest founded Russian settlements, had already declined at the time of Arsenyev's visit in 1906.

The Russian Cossacks and peasants advanced into a region that was moderately occupied by Chinese and Korean settlers. Between 1845 and 1850, the Primorye was inhabited by a sparse Chinese population; there were farms and villages in the Udege area, Hei-Shan-Wei (Vladivostok), and Shim-pun (Kotka). Richard Andree, a German traveller who visited the region in 1867, estimated the number of Chinese to be about 1,000 (Andree 1867: 219). That changed rapidly in the decades following the Russian accession. Several push and pull factors led to an increase in the number of Chinese settlers. During the early 1860s, Chinese immigration increased mainly because the rebellion in Manchuria during 1864-66 led to a rise of Chinese refugees in the region; and because the steady stream of Russian settlers into the region made it increasingly lucrative for Chinese merchants to establish trading posts in Russian settlements. In the 1890s, the construction of the Trans-Siberian Railway and gold mining in the Amur basin attracted manual labour from China (Siegelbaum 1978: 311). During these decades, Chinese agricultural settlements spread quickly along the Zeya and Suifun river valleys and on the Khanka plain. The Treaty of Beijing, which finally settled the border issue between China and Russia, declared that all Chinese in Ussuri region remained under China's jurisdiction as a tributary to the Bogdychan of Outer Mongolia. The political status of the indigenous population remained unclear; nevertheless, Chinese farmers and traders considered themselves subjects of the Chinese Empire.

The number of Chinese rose rapidly to over 40,000 in the 1890s.[6] The aforementioned special political status of Chinese nationals in Priamur and Primorye Region provinces led to the creation of several semi-autonomous settlements with a high degree of self-government. Arsenyev stated that, 'between 1911 and 1917 no Russian village in the Ussuri and Priamur region existed without a Chinese trading post' (Arsenyev 1926: 178). For the Ussuri region, which included the city of Vladivostok, Khabarovsk, Ussurisk, and Nikolaevsk, Arsenyev's demographic calculations of Chinese based on local municipal and police registers between 1905 and 1910 counted 130,000 merchants, 200,000 farm workers, and 15,000 hunters and trappers (Arsenyev 1926: 58).

At the end of the nineteenth century, three different groups of Chinese migrants can be distinguished: merchants, farmers and field hands, and hunters and trappers.[7] Economic activities of Chinese migrants were characterized by a high degree of seasonality in the Ussuri region – farming during the summer months and fur trapping during the fall and winter. At the beginning of fall, sable hunters came in large numbers from Vladivostok, Nikolsk, Khabarovsk, and China to the Ussuri region (Arsenyev 1926: 55).

Chinese farmers were referred to as *mansy* (or Chinese *man-zhi*). This was originally a term used for the mixed population of Han Chinese and local tribes in southern China, but was later applied to settlers in China's borderlands. The *mansy* did not built compact villages, but rather settled in loose accumulations of individual farms. These farms, called *fansy* in Russian (sg. *fansa*), consisted of a main building and several smaller, outlying farm sheds. The walls of the main building were clay-plastered twig, the roof was straw or reed, and there was a single wooden chimney. The economic unit was centred on the *zaitun* (landlord), who together with partners and workers tended to the surrounding fields. On a seasonal basis and employed for a limited time, groups of migrant workers tilled the fields for particular landlords. The Chinese placed their settlements strategically in the mountain river valleys where fertile soil allowed for profitable agriculture (mainly wheat and opium), and at the same time provided close access to indigenous hunting and fur trapping areas. The storehouses of Chinese fur merchants were normally situated at the confluences of rivers.

---

[6] High mobility of the population and unhindered cross-border travel from Manchuria make it difficult to calculate accurately, but all estimates of the Chinese population in the Russian Far East show a rapid increase at the end of the nineteenth century: 6,000 (1878), 14,500 (1885), 40,000 (1890s) (Landgraf 1989: 506).

[7] V. V. Grave, an official representative of the Russian Foreign Ministry, distinguished three different groups of Chinese on his journey through the Priamur Region in 1910: (1) merchants, (2) seasonal workers, (3) hunters and gatherers, criminals, and brigands (Grave 1912: 27).

In the early years of Russian rule, Chinese farmers were renowned for being more successful than the Russian colonists (Arsenyev 1926: 60). For instance, Wirt Gerrare, a British writer who travelled the region in 1902, noted, 'It is the Chinaman above all who stoops the *petite culture* of the spade, and raises vegetables as though his farm were a garden [...] He can raise more on a rood of ground than a Russian farmer will grow on an acre' (cited in Siegelbaum 1978: 314). Chinese farmers supplied produce to the steadily growing settlements of Blagoveshchensk, Khabarovsk, and Vladivostok. The Priamur was also a major recipient of Chinese agricultural exports, like soy and grain, which were shipped into the territory through Vladivostok. Between 1911 and 1917, Russia imported from China nine million kilograms of soy and seventeen million kilograms of grain (Wishnik 2005: 70).

The Ussuri and Amur regions presented opportunities for a range of different venturers – brigands, ginseng collectors, gold diggers, fugitives, and alcohol smugglers (Lee 1970). Brigands from Manchuria, the *khunkhusy*, operated mainly along the coast, yet Russian settlers along the Amur and Ussuri rivers were also frequently targeted by bandits who crossed the border from China (Arsenyev 1926: 149). The gold strikes along the Amur and later on the Island of Askhod attracted Chinese gold diggers, so that between 1890 and 1916, 20 to 40 per cent of the annual gold production was sent to China, while Cossacks profiteered from the export as middlemen (Stephan 1994: 73). The harvest and gathering of plants and animals for culinary and medicinal purposes was another profitable activity for many Chinese seasonal workers. Arsenyev estimated the annual number of Chinese ginseng collectors in the Ussuri region to be around 30,000 at the beginning of the twentieth century (Arsenyev 1914: 123). Along the coast, Chinese *trepang* (sea cucumber) collectors were also highly active. Arsenyev's observations led him to denounce the ease by which Chinese harvested local bio-resources. He described their general attitude in the following words, 'Why dig up the ore from underneath the ground, if the great richness is scattered on the surface, where one only has to pick it up' (Arsenyev 1914: 121).

Plate 3. Sea cucumber (*trepang*), wild ginseng (*zhen'shen'*), and antler velvet (*panty*), clockwise from top (in Arsenyev 1926: 120).

Koreans, who started to migrate in small groups into Priamur at the beginning of the 1860s, constituted another ethnic group that had an impact on the region. Officially, it was forbidden to leave the Korean Kingdom, but bad harvests, a steady population increase, and autocratic repression forced many peasants to flee northwards into Russian territory. In 1869, heavy rainstorms destroyed a large percentage of Korea's harvest, which resulted in the immediate immigration of at least 7,000 Koreans into the southern Ussuri region (Landgraf 1989: 520). Several Korean settlements were founded in the south of the Maritime Region around Poset Bay, and along the Suifun River north-west of Vladivostok. Like the Chinese farmers, Korean farmers supplied Russian settlements with agricultural products; millet and beans came from around Poset and Koreans harvested kelp along the coast. The Russian government encouraged this early Korean immigration for several reasons. Koreans were seen to counterbalance the influence of the Chinese; they were popular among Russian consumers because they sold crops at a good price, and they provided welcome cheap labour (Landgraf 1989: 519). Koreans were also known for their willingness to assimilate; they learned Russian and baptised their children in the

Orthodox Church. After 1884, one-quarter of the Koreans had Russian citizenship. Korean immigration into Primorye swelled after the Japanese annexation of Korea in 1910. In 1900, there had been 24,000; by 1914 there were 64,000 (Stephan 1994: 79).

Korean migrant workers were organized in brotherhoods of 100-150 people, who entered work contracts as a group and were paid under a common account. They worked mostly as miners, lumberjacks, gold washers, and boatmen. In 1894, ten per cent of Primorye's population was Korean (Landgraf 1989: 666). Korean communities had a form of local self-government in that village headmen and elders guaranteed a certain degree of political autonomy. Yet, this self-governance raised suspicion among Russian officials. For instance, Military Governor Pavel F. Unterberger (1888-97), who was also the *ataman* (supreme military commander) of the Ussuri Cossacks, accused the Koreans of 'creating a state within a state' (cited in Stephan 1994: 79).

Prior to the arrival of the Chinese, Koreans, or Russians, the remote river valleys and mountains of the Maritime Region had been settled as early as the fourteenth century by Manchu-Tungus peoples. At the turn of the twentieth century, the total of the various groups (notably Nanais, Udege, Orochi) numbered approximately 10,000 people.[8] Chinese cultural influence on the Manchu-Tungus groups was strongest among the Nanais, with whom the Chinese had established trading links in the fourteenth century (Forsyth 1992: 212). The Nanais had traded furs, ginseng, and antlers for textiles, guns, flour, rice, tea, and tobacco. The Nanais lived mostly along the middle Amur, Ussuri, and Sungari rivers. In addition to fishing, trapping, and hunting, the Nanais domesticated pigs and chickens, and cultivated fields of millet and maize. Less sedentary groups lived in the Sikhote-Alin Mountains. The Orochis lived in the northern reaches, concentrated around the mouth of the Tunim River. Mostly hunters, the Orochis only began to cultivate gardens and small fields at the beginning of the twentieth century (Levin and Potapov 1964: 750). The southern part of the Sikhote-Alin Mountains, from the coast to the Ussuri River, was populated by Udege fishing and hunting communities. Fur trapping (mostly sable and black squirrel) for Chinese middlemen had become a dominant economic activity among the Udeges at the end of the nineteenth century.

Before the Russians established themselves in Primorye, Chinese traders and settlers dominated the region and had monopolized the trade with the indigenous population, which left little room for small Russian businesses. Chinese merchants had established a system of debt peonage and

---

[8] The 1926-27 Soviet All-Union Census recorded 5,757 Nanais; 1,357 Udeges; and 405 Orochi (Levin and Potapov 1964: 694, 737,750).

exploitation, forcing indigenous communities into compliance with the trader's demands (Landgraf 1989: 506). Renowned and feared for their exploitative activities, these Chinese merchants were known among local groups as the 'spiders of the taiga' (von Zepelin 1911: 63), a metaphor which also alluded to their widespread economic networks. Chinese hegemony in the Ussuri region was based on a highly organized economic and political structure that encompassed Chinese farmers, traders, and trappers alike. Arsenyev's inquiry into and description of Chinese self-government in the Sikhote-Alin Mountains presents a revelatory picture of the inner workings of these structures.

Plate 4. Russian game wardens destroying huts of Chinese poachers (in Arsenyev 1926: 98).

The commodity flow in and out of the country was strictly controlled by different organizational layers (see Figure 3). On the lowest level were indigenous trappers and hunters or working brigades of Chinese fur trappers, ginseng collectors, or deer hunters who were supervised by a local headman. On the next level was a district landlord, the *zaitun*, who controlled the commodity flow in and out of the respective valley district. The *zaitun* was also a middleman between the district and the next level of organization, which was a Chinese trading society or guild in one of the larger cities. The umbrella organization was a trading house of a secret society based out of China, namely Shanghai.[9] To protect their interests and to control native trading partners, the Chinese trading societies had their own intelligence and enforcement service (Arsenyev 1926: 180).

In addition to what he drew from observations and conversations with Chinese, Russian, and indigenous people, Arsenyev based his description of Chinese self-rule on several documents he obtained in the course of his travels. In 1906, Arsenyev acquired two scrolls containing information on a valley district court meeting and a collection of statutes governing the district's Chinese community. The documents dated from 1898 and detailed a meeting that occurred every three years to re-evaluate and, if necessary, rewrite existing laws that governed the constituency of the *pao-tou* (hunters' federation) which controlled the district. The hunters' federation was subdivided into several units, each composed of five to sixteen hunters specialized in deer hunting, fur trapping, and ginseng collecting. The court meeting was attended by a group of judges, prosecutors, jurors, and attorneys. A central role in the court was played by the *da-je* (village elders) who acted as jurors in the proceedings. The scrolls give a detailed account of a law codex governing the economic and political life of the Chinese-controlled valley. Geared to protect the sovereignty and property of the federation, the codex also included statutes that explicitly protected the economic monopoly of Chinese ginseng and fur traders (Arsenyev 1926: 161). In addition, the codex included specific laws of hospitality for Chinese farmers and merchants and provisions for engaging in hostility any strangers who travelled through the territory. The penal code detailed rules for monetary compensation and included draconian punishments such as flogging, drowning, and burying alive. The laws protected the control and monopoly of the local landlord: they secured a monopoly on gambling; prescribed the death penalty for theft of sable, fur, and ginseng; placed all hunting, trapping, and trading activities under the strict control of the landlord; pre-empted illegal trade among members, non-members, and natives alike; set taxes for imports into the valley district; prohibited the formation of alternative secret societies or brotherhoods; and strictly regulated native economic activities (Arsenyev 1926: 177).

---

[9] At the beginning of the twentieth century, Chinese Chambers of Commerce replaced the secret society trading houses (Crissman 1975: 290).

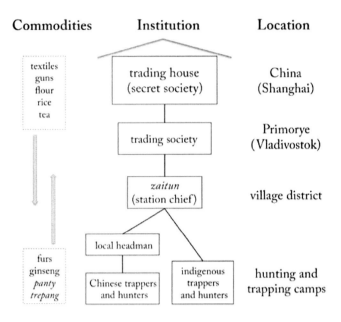

Figure 1. Organization of Chinese trading guilds and commodity flows during the nineteenth century, Primorye Region.

The Chinese district societies in the valleys of the Sikhote-Alin Mountains were part of a larger system of Chinese self-government in the Amur and Primorye Regions that was modelled after Chinese secret societies of the nineteenth century.[10] Larger Chinese societies in the cities, comparable to trading guilds, complemented the district societies on a higher organizational level. Membership of the trading societies in the cities included wealthy and influential local Chinese as well as the majority of Chinese merchants. Village societies were thus supplemented by trading societies in the cities, a fact that made Arsenyev suspicious, 'At a closer look, we find a compulsive cohesion [among the Chinese] and inclusion into a larger system, which does not seem conspicuous for the outsider' (Arsenyev 1926: 178). He suspected that the three Chinese societies in the Primorye Region, based in Vladivostok, Khabarovsk, and Nikolsk Ussuriski (modern-day Ussurisk)

---

[10] 'Overseas Chinese', especially merchants, regularly joined secret societies for protection and trade benefits. Secret societies originated in China in the seventeenth century as a form of opposition to the Manchu warriors who had dethroned the Ming Dynasty. Anti-governmental (i.e. anti-Ch'ing) in nature, the original societies were based on the ideas of brotherhood and fictive kinship (Chin 1990: 16).

were orchestrated by an umbrella organization located in Shanghai, which set prices for raw materials and controlled the trade to Vladivostok. Arsenyev described the main functions of Chinese trading societies as, 'investigation and prosecution of criminal behaviour among themselves, the levying of taxes to strengthen their own means, the support of economic trade goals and the continuation of the equilibrium of the economic fight against the Russians' (Arsenyev 1926: 180). Arsenyev's analysis was accurate: one of the main functions of the societies was to control and organize the Chinese trade with the Russian Far East, especially by establishing a trading monopoly with the indigenous population in the backcountry.[11]

The lack of Russian state control in Priamur and Primorye Region, especially in the remote areas of the Sikhote-Alin Mountains, along with the provisions stated in the Treaty of Aigun created autonomous enclaves that were essentially under Chinese control.[12] Furthermore, the profitable economic activities of Chinese trading guilds in the Russian Far East raised the suspicion of Russian authorities and led to several measures to curb their widespread activities. Arsenyev, for instance, accused these societies as constituting, 'a state inside the state [...] independent outposts of China's secret foreign policy disguised as trading and mutual aid societies' (Arsenyev 1926: 181-82). This might be an exaggeration, but nevertheless gives an insight into the extent of the perceived threats to Russian control over the territory. Officially, the Chinese societies were outlawed by Russia in 1897, yet existed at least until 1917. The Russian Revolution, which continued until 1923 in the Russian Far East, led to the final dissolution of Chinese merchant houses and trading societies, as outlined in the next section.

---

[11] The monopolization of trade was a central objective of Chinese secret societies throughout Asia. For instance, the main goal of Chinese secret societies in the European-controlled Malaysian Straits Settlements (Malacca) was the monopolization of specific key occupations. Chinese secret societies existed in Malacca under British and Dutch rule as early as 1825 and were intrinsically tied to the 'indirect rule' policy of the colonial powers that encouraged self-rule through such secret societies (Fong 1981: 21).

[12] Chinese secret societies in Asian port cities under European control, i.e. the French Concession of Shanghai, fulfilled a range of functions, from security providers to sources of real political power. Brian G. Martin argued that 'secret societies were resilient social organizations that not only could adapt successfully to the complex environment of a modernizing urban society but could emerge as powerful sources within that society' (Martin 1996: 3).

City

> 'Vladivostok is far away, but nevertheless this city is ours'.
> – Vladimir I. Lenin, 1922 (quoted in *Pravda* 1964)

In 1872, Russia transferred its main civilian and military port on the Pacific (i.e. the base of the Siberian Fleet) southward from Nikolaevsk (at the mouth of the Amur River) to Vladivostok.

At the time, Vladivostok had been established for only twelve years as a small free port and military outpost of the Russian Empire. Nevertheless, many things had changed in this short amount of time.

Before 1860, Vladivostok's bay had been a popular catching ground for sea cucumbers, hence its Chinese name – *Hai-Shan-Wei* (Sea Cucumber Bay). During the summer, Chinese fishermen set up their camps along the shores of the bay and retreated at the beginning of winter with their valuable catch to Chinese ports. The Russian occupation of the natural harbour, which began with the arrival of the three mast steamboat *Manchur* in the summer of 1860, started the first permanent settlement. Under Russian rule, Sea Cucumber Bay was renamed the Golden Horn Bay in an allusion to Constantinople's Golden Horn. The bay was thought of as the *Bosfor Vostochnyy* (Eastern Bosporus) because it represented new access to world trade. Routes through the Far East were envisioned as a replacement for the blocked access to the Mediterranean after Russia's defeat in the Crimean War (Zabel 1904: 126).

In the twelve years between 1860-72, barracks, an officers' club, bathhouse, workshops, and storehouses were built. These were soon followed by additional barracks, a hospital, and a small Orthodox church. On the hills, which surround the bay like a chaplet, heavy cannons were entrenched behind earth walls. Russia was aware of the precarious location of this harbour. The name speaks for itself – Vladivostok means 'to rule the East'. The town's status as a free port soon attracted civilian entrepreneurs, attentive to the peculiar strategic position of the harbour. Vladivostok was Russia's new gate to the Pacific Ocean. Most of the newly founded settlements and military outposts in eastern Siberia were more easily accessible from the sea side than by the long overland routes. Two young entrepreneurs from Hamburg, Gustav Kunst and Gustav Ludewig Albers, were among the first to understand this fact. For decades to come, their business house would play a central role in the economic life of Vladivostok and the Russian Far East (Deeg 1996).

The settlement grew and the foundation of a city was soon laid. Private houses, governmental buildings, a sawmill, five brickyards, a brewery, and a grain mill rose along the narrow but even stretch of ground between the bay and the surrounding hills. By 1872, Vladivostok was more than ready for its new role. A year earlier, Copenhagen's Great Northern Telegraph Society had laid an underwater cable from Vladivostok to Nagasaki and further on to Shanghai. During the same year, a telegraph line across Russia was completed, running from Vladivostok, through Siberia, to St. Petersburg. Vladivostok was already well-connected for communication as the ships arrived en masse.

The first ship to arrive was the steam corvette *Amerika*, carrying Admiral A. E. Crown, the commander of the Siberian Fleet. It was not the ship's first journey into these waters. In 1859, under the direction of Nikolay Muravyov-Amursky, the Governor-General of Eastern Siberia, the corvette had participated in the surveying and mapping of Peter the Great Bay in the search for a suitable port for the nascent Siberian Fleet (Sushkov 1958: 25). The *Amerika* was soon followed by the larger frigate *Svetlana*, which carried on board an even more important dignitary, the Grand Duke Aleksey Aleksandrovich. Throughout 1872 and 1873, the remaining 20 ships in the Siberian Fleet arrived.[13]

As in its earlier history as a sea cucumber harvest point, Vladivostok was a multi-ethnic melting pot in the early 1900s. Chinese, Koreans, and Japanese intermingled with Russians, Europeans, and Americans in the harbour, on the streets, and in the parlours of the steadily growing port city. Especially during the Russian Civil War, the city was a multinational melting pot and place of encounter between East and West. Vladivostok was the last stand of the Whites (the troops loyal to the dethroned tsar) and a large contingent of refugees fled from Vladivostok to Shanghai in 1923. Konstantin Kharnsky described in 1919 the city of Vladivostok with an almost surrealist staccato of words: 'Morphine, cocaine, prostitution, blackmail, sudden riches and ruin, dashing autos, a cinematic flow of faces, literary cabals, bohemian lifestyles, coups and coutercoups, Mexican political morals. Parliaments, dictators, speeches from balconies, newspapers from Shanghai and San Francisco, "Intervention girls", uniforms from every kingdom, empire, republic, monarchist club, leftist rallies, complete isolation from Moscow' (cited in Stephan 1994: 126). Another traveller, Mary Gaunt, who arrived from Harbin, China in 1914, was equally astonished by Vladivostok's cosmopolitan character: 'I thought all the races of the earth met in Kharbin, but ... this port does run it very close. There were Japanese, Chinese, Russians, Koreans in horsehair hats and white garments; there were

---

[13] This period of Vladivostok's maritime history is reflected in the renaming of Vladivostok's main street, which has had three different names throughout its history: first it was Ulitsa Amerikanskaya, then followed Svetlanskaya, during Soviet times it was renamed as Leninskaya, and finally since the early 1990s it has been Svetlanskaya again.

aboriginal natives of the country and there were numberless Germans' (Gaunt 1919: 157).

Vladivostok's population grew rapidly from 510 in 1868 to 45,300 in 1903 (Pozniak 2004: 223). The city's peculiar geographic position made for an ideal trading hub that attracted a variety of European and Asian traders and merchants. On the one hand, the city was a centre for the export of local resources to Chinese ports. On the other hand, Vladivostok's port functioned as an import hub for overseas commodities destined for consumption mainly by the steadily growing Russian settler population in the Far East backcountry. These economic opportunities lured many international venturers to the city. In 1897, approximately 40 per cent of Vladivostok's total population was of foreign nationality.[14]

The growing Japanese influence in Manchuria at the turn of the century led to an influx of Japanese merchants and workers in the service industry. They worked especially as barbers, carpenters, launderers, and photographers.[15] But, as in the backcountry, the Chinese dominated the city's economic life. The city depended heavily on unskilled Chinese labour and the services of Chinese traders (Richardson 1995: 53). V. V. Grave, an official representative of the Russian Foreign Ministry, estimated that more than 50,000 Chinese, the majority of them unskilled workers, lived and worked in Vladivostok.[16] Unskilled labour was of particular demand in the port area and in the city's construction business.[17] A representative in the city duma of Vladivostok exclaimed already in 1884, 'The Chinese play such an important role in the life of our city that their removal at this point would put great hardship on our [Russian] citizens. The Chinese are horse traders, sellers of hay and oats, craftsmen, gardeners, fishermen, and grocers' (cited in Landgraf 1989: 604). Indeed, Chinese economic dominance was especially visible among small-scale traders; in 1910, they managed almost 80 per cent of the local small stores (Grave 1912: 33).

The Russian authorities tried to control the influx of Chinese traders, which they saw as a competition for the nascent Russian merchants, with only meagre success. Registration and taxation laws enacted at the beginning

---

[14] Of the 12,577 foreign residents counted by the first Russian census in 1897, 167 were European, 9,878 Chinese, 1,249 Japanese, and 1,283 Korean (Pozniak 2004: 223).

[15] The Japanese Army recruited spies on a regular basis from among Vladivostok's Japanese population. Japanese prostitutes (the so-called rice ladies) and brothels (the first opened in 1883) functioned as espionage havens for data and shelter (Stephan 1994: 77).

[16] Chinese were particularly popular as hired workers, mainly due to their willingness to work for half of a Russian's wage (Grave 1912: 125).

[17] In 1900, 90 per cent of the workers in Vladivostok's shipyards were Chinese. In addition, contractors recruited Chinese coolies for the Amur goldfields and railroad construction (Stephan 1994: 73).

of the twentieth century are an indirect sign of the felt need to regulate coastal boat travel. Vladivostok's governor reacted with the introduction of landing permits for Chinese vessels and a ban on the transport of Chinese without valid passports on steamships. The policy was not very effective, largely because most of the goods and passengers travelled on sailing boats. Looking from one of Vladivostok's numerous hills Arsenyev observed that, 'on clear days the water is shimmering up to the horizon with sails. Almost exclusively Chinese schooners, sloops, and junks' (Arsenyev 1926: 178). Another problem was that Chinese ships, mostly smaller sailing boats, did not unload in the main harbour of Vladivostok, but in Millionka. Millionka was the city's Chinese quarter and had a population of up to 20,000 Chinese at the beginning of the twentieth century (Ivashenko et al. 1997: 301). Russians were almost completely excluded from Millionka's trading activities, and thus most of the imported goods from China arrived unaccounted into the Primorye. With its winding alleys, hidden backyards, street markets, gambling houses, and opium dens, Chinese-dominated Millionka was a constant problem for Vladivostok's Russian authorities. In 1910, V.V. Grave and the chief of the city's Health Department visited Millionka. Grave reported:

> I was astonished by the picture that opened in front of my eyes. Filth, horrible stench, overcrowding, I was reminded of the worst quarters of the Chinese part of Beijing [...] The Chinese masses constantly dash about in the alleys, scream, trade, eat, and follow all their natural needs. In the evening, all this is illuminated by paper lanterns and presents itself as a picturesque painting, as if the traces of filth had vanished in the dark (Grave 1912: 126).

In addition to posing sanitary problems for the city, Millionka was a criminal hotspot. Thousands of illegal Chinese residents lived in Vladivostok at the beginning of the twentieth century. For instance, in May 1912, Vladivostok's town council was informed by the city police of 9,500 arrested persons during the first half of the year – 5,300 of the detained were Chinese without valid documents.[18] Passport forgery was rampant. The local newspaper *Dal'ekaya Okraina* stated in 1910 that 'the majority of Chinese live without any passports or with forged passports that are sold on the Semenovskii Bazaar [another name for Millionka] for 50-75 Kopeks, as anybody knows'.[19] To control the criminality among the residents of the Millionka district, the city's authorities increasingly reverted to Chinese police patrols. Although this measure of indirect-rule relieved the city police from patrol

---

[18] Vladivostok City Police Report, May 1912, 'Muzei Vladivostokskaya Krepost' (Vladivostok Fortress Museum), accessed in the museum, 30 November 2004.

[19] 'Bespasportnye Kitaytsy', *Dal'ekaya Okraina* 921 (1910), 4.

duties in Millionka, it led to the formation of a semi-autonomous Chinese police force that was chronically plagued by corruption.[20] Despite all measures, the numbers of Chinese grew steadily. In 1916, almost 40,000 Chinese lived in Vladivostok, composing almost half of the city's total population (Pozniak 2004: 223).

At the beginning of the twentieth century, the Russian discourse about Chinese migrants was framed by two catchphrases: *zheltaya opasnost'* (yellow peril) and *zheltyy vopros* (yellow question). A major problem for the Russian authorities was the economic competition that was represented by Chinese workers and traders. Grave stated in his report that important key occupations (retail, fishing, carpentry, smithing, and dock work) were completely in the hands of Chinese and represented Vladivostok's *khronicheskiy nedug* (chronic disease) (Grave 1912: 232). The causes for this 'disease' were obvious to him – under representation of the Russian population, a weak border, and too many Chinese. The cure was equally obvious: forced Russian settlement, infrastructural improvements, incentives for Russian and European investments, increased border security, and a strengthening of the local administration (Grave 1912: 233). Grave concluded his account with pessimistic undertones, 'During my travels in the Amur Region, one could hear that all the Russians went bankrupt; and to the question of who got rich one would receive a stereotypical answer: the Chinese' (Grave 1912: 235).

The situation of Chinese traders in the Russian Far East changed dramatically after the Russian Revolution. Trading houses were closed and Chinese property was confiscated. Many Chinese left the city voluntarily in the following years. Drastic measures were proposed to remove those who remained. For instance, Arsenyev reported to the office of the Far Eastern VKP (All-Russian Communist Party) in 1928:

> We don't have time to turn people into Soviet citizens and wait until they change their opinions and characteristics. With our close connections to Manchuria and Korea we have a danger of conflict on our borders with the Korean and Chinese people. The struggle against this includes the possibility of bringing many people from the European part of the USSR and Western Siberia without regard to their nationality. But the Koreans or Chinese must be resettled to the center of our country, and/ or to the West and North of the Amur (cited in Khisamutdinov 1993: 119).

Nine years later, Arsenyev's recommendation was rigidly enforced. Korean displacement started in September 1937. Under the pretext of Japanese

---

[20] Aleksey Buyakov, 'Kashdy kitaets mechtal' stat' politseiskii', *Vladivostok*, 19 April 1999.

espionage, Korean settlements were cordoned off, the entire population arrested, and subsequently deported to Central Asia. The *Kitayskaya Operatsiya* (Chinese Operation) followed. Conducted by the NKVD (People's Commissariat for Internal Affairs), the operation's goal was to arrest all Chinese in the Russian Far East and forcefully deport them to China. The operation was completed in three rounds – December 1937, February 1938, and March 1938. Vladivostok's Chinese population was arrested during the final round (Khisamutdinov 1993: 121). Russia's Chinese question was swiftly resolved, at least for the next fifty years.

Chapter 3
Urban Informality: Open-Air Markets and Ethnic Entrepreneurs in Vladivostok

Vladivostok, summer 2004. I step into one of Vladivostok's Chinese markets. This one is part of the larger Sportivnaya Market, which also has Russian sections. '*Dollary, dollary*', mumble the money exchangers at the congested entrance of the market, kneading thick money bundles in their hands. Russian pop music drips from the rattling speakers of a little shop that sells music tapes. With a few steps I enter a different world. The urban horizon of house fronts and traffic arteries disappears. The world is now a narrow labyrinth of metal shipping containers transformed into improvised shopping stalls. Blue plastic tarps span the contracted alleys and shower them with a dim light. The music fades. I let myself get carried away by the crowd, which moves along the stands and spills me into a free space in front of a small shop. The Chinese owner eyes me full of expectation and points to his vast assortment of leather shoes, hung on a wire frame that covers the inside of his container. His shoes cost approximately US$10. In broken Russian, the seller tries to convince me to buy a pair because of their superior quality, of course. Rejecting his offer with a smile, I step back and get swallowed by the crowd again – I drift along.

A Chinese woman pushes her small hand cart loaded with plastic cups and several thermoses of hot tea through the crowd. She praises her tea to the traders, '*Chai, chai, chai*'. Booth after booth is stuffed with a varying array of merchandise: shoes, leather jackets, jeans, underwear, dresses, and track suits. All of the commodities are Chinese imports, a dazzling assortment. Over and over, I can hear the phrase '*skol'ko*' (how much), uttered by the shoppers as a casual question thrown towards the trader, accompanied by a swift, indicating motion of the hand. The customers are selective and have learned haggling skills in a short time. Several Chinese crouch in a quiet corner around a game board and sip tea. The container behind them is closed shut with a large padlock. In one of the open containers further down the alley a Russian woman tries to fit into a small tank top. The Chinese trader holds a large blanket in front of her, as a privacy shield. Querying, the Russian looks to her friend, who shakes her head in denial. The trader nods approvingly. I don't catch the final decision – I am part of the crowd again. The dim blue light under the plastic tarps has a strange effect, enclosing me like a bubble. Sometimes it appears to me that the mass of people stands still, and the celestial blue container stalls are actually moving, like they are strung on a conveyor belt. The crowd is immobilized and the commodities flow by, in endless repetition.

The canopy ends and the alley opens into a larger space. I am blinded momentarily by the bright beams of the midday sun. The rays lighten up an assortment of toys on the next stall. Plastic cars in neon, futuristic looking model rifles, and a wide array of other coloured toys are piled on a large table – all made in China, of course. Gigantic stuffed toys dangle from the roof. The metallic voice of a battery-powered monkey caws something unintelligible. Another mechanical teddy bear has run almost out of power, and shakes its head grindingly. The neighbouring stand is crammed with kitchen equipment – plastic plates, salt shakers, toothpicks, dustpans, and batteries. The stands enclose a little square, a transit zone. Beyond, new alleys extend, full of clothes and shoes. I enter.

The Russian sector of the market begins here. The goods for sale are almost identical to those of the Chinese traders and even the containers are painted in the same blue. Yet all the salespersons are Russian women. The atmosphere is less dense than in the Chinese part of the market; the alleys between the containers are broader, and the spanned tarp is missing. Compared to the Chinese, the Russian traders look almost shy. Some smoke, drink tea, or exchange a few words with their neighbours. Like in the other part of the market, a similar assortment of merchandise is displayed: tracksuits, leather jackets, underwear, and fashionable shoes. In between, a booth with glaring plastic flowers and hanging synthetic ivy stands out. Another one offers glittery wigs. A trader specializing in socks tries to convince a potential buyer of the superior quality of her merchandise, 'These are ours, Russian made', she says, stretching the sock and holding it against the light. I continue, then slip between two containers and a hole in the fence behind them to arrive into the centre of the market.

The space opens into vacuousness. Silence engulfs me and a gust of wind blows fine dust into my eyes. The market, with its Chinese and Russian sectors, rings the oval of a former sports stadium that lies like a withered eye at its centre. The stadium gave its name to the market, 'Sportivnaya', but little else remains. There are no seats, only the concrete steps leading down. An old man, dressed in a suit and carrying a black plastic bag in his hand, walks slow laps on the chapped, asphalt sheeted track below. The track runs around a soccer field with two slanted goals crowning its ends. Bare earth surfaces at some spots. Rusty floodlight towers with broken lamps reach into the blue sky. Seagulls, attracted by the discharge of the market, circle in the air above. The acrid smell of burned plastic is all around. Gusts of wind spin screw caps of vodka bottles over the concrete arena and jitter long strips of magnetic tape caught in the ground fixtures of the former seating. Nothing remains here of the hustle and bustle of the surrounding market; like the eye of a storm. The seamlessly arranged containers surround the stadium like a fortress. A black plastic bag flies by. The seagulls scream. The man in the suit is gone.

Plate 5. Inside the maze of Sportivnaya Market, 2012.

I exit the stadium at another spot and enter the market's food section. Vegetable stands alternate with improvised storefronts built on the flat beds of small trucks. I can hear the thudding sound of a butcher preparing meat on a wooden chopping block. Glass jars filled with honey are lined up for sale on the wooden table of a Russian beekeeper. At the neighbouring stand, plastic buckets filled with potatoes are on offer, each bucket containing the equivalent of five kilograms. Chinese sell fresh vegetables and red radishes sealed in plastic. Traders from Central Asia offer dried fruits from large linen bags. I buy a package of green tea from a Chinese woman who struggles with her sunshade, about to be blown away by strong gusts of wind. The booth of an Azeri attracts my attention. The lemons cost only eight rubles here, two less than at the stands of other sellers.[21] I stop and immediately have his full attention. 'The tomatoes are also of exceptional quality', he explains and wiggles one right under my nose. I ask him where the tomatoes have been imported from, 'Are they from China?'. 'No, they come, of course, from the kolkhoz [former state farm]', he answers with a smirk that reveals his golden front teeth. I do not believe him, but nevertheless buy a kilogram. 'You are already the second time at my stand'. That is true. Parting, he presses my hand with force, 'You should stop here again'. Once more, his golden, shiny teeth strike me.

The vegetable stands merge again into container booths selling pre-packed foods and kitchen supplies. Even though they are of the same type as in the clothing section of the market, these containers have been refurbished to become small kiosks. Display cases are mounted on the inside of the swinging doors and the interior walls are also lined with showcases. The salesperson sits in a little booth crammed inside the container. Every kiosk has its own unique assortment of goods to offer. One offers sugar, oil, noodles, and rice; another shampoo, detergents and soaps; yet another, tea, coffee, and cigarettes. The sellers are Russians. A few kiosks further down the line, long rows of meat and fish sellers extend. I can already hear their shouting.

I turn into a small side alley that runs parallel to the edge of the market. On the one side, stalls of Chinese vegetable and food sellers are located, including a video store with exclusively Chinese films. Mainly local Chinese buy their supplies here. The large tables are filled with pickled vegetables, dried mushrooms, instant noodle soups, a variety of soy sauces, and special ingredients for Asian cuisine. The Chinese language surrounds me. On the other side of the alley, half a dozen shops offering hot food have been created out of double-sized shipping containers. I enter the shop called *Druzhba* (Friendship), its name printed in large letters on a front board. One half of the container is furnished as a dining room; the other half is a small kitchen. An open hatch connects the two. The sound of sputtering oil comes from the kitchen. The cook smiles and points to a free table. I sit down and study the menu, which is written in Chinese and translated into faulty Russian. Soups (*supy*) are called teeth (*zuby*). I order one. At the neighbouring table sits a group of Vietnamese. Their dusty and torn work clothes reveal their profession as construction workers. The group

---

[21] In 2004, 28 rubles equaled approximately US$1.

communicates in simple Russian with the proprietor, crack their chopsticks, and hunker down over what must be an opulent lunch. My thick noodle soup tastes excellent. A warm feeling spreads in my stomach. In the background, some dishes clatter, otherwise it is silent. I recline, enjoy the tranquillity, and observe the moving crowd through the windows. Without sound, the agitated scene outside has an almost cartoonish quality. Mutely, a Russian customer haggles with a Chinese trader. He is apparently unsuccessful, as the Russian holds the bundle of garlic threateningly into the air, then places it back on the table, and turns away with a disgusted expression on his face. Rays of the afternoon sun fall on the displayed produce and illuminate them in full colours. I have left the Russian city and am now in a market in Asia. The proprietor brings some tea, which is free and tastes of jasmine.

Chinese Markets

In the early 1990s, *kitayskie rynki* (Chinese markets) opened in the cities of Primorsky Krai. These open-air markets sell a wide variety of imported goods from China and upon entering one is initially overwhelmed by the sheer quantity of goods and the seemingly chaotic labyrinth of alleys and bazaar culture. Retailers with handcarts full of packed goods, shoppers laden with their purchases, and people out for a stroll make up a steady stream rushing in, through, and out of the market. The loud calls of Chinese traders blend with the Russian pop music blaring from crude speakers at kiosks selling pirated music tapes. It is as though Asia's commodities have been crammed in small-format under blue tarps and inside shipping containers. The market stands are improvised shop windows onto a world of Chinese electrical appliances: radios, alarm clocks, animated plastic toys, surveillance cameras, portable television sets, and other marvels. Even more goods are piled on tables and fluttering in the air: leather jackets, fur coats, jeans, dresses, casual wear, sneakers, and fine leather shoes. Steam rises from the hot pots of food on a handcart that Chinese women manoeuvre through the crowd.

On closer look, certain patterns are revealed. There are some Korean, Central Asian, and Russian traders, but Chinese and Vietnamese dominate. Ethnic Russians provide the administration, protection, and security services in the market. Most of the customers are Russians.

In this chapter I focus on Vladivostok's post-Soviet open-air markets for several reasons. First, as an institution of the economic transition period in post-Soviet Russia, open-air markets are economically vital sites but subject to constant change. In this respect, they incorporate and express the very essence of the transition period and the creative adaptation of entrepreneurs and consumers alike. Second, open-air markets in Vladivostok are public spaces where different ethnic groups interact, and they are sites where the paths of people and commodities interlink in a visible form. The surfacing of transnational commodity flows in open-air markets make an otherwise elusive subject observable, revealing its features and qualities to the anthropological gaze. Third, open-air markets operate in a distinctively grey economic zone where formal economic practices blur with informal strategies. Open-air markets offer a window on the social reality of a shadow economy and offer a privileged view on the underlying social mechanisms.

The term 'Chinese market' might seem to imply that a market completely run by Chinese. In fact, different ethnic groups are actually sharing the same locality. The markets are organized according to ethnic groups, each occupying a particular niche. As a first methodological step, I systematically mapped and recorded the inventories of three major Chinese markets in Vladivostok. The spatial groupings of foreign traders and their commodities revealed a highly structured and organized economic sphere, although often on the brink of illegality. In-depth interviews with vendors, suppliers, market administrators, and clients completed the picture of a complex and condensed niche economy in which different ethnic groups occupy marked spatial positions and monopolize whole categories of consumer goods. Entrepreneurs from China and the former Soviet republics of Central Asia and the Caucasus dominate the markets and their supply routes. Family relationships and ethnic ties play an important role in the transactions among ethnic entrepreneurs. The ethnic entrepreneurs rely heavily on each other and form enclosed groups according to their ethnicity.

To present a picture of the bazaar ecology and the underlying spatial and social order in Vladivostok's Chinese markets, I will proceed in several steps. First, I describe in detail the spatial layouts of the markets and delineate different commodity niches occupied by specific ethnic groups. Second, I place Vladivostok's Chinese markets in the wider context of open-air markets throughout the former Soviet Union, with a special focus on consumer perceptions of markets, traders, and commodities. Third, to understand the phenomenon of open-air markets in the former Soviet Union in the context of recent labour migration flows, I briefly address the general major migration flows into Primorsky Krai, specifically focusing on Chinese migration and local perceptions of Chinese migrant workers. Finally, to provide an insider view of Vladivostok's Chinese markets, I present the story of a trader from Uzbekistan, his extended kinship network, and his specific strategies in the market's shadow economy.

Bazaar Ecology

> 'On the territory of our market, organized crime exists only in the form of the administration'.
> – Vice-director of Balyaeva Market

Vladivostok's four major Chinese markets – Vtoraya Rechka, Balyaeva, Lugovaya, and Sportivnaya (see Figure 4) are the subject of the following pages. Despite their differing histories, appearances, and layouts, these markets have certain common characteristics. All four are located next to major transportation hubs: Vtoraya Rechka, in the northern part of Vladivostok, was established next to the long distance bus station; Balyaeva Market, one of the oldest in the city, is located at a major intersection on the city's margins; Sportivnaya Market, along with the adjacent Lugovaya Market, are situated close to a central bus station at the end of Svetlanskaya Street. The specific locations of the markets were also constrained by the limited availability of open space in Vladivostok's condensed cityscape.

Map 3. Chinese markets in Vladivostok.

All four markets share similar architectural elements. The 'buildings' are of three main types: containers, kiosks, and improvised stands. Flatbeds of trucks or open vans are also used as temporary selling booths, and there are some individual pavement traders. The use of standard metal shipping containers, approximately 3x3 metres, is one of the distinctive features of Vladivostok's Chinese markets. During opening hours, the vendor displays his merchandise on the container's inner walls and often sits or stands inside. At night, the container is closed and locked to function as a storage space. To adapt to spatial constraints, some of the containers, the ones used solely as storage, are stacked on top of others. Additional construction elements, like tarps, boardwalks, and galleries, are occasionally added, combining dozens of individual containers into clusters that resemble narrow bazaar alleys. Inside the maze of containers, customers and vendors are protected from cold winter storms and blazing summer heat.

Kiosks and open stands are the other major architectural style visible in the markets. Some kiosks were shipping containers that have been remodelled with the addition of windows, doors, and hatches; other kiosks are custom-made. Improvised open stands, such as *lotki* (tents) or *prilavki* (counters), are yet another category of shopping booths found at the markets. Although their appearance can greatly vary, these stands consist normally of a simple board resting on a pair of trestles; protection from sun and rain is provided by tarps stretched above the tables.

The core of the market is constituted by containers and kiosks that are arranged along lanes. The open stands mark the inner periphery of the market, but the true outer periphery is marked by pavement traders who use improvised stands often consisting of no more than a little bench or blanket spread out on the pavement. On the streets and walkways that surround the markets, ethnic Russians of retirement age sell home-grown produce (flowers, potatoes), gathered foods (mushrooms, ferns, berries), and second-hand goods (clothing, toilets).

Balyaeva

Balyaeva is one of the oldest Chinese markets in Vladivostok. Balyaeva mostly specializes in the sale of non-perishable goods imported from China, such as apparel and shoes. It also offers a broad variety of kitchen hardware, household goods, and electronic items (see Figure 2, Appendix). Balyaeva Market also partially functions as an *optovaya baza* (wholesale centre) for other open-air markets in Vladivostok.

Founded in 1994, Balyaeva has retained its original small size and relatively simple structure. Its growth is constrained by the two major expressways leaving the city to the west and north. Several rows of containers form the main shopping area; open stands ring the main area. Storage space is provided by a second floor of containers that are stacked on top of the shopping stalls. In the market's north-western corner, several food stands run by Azeris cater to vendors and customers. The whole market is surrounded by high walls, and it is easily closed at night. A new, multi-storey *torgovyy tsentr* (shopping mall) was recently built adjacent to the market. In 2004, two of the mall's floors were in operation, offering rental boutiques for apparel traders.

Managed by the company Vostochnyy Dvor, Balyaeva Market houses approximately 600 sellers. Of these, roughly 300 are of Russian nationality, 200 are Chinese or Vietnamese, 50 are ethnic Koreans (with Russian citizenship), and 30-40 are from Azerbaijan. Stand owners also own the merchandise, but they may employ other people to do the selling. According to the vice-director of the market, for instance, most of the Azeri stand owners employ Russians as salespersons. In the case of Chinese and Vietnamese traders the picture is more complicated as the vice-director explained:

> There is a hierarchy among the Chinese and Vietnamese traders. Among the Vietnamese it is more hidden, not really noticeable. But the Chinese, for instance, have between two and three bosses (*nachal'niki*) for every 150 traders. In Vladivostok there are approximately three companies that set up the traders in the markets of Vladivostok. Those companies take care of the documents and other formalities. These broker companies (*firmy-posredniki*) do not own any goods, they just take care of documents, arrange work at the markets and other places in town. There are also smaller groups, three to five people, who work on their own. Approximately 50 per cent of the traders in our market own their merchandise, which they buy at the wholesale bases in Ussurisk or Suifenhe.

The vice-director's comment hints at the subtle, informal hierarchies that exist in the markets and the crucial role of brokers in facilitating the trade.

Open-air markets have become a lucrative business not only for the stand owners, but also for the market administration and a range of involved businesses, like the above mentioned middleman companies. In addition, the open-air markets attracted racketeering groups who tried to force *kryshi* (lit. roofs, i.e. protection arrangements) on the sellers and stand owners, sometimes with deadly results. In September 2000 the director of Balyaeva Market, Valerian Vachurin, was fatally injured by assailants in an apparent contract hit.[22] When I interviewed the vice-director in 2004, he was already well accustomed to these problems and showed a pragmatic attitude to organized crime on the territory of his market:

---

[22] 'Vo Vladivostoke ubit direktora kitayskogo rynka', *Vladivostok*, 19 September 2000.

> We have the saying: On the territory of our market organized crime exists only in the form of the administration. Behind the limits of our market you can do whatever you want, build a roof (*krysha*) or whatever. But if some roof comes to us, any roof, we take the entrepreneurs together with their roof and just throw them out of the market, and so put a stop to their dealings. If I remember rightly, that happened twice. The Chinese [who were involved] are not here anymore, they retreated and it didn't happen again.

Stiff competition on the market has led to sometimes extraordinary measures by influential competitors. The vice-director recounted a different kind of incidence that had occurred in 1996, instigated by a private entrepreneur with considerable influence in the local power structures. The entrepreneur wanted to expand the offerings at Sportivnaya Market, and effectively stole the documents of Chinese traders at Balyaeva to force them to relocate:

> In 1996, OMON (Special Forces of the Interior Ministry) appeared in four buses, surrounded our market, herded all the Chinese traders together, confiscated all their passports, shipped them to Sportivnaya, and told them: If you start working here, you will receive your passport back. Until this time, there had been only a produce market at [Sportivnaya], that's why they send the Chinese over there.

Most of the Chinese returned eventually to Balyaeva after a short amount of time, but the seed for a new market was already planted. By 2004, Sportivnaya Market had become the largest open-air market in Vladivostok.

Sportivnaya

Compared to Balyaeva, Sportivnaya Market offers a broader variety of goods and presents a more complex structure. Surrounding a former sports stadium, this large open-air market housed approximately 1,600 shopping booths in 2004. The booths are sometimes shared by two sellers, bringing the number of traders to over 2,000. The offered commodities range from construction materials, to apparel and food, to electronic goods (see Figure 3, Appendix).

The economic centre of the market is located on the western side of the stadium (Area 1). Hundreds of shipping containers form narrow alleys that are covered by tarps. This zone is exclusively used by Chinese and Vietnamese traders who sell apparel and shoes. Similar commodities are offered by ethnic Russian sellers, usually women, in less crowded spaces to the north and south of the stadium (Area 2 and 6). At the northern end of the market is a larger accumulation of kiosks and containers staffed by Russian salespersons (area 7). These closed booths feature vegetables, meat, fish, and pre-packed food items. Adjacent to this zone, is a small alley with approximately ten shops offering cooked Chinese dishes (area 9). The individual shops are equipped with a small kitchen and provide room for two to four tables. In addition, several Chinese cater to the produce and food demands of Vladivostok's Asian communities. In the north-western corner of the market, easily accessible by car or van, Chinese traders advertise large household items, like rugs, furniture, and electrical appliances (area 10). Several smaller warehouses function as storage and display areas. To the east of the stadium (area 5), remodelled containers and kiosks line an alley that runs parallel to the stadium's perimeter. Russians sell here vegetables and pre-packed food items. Some Central Asian and Chinese fruit and vegetable dealers are also among them. Between this zone and the stadium is another niche (area 8) where Chinese traders offer electric appliances and household goods from large, tarp-covered tables. Adjacent to the south end of the market is a zone characterized by open and improvised stands (area 4), which are normally disassembled at the end of the market day. Russian, Azeris, and Central Asians sell here seasonal fruits and vegetables. This area is accessible by road from two sides, thus easing the delivery of larger vegetable and fruit quantities. Just left of this area is a zone used at the beginning of the winter season by Russian traders to sell fur hats (area 3).

Vtoraya Rechka

Vtoraya Rechka Market is located in the northern part of the city, adjacent to the long-distance bus terminal and close to the main traffic artery that runs northward from Vladivostok towards Ussurisk, where the main wholesale base for Chinese goods in Primorsky Krai is located. Like Sportivnaya, Vtoraya Rechka consists of different zones; economic niches that are occupied by different ethnic groups offering specific commodities (see Figure 4).

As in the case of the other two Chinese markets, this market's core zone consists of Chinese and Vietnamese traders, selling Chinese apparel and shoes from shipping containers that are arranged to form several narrow alleys (area 1). Smaller booths line the front of the market (area 2). Chinese and Vietnamese traders sell electric appliances, household utensils, and a variety of hardware. A similar assortment can be found at the backside of the market (area 3). At large stands, Chinese traders sell plastic toys, hardware, and home improvement materials. One side of the Chinese zone is lined by Russian-operated kiosks and container booths which offer pre-packed food items, meat, and milk products (area 4). Although spatially part of the same market, this zone is managed by a different company from the rest of the market, which has its own administration.

The periphery of the market, which is a larger boardwalk between the actual stands and an access road, is occupied by pavement traders (area 5). From makeshift tables along the road, Russian women sell fresh herbs and other products from their small subsistence gardens, *semichki* (sunflower seeds), and music tapes. Similar to the situation at Balyaeva, a multi-storey shopping mall has been erected recently next to the market zone (area 6). In 2004 it was still under construction.

Despite the different layouts of the three described open-air markets, similar features appear in each of the sites. Different ethnic groups specialize in certain commodities and occupy a specific space in relation to the overall market. In addition, these economic niches are characterized by distinct architectural features of the respective sales stands. The figure below outlines these similarities in an exemplary and ideal-typic form (Table 1).

Table 1: Spatial order of a Chinese market

Commodity or Service	Architectural Feature(s)	Location within the Market	Ethnic Group
Clothes Shoes Electronic appliances Plastic toys Kitchenware Household goods (products all made in China)	Covered container stands or semi-permanent building blocks; Thematically ordered 'streets'; Combined and covered by blue tarps	Centre (Clothes are more central, electronic appliances tend to be more peripheral)	Chinese, Vietnamese, and Russians (mostly Chinese stand owners)
Shoe repair	Small improvised stands	Periphery of the Chinese section	Chinese
Dried fruits and nuts	Open stands	Periphery	Azeris, Armenians, occasionally Central Asians
Restaurants/ bars (*shashlik/ shurma*)	Small buildings	Periphery, mixed in between	Azeris, Armenians, Russians (as employees)

Chinese food (rice, *noodle soup*, etc.)	Small bicycles with front hanger	Cruising between the Chinese stands and catering to Chinese sellers	Chinese
Vegetables (in winter: Chinese origin; in summer: sometimes local)	Open, sometimes tarp-covered stands	Periphery	Russians, Central Asians
Packed goods (*produkty*) (Russian or European origin)	Container kiosks	Separate market section/ street, separate part of the market	Russians
Music cassettes, CDs	Open small stands or tables	Periphery or mixed in between (depending on space)	Russians
Pickled cabbage (*kimchi*)	Covered stands	Close to Russian food stands	Russian Koreans
Second hand goods in small quantities (household goods, electronic parts)	Tarp or small table on the street	Outer periphery	Russians (older women or men)
Snack food (*belyashi, pirozhki*)	Small, often improvised shops	Mixed in the Russian section of the market	Russian women
Nuts, seeds (*semichki*)	Tarp or small table on the street	Outer periphery	Older Russian women (*babushki*)
Seasonal products in small amounts – pickles, mushrooms, berries (dacha products or gathered foods)	Small stand, or small table on the street	Outer periphery	Older Russian women (*babushki*)

Lugovaya Square

The foregoing descriptions and topographic sketches of the largest three open-air markets in Vladivostok (Balyaeva, Sportivnaya, and Vtoraya Rechka) are of course only momentary snapshots of a highly dynamic market system in constant flux. Traders leave the markets on a regular basis, seasonally or permanently; new entrepreneurs arrive; formerly employed sellers advance to stand proprietors; and new groups move into vacant economic niches. These changes are reflected in new spatial and economic structures as well as in a transformed market topography.

Plate 6. Rows of container kiosks, Lugovaya Market, 2009.

Beginning in 2003, for example, the construction of new shopping arcades began to alter the appearance of some of Vladivostok's markets. These shopping centres offer stores and boutiques for rent to prospective traders in multi-storey buildings, and are part of a process of formalizing and ordering the informal trade of the open-air markets. According to the vice-director of Balyaeva Market, it is only a matter of time before the open-air markets will eventually disappear and the former street traders will settle into the new shopping centres. The vice-director concluded, 'then we will have eventually a civilized trade'.

In 2004, this transformation was already well advanced at Lugovaya Square. This market is located at an infrastructural hub at the eastern end of

Svetlanskaya Street. It is an apt example of the rapid transformation of a Chinese open-air market into a shopping centre. Lugovaya Square hosted one of the oldest open-air markets in Vladivostok. Relatively small in size, it nevertheless offered Chinese commodities and food items at a central location in the city. The market featured a central Chinese garment section, kiosk with food items, and an open-air vegetable market. In addition, at the northern end, the market incorporated several larger buildings, which housed meat and dairy stands, a small indoor vegetable market, and storage areas (Figure 5, sketch 1).

Construction work on the shopping centre began in 2003. The centre is a multi-storey building with a pedestrian overpass to enable safe crossing of the heavily frequented streets around the square and to provide access to Lugovaya bus station from Svetlanskaya Street. The new centre reduced the size of the market's Chinese section considerably, and more changes followed (Figure 5, sketch 2). In mid-August 2004, flat-bed trailers and cranes arrived at the square. A decision by the newly elected city administration asked for the removal of kiosks and booths from the square to clear the space around the newly-built shopping centre (Figure 5, sketch 3).[23] For several days, kiosks, containers, and ramshackle stands were attached to steel cables of large cranes and heaved onto the flatbeds of waiting trucks. After one week of work, the square around the shopping centre was entirely clear except for four rows of kiosks. It was as if nothing had ever obstructed the view onto the new shopping overpass. Vietnamese pavement traders began to reclaim part of the square almost immediately. Selling clothes from big heaps that were spread on blankets covering the ground, these highly mobile traders offered their merchandise at sell-out prices, attracting large crowds of shoppers. A chaotic shopping frenzy went on for several days, a last rise against the new order. Several weeks later, the last kiosks were removed, an additional store building was rapidly constructed, and the square was cleaned of the leftover debris (Figure 5, sketch 4).

In addition to the topographic changes of the markets, increased consumer demand, higher wages, and changed consumption behaviour led to a qualitative change in the merchandise offered in the markets. During the 1990s, merchandise imported from China to the open-air markets of the Russian Far East was of lesser quality. By the 2000s, Chinese goods of a better quality and with a higher price tag could be found in all of Vladivostok's markets, especially in shopping centre boutiques.

I talked with Marina, a 34-year-old flower seller, in one of the boutiques in the main building of the newly-built shopping centre. The

---

[23] Viktor Kudinov, 'Ploshchad' Lugovaya stanet vyshe', *Zolotoy Rog*, special issue 'Stroim Gorod', 19 October 2004.

building's basement level had a flower section; Marina ran a little shop there and paid a monthly rent of US$300. Her flowers were imported from Moscow by an Azerbaijani wholesale trader, and delivered to her shop where she arranged them into bouquets. Marina complained about the high rents in the new centre; the boutiques in the overpass cost an average of US$500 per month. These rents were high compared to the cost of stands at the open-air markets, and Marina thought it would not be affordable for many market traders to relocate to the new centres. Small-scale traders on Lugovaya Square were clearly disadvantaged in the new business climate, faced with eviction from the open-air market, but unable to afford the higher rents of the shopping centres. Marina saw the changes in Lugovaya Market as a general trend in Vladivostok:

> More and more small-scale traders have begun to disappear from the markets. Chinese and Azeris are moving into the gaps. If you want to start your own little business, you have to know all those different laws, pay very high taxes and take care of all those special requirements, like building codes or sanitary inspections. If you do not know the laws, you have to pay. Not knowing the laws is one of the main problems for us small-scale traders.

In her assessment, Marina hinted at another, more hidden aspect of the markets' transformations. When open-air markets started in Vladivostok and the Russian Far East at the beginning of the 1990s, almost all of the traders and sellers were Chinese nationals. At the end of the 1990s, the markets included Russian and Vietnamese sellers, and these nationalities had begun to replace Chinese in the storefronts. Chinese traders moved into the background of the market as stand owners, wholesale traders, and importers, thus establishing themselves as a middleman minority in the Russian Far East. Similar effects of market consolidation and saturation in which Chinese market vendors changed into distributors and importers were also documented in Hungary during the 1990s (Nyiri 2006: 541).

By 2004, the position of the Chinese in market relations was particularly complex. As a middleman minority (Blalock 1967), they filled several roles necessary to link producer and consumer, employer and employee, and owner and renter. Moreover, some Chinese traders had accumulated enough capital to move 'upwards' in the organizational and social hierarchies of trade and commerce (see also Yalçın-Heckmann 2014). These traders had created enough venture capital in the 1990s to invest it in wholesale trade and permanent stores in the 2000s. Though the new stores often appeared to be operated by Russians, the salespeople were often the employees of a Chinese store owner. In some cases, especially in the new shopping centres, the Russian salesclerks provided a legal 'front' for the non-Russian owners. In the new centres, stricter rules are applied to documenting employment conditions and ownership; when the owner does not have all the necessary documents, or simply for expediency, everything may be registered under the name of a Russian employee. As the manager of Balyaeva Market explained, 'Russians run the trade only on paper, in fact, Russian nationals are just the regular salespersons. The whole profit is made by the Chinese'.[24]

Open-Air Markets in the Former Soviet Union

> 'Nowadays, the whole Lugovaya has been reduced to a vast, rough, and dirty bazaar'.
>
> – Journalist, Vladivostok

In 1988, China signed an agreement with the Soviet Union to allow visa-free cross-border travel that allowed for a limited flow of goods across the border. Thus even in the last years of the 1980s, Chinese traders began to export food products and consumer goods to the Soviet Union. Initially, these imported goods supplemented the Soviet economy, and alleviated some of the torment of its chronic shortages (Alekseev 1999a). In the early 1990s, open-air markets dominated by Chinese nationals were opened in the larger cities of the Maritime Province (Vladivostok, Ussurisk, and Nakhodka) selling a wide variety of imported goods from China. According to one retail trader I interviewed in Nakhodka in 2002, the profit margin for Chinese traders in the 1990s was around 80 per cent. In the early 2000s, profits had dropped, but they were still at a substantial 50 per cent.

Beginning in 1994, Chinese economic activities in the Far East and Siberia were curbed by the Russian state, and a crackdown on all foreign retail traders followed (Humphrey 2002: 92). Around the same time, Chinese economic activities were consolidated, as an increasing number of traders moved their capital from retail into joint ventures with Russian companies. The number of Russian and Chinese joint ventures increased substantially after 1994 (Alekseev 1999b: 2). After 1996, the number and revenue of these joint ventures gradually declined (Alekseev 2000: 5).

Though not often discussed as an integral part of socialist economies, open-air markets existed across the Soviet Union and eastern Europe. Petty trading at open-air markets was practised in Hungary during the 1970s, and the first 'suitcase traders' appeared in Poland during the 1980s (Williams and Balaz 2005: 535). Petty trading under state socialism took advantage of rising consumer demand and restricted trade. During the 1970s and 1980s,

---

[24] Yuri Nurmukhametov, 'Tvoya moya pomogay', *Zolotoy Rog*, 20 July 2004.

ethnic minorities settled successfully in this economic niche, taking advantage of their international social networks to acquire merchandise that was in high demand in their host country (Nyiri 1999). For instance, during the 1980s in Czechoslovakia, Vietnamese traders specialized in the manufacture of jeans and sportswear. They organized the shipment of raw materials from Vietnam, sewed the clothing, and then sold it in informal street markets (Williams and Balaz 2005: 538).

The breakdown of the Soviet Union led to an explosive rise in open-air markets in the successor states. Part of the rise can be explained as a result of the further weakening (and breaking) of the Soviet Union's chronically deficient systems for distributing consumer goods. The weakened retail sector and inefficient wholesale trade led to alternative strategies for distribution and sale. Informal trade networks flourished in the absence of strong formal economic organizations. For consumers, open-air markets presented a considerably cheaper alternative to regular shops. In 2004, produce sold in Vladivostok's open-air markets still was priced 20 to 30 per cent less than that in the city's food stores and supermarkets.

The rise of open-air markets can also be explained in relation to the development of new consumer demands in the post-Soviet economic sphere. As Endre Sik and Claire Wallace have observed, 'open-air markets are the bridge between low or declining incomes and rising consumer aspirations in countries where large parts of the population have been plunged into poverty at the same time as being offered greater "freedom" to consume' (Sik and Wallace 1999: 712). Open-air markets allowed post-Soviet consumers to buy new items, styles, and fashions that they would otherwise have been unable to afford. For example, in the markets one could find brand-named clothes (albeit often counterfeit) at a fraction of the normal price. Petty traders could also quickly react to fashion trends and changing consumer demand because they dealt with relatively small volumes of merchandise.[25] In the case of Vladivostok, the relatively short supply lines from Chinese production sites and wholesale markets further decreased sellers' reaction time to new demands.

In the 2000s, the open-air markets of the former Soviet Union shared common characteristics, particularly in terms of the kinds of informality they engendered. Although open-air markets had become long-term institutions in the successor countries, they were informal institutions, especially in terms of taxation. Companies operating large open-air markets (like the four described above) usually paid federal taxes on the income they gained from

---

[25] Immigrant garment firms in urban centres of the United States, for instance, succeed by specializing in short-run products that larger firms cannot handle effectively (see Morocvasic et al. 1990).

rent, but the traders themselves were normally beyond the reach of tax authorities. The informalities made open-air markets especially attractive for investment-poor traders, as well as (potential) immigrants who lacked other employment options.

By 2004, open-air markets across the Soviet Union, and in Vladivostok, were regarded with distrust and seen as a source of disorder among the local population, even as they continued to be heavily frequented.[26] Limited room, improvised sale booths, and crowded shopping alleys evoked the image of a chaotic space devoid of order and regulation. A local newspaper journalist announced her complaints about this chaos with the headline, 'Nowadays, the whole Lugovaya has been reduced to a vast, rough, and dirty bazaar'.[27]

Beyond the value judgments on the physical appearance of the markets, the negative evaluations are also based on the experience of buying in a market. In the open-air markets, transactions between sellers and buyers are conducted through asymmetrical relationships (see Geertz 1963: 34; Fanselow 1990: 251). In addition, flexible price categories were a new phenomenon in post-Soviet Russia. Consumers had to acquire new skills, like persistent haggling and rigid price comparison. Shoppers generally suspect that they will be cheated at the open-air markets. One customer at Sportivnaya Market said to me, 'I have problems with people from the Caucasus and Central Asia, they cheat you all the time. You buy a kilo of vegetables from them and they cheat you by 300 grams'. Rigged scales, a common phenomenon among vegetable traders in Vladivostok's markets, have only accentuated consumer mistrust towards trading minorities.

In the post-Soviet economic environment, where most of the consumer goods on local markets are provided by Chinese or originate in China, xenophobic sentiments are closely connected to consumption and everyday encounters in open-air markets. These markets represent vital sites of social interaction and places where the local Russian population interacts on a daily basis with members of different ethnic groups – traders from the Caucasus republics, Central Asia, and China.

The quality of goods originating from China is a much-discussed topic among regular market shoppers, a fact that has been observed in similar open-air markets of the former Soviet Union that offer cheap Chinese or

---

[26] Trading minorities are often made responsible for creating the 'disorder' of the markets (Humphrey 2002: 90). Following a similar logic of immediate causality, foreign traders are directly associated with the unsanitary conditions prevalent at street markets (see Hann and Hann 1992: 4).

[27] Svetlana Zhukova, 'Ploschad bedy: Segodnia vsia Lugovaya prevratilas' v orgromnoe griaznoe torzhishche', *Vladivostok*, 6 June 2001.

Turkish commodities (Pelkmans 2006: 186-89). Chinese merchandise, especially clothes and shoes, are usually regarded as being of lower quality than Russian or Western products, yet this view is not applied indiscriminately. Russian traders with personal experience of wholesale markets in China often stress the high quality standards that Chinese apparel manufacturers have adapted in recent years. As one experienced Russian stall owner noted, 'The quality of Chinese merchandise can be very good, although most of it does not make it to Russia; it is sold in China or in the West'.

Nevertheless, a variety of stereotypical images of Chinese nationals and commodities persist in the media as well as in everyday discourse. Negative stereotyping of Chinese in local media was especially prevalent in the 1990s, when the region was going through the extremes of economic transition. During that time, journalists as well as intellectuals in Primorsky Krai framed their fears of an overwhelming Chinese economic domination by depicting Chinese individuals and companies as predatory resource extractors (Lukin 1998: 823). Chinese were regularly featured in the local media as predatory consumers of precious commodities, from local bio-resources to Russian women. They were also seen as the importers of poisonous commodities that threatened the health of the Russian population.

During the 1990s, images of a hungry neighbour, posed to consume the Russian Far East, ran like a thread through the press coverage of Chinese-Russian relationships. These images were still common in 2004. Chinese were imagined as an amorphous mass; the common metaphors of the Chinese as migrating birds, locust, or cockroaches suggest the image of a threatening swarm of pests ready to consume its helpless host.[28] The fear of the Chinese is naturalized through these metaphors, and the Chinese presence in the Russian Far East is imagined to present an unavoidable and spreading biological danger. Incidents of polluted rivers, caused either by Chinese industrial accidents or by Chinese poachers who occasionally poison rivers to kill and catch frogs by the thousands, only underscore this perception of ecological threat. Poachers are even referred to as 'environmental terrorists'.[29]

The amorphous mass of Chinese bodies is also regularly accused of spreading cholera and other contagious disease among the Russian popu-

---

[28] Such imagery appeared, for example, in Vladimir Oshchenko, 'Kogda uezzhaiut kitiatsy, ostupaiut morozy', *Vladivostok*, 30 January 2001; Iulia Ignatenko, 'Zhuravly v Podnebes'e', *Vladivostok*, 25 July 2003.

[29] As for example, Ekaterina Liukonina, 'Sosedi traviat primortsev kak tarakanov', *Vladivostok*, 23 January 2007.

lation.³⁰ Chinese imports like children's toys, cooking utensils, and household items are suspected of containing dangerous and poisonous substances. Chinese are thus conceptualized as contagious bodies and polluters who endanger the very health of Russian society. The threat of a polluted environment and xenophobic fears are fused into a general anxiety of a border environment occupied by polluted (and polluting) bodies and commodities.³¹

The conceptual intermingling of migrating bodies, commodity flows, and pollution comes as no surprise. In her study of cultural conceptions of contamination, the anthropologist Mary Douglas showed that pollution is essentially 'matter out of place' (Douglas 1966: 40). The multiple transgressions of borders in the Russian Far East thus create a multitude of objects and bodies that are out of place which are perceived as polluting agents that endanger the very foundation of society. Xenophobia in the Russian Far East can thus be seen as a moral discourse accompanying rapid economic and political change, and as a local comment on recent transnational commodity flows and labour migrations. Objects and bodies are transformed to contagious substances and perilous strangers, not only by transgressing borders but also by blurring borders (Bauman 1997: 25-26).

The negative notions and preconceptions towards Chinese traders and migrants that regularly spin in the media find their equivalent in everyday talk. On numerous occasions I was confronted by local Russians with blunt views on the Chinese. They would tell me, 'The Chinese eat everything', or 'the Chinese take away our resources and leave us nothing but trashy commodities'.

There are also negative judgments about vegetables from China, which are alleged to be highly contaminated by pesticides. During the winter months almost all of the vegetables in local food markets are imported from China. Only during the summer season does local produce appear, albeit intermittently, as one 63-year-old Russian woman who runs a little vegetable stall in one of Vladivostok's open-air markets explained to me:

> Because of the foreigners our people do not plant their own gardens. They beat us down with the price and that is why our fields are empty, although we have a lot of farmland here in Primorsky Krai. And even if they [local farmers] come here to the market, the transportation costs are too high and they are not given a place in the market. That I know for sure. The people who come from the

---

³⁰ For instance, Nikolay Kutenkikh, 'Myaso iz Kitaya zarazheno yashchurom?' *Vladivostok*, 28 August 1997; 'Kitayskie kerosinsckie radiyatsiey', *Vladivostok*, 14 February 1997.

³¹ Sarah Hill (2006) has documented a similar conflation of environmental perceptions and negative reactions to migrants along the US-Mexico border.

Caucasus [Northern Caucasus, Armenia, and Azerbaijan], they are nice people, I like them personally, but our people cannot compete with their prices. [This is so] even though our agricultural possibilities are not worse or even better than theirs.

Consumers are very conscious about the origins of products and food items offered at the open-air markets. Questions on the origins of certain produce are asked regularly. '*Eto nashi?*' (is it ours?) is a common question that guides the customer through the market's maze of foreign commodities.[32] Compared to Soviet times, where the consumer was located at the receiving end of a state-orchestrated economic distribution system, in post-Soviet times product choice is at the centre of consumption behaviour (Humphrey 1995: 45).

Although a general animosity towards foreign traders and their commodities exists, xenophobic notions are usually weighted against economic incentives and advantages. The following responses of ethnic Russian consumers, aged 16-50, interviewed at Sportivnaya Market reveal these conflicting views:

> I do not like the Chinese in the market; they are too aggressive, always trying to push their goods on us. But if we would buy all our clothes in the shops, our money would not be enough.

> I do not like the Chinese, there just too many here in Vladivostok. If you go to the market, you do not see any Russians anymore, just Chinese or people from the Caucasus.

> I do not like that the Chinese make so much money here and the Russians stay without jobs. But what would we do without the Chinese here?

> Of course, the quality of vegetables from China is lower, but what can you do here in the winter? There are no other vegetables in the winter beside the ones from China. The Chinese feed us. You see, I have nothing against the Chinese, they just work here and they are good workers.

> There are a lot of foreigners in the market, but we depend on them. The Russian products are just more expensive; even the Chinese

---

[32] Melissa Caldwell has shown clearly how Russians are strongly guided in their consumption strategies by the dichotomous concept of *nash* (ours) and *ne nash* (not ours) (Caldwell 2002: 309-11). This dichotomy has a long history in Russian thought that traces back to Soviet times (Yurchak 2006: 103).

products that are sold by Russians are more expensive. [With the Chinese vendors] I can even bring back and exchange jeans that I have bought and that do not fit well.

What is interesting in all of these statements is the sense of dependency that Russian consumers feel towards the Chinese migrants.

Labour Migration into the Russian Far East: Perceived and Real Threats

'Throughout the history of economics the stranger everywhere appears as the trader, or the trader as stranger'.
– Georg Simmel, 'The Stranger'

Labour migration after the breakdown of the Soviet Union into the Russian Far East involved ethnic groups that arrived in different immigration waves. Labour migrants in Primorsky Krai concentrated mostly on the larger cities, like Vladivostok, Nakhodka, Artem, and Ussurisk. The latter played a major role as a migration hub, especially for Chinese migrant workers. Due to its proximity to China and its central location in Primorsky Krai, Ussurisk functioned as a reception camp for labour migrants. Several waves of labour migration into Primorsky Krai can be distinguished.

The first large-scale migration from the Caucasus region was composed of Armenians and Azeris and began during the 1980s. Several push and pull factors were responsible for this wave of Armenian labour migration during Soviet times. Mubaris Akhmedov distinguished three main reasons for labour migration among Azeris: (1) a general military draft during the Soviet Union that dispersed Azeris widely across the former Soviet Union; (2) job vacancies in the merchant marine and fishing ships; (3) the deteriorating economic situation in Azerbaijan after the Nagorno-Karabakh conflict started in 1988 (Akhmedov 2000: 190 92). The regional conflict and war between Armenia and Azerbaijan that lasted until 1994 led to the latest subsequent wave of immigrants.

In general, migration from regional conflicts and wars after the breakdown of the Soviet Union has played an important role in recent migration flows to Russia. In 1994, approximately 500,000 refugees from territories of the former Soviet Union found shelter in Russia (Mukomel 1999: 66). In 2000, according to leaders of the diaspora groups, there were 25,000 Armenians and 21,000 Azeris resident in Primorsky Krai (Vashchuk 2000: 159).

During the early 1990s, another wave of migrants came to the Russian Far East. Russian Koreans arrived by the thousands in Primorsky Krai between 1991 and 1994. After their deportation in the 1930s to Kyrgyzstan, Kazakhstan, and other parts of Central Asia (see chapter 2), most Koreans were heavily Russified. Those who have returned to the Russian Far East are native Russian speakers and see their migration as a return home. Approximately 26,000 of these Russian Koreans are currently living in Primorsky Krai (Vashchuk 2000: 159).

Russian Koreans should be distinguished from North Korean migrant workers who also arrived during the early 1990s. In 1995, there were 3,956 registered migrant workers from North Korea in Primorsky Krai, employed in construction business and as agricultural farm labour. In 1995, the former governor of Primorsky Krai, Yevgeniy Nazdratenko, signed a contract with the North Korean government to employ up to 10,000 North Korean workers in the region. Despite this political effort, the numbers of North Korean workers dropped each consecutive year to total only 2,373 in 1999 (Vashchuk 2000: 198). In 2004, most of the North Korean labour migrants were employed in the construction business, earning only US$20 to US$100 per month. The very presence of these workers was mostly visible along Vladivostok's Svetlanskaya Street, where the facades of classical buildings were remodelled by North Korean construction teams.

Another group of Asian migrant workers is composed of Vietnamese nationals who arrived during the late 1980s. As *sotsialisticheskii gastarbaiteri* (socialist immigrant workers), they were under strict state control and used to fill gaps in the local labour market, especially in construction and the textile industry (Vashchuk 2002: 197). As state controls relaxed with the end of the Soviet Union, workers switched their occupation and began to work as traders in the open-air markets.

Recent Chinese migration into the Russian Far East can be divided into four stages. The first wave of migrant workers arrived from China during the mid-1980s (Larin 1998: 107). During that time, a legal pretext was created through which Russian state enterprises could sign contracts with Chinese partners. Chinese workers were mostly employed as construction workers and farm labour in Primorsky Krai. With the dissolution of the Soviet Union, a second wave of migrants arrived. The number of border crossings increased by a factor of almost five.[33] This stage was characterized by almost no state control of the immigration flow and a steady increase of entrepreneurs and traders who entered the Russian Far

---

[33] The most frequented border crossing in Primorsky Krai, the Grodekovo border post near Pogranichnyy, registered 46,000 border crossings in 1991. In 1992 the number of crossings was 200,000. Although these numbers include the frequent and multiple border crossings of Chinese tourist traders, they nevertheless illustrate the substantial increase in border traffic between Russia and China (Vashchuk 2002: 200).

East under the disguise of tourism. During the third stage, which lasted between 1994 and 1998, the Russian state tried to curb and control the migration flow, especially those who overstayed on tourist visas. During this time, an occupational shift occurred in the Chinese migrant population. More Chinese migrants started to work as traders than in the construction or agricultural sector (Barineva 1997: 15). In addition, well-educated and connected Chinese entrepreneurs arrived and founded an increasing number of import-export companies in Primorsky Krai. The devaluation of the Russian ruble in 1998 induced the fourth wave of Chinese migrants. During the following summers of 1999 and 2000, the Russian Far East and especially Vladivostok saw a large increase of Chinese tourists from neighbouring Heilongjiang Province. Despite reduced local purchasing power after the financial crisis, many Chinese businessmen had already established profitable import and export businesses, ranging from wholesale import of Chinese merchandise to the export of Russian timber.

The migration of Chinese traders into Russian cities, the mushrooming of open-air markets, the influx of foreign goods, and the development of new political structures led to fundamental transformations in post-Soviet Russia (Vitkovskaya and Zaionchkovskaya 1999). The total number of Chinese nationals visiting Primorsky Krai increased from 40,000 in 1994 to 73,000 in 1998. Although the region's economy has benefited from Chinese traders who provided urgently needed food supplies and consumer goods, the cross-border flow of people, goods, and services created security concerns and socio-economic grievances among political elites and local residents (Alekseev 1999b: 1). Public and official perceptions of these processes are framed and summoned in reference to a new 'yellow peril' (Larin 1995; Vitkovskaya 1999a).

Official agencies and the Russian press are increasingly alarmed over the problem of migration from China. The fear is that mass resettlement from China will intensify competition on the Russian labour market, drain the country of hard currency, create social problems, increase crime, and endanger the health of the Russian population. This fear is only intensified by demographic trends among the Russian and other Slavic populations: negative population growth, growing unemployment, and emigration to more central regions of the Russian Federation. Those who see the Russian Far East as being negatively affected by demographic pressure from China gain strength from pointing to these trends.

Viktor Larin, director of the Vladivostok Institute of History, analyzed print media coverage of Chinese migration into Russia between 1993 and 1995 and counted more than 150 articles referring to a 'yellow peril' in the Russian Far East (Larin 1998: 74-75). Some of these articles claimed that up to 150,000 illegal immigrants were settling in Primorsky Krai, as part of a total of up to 2 million Chinese nationals in the Russian Far East. A report published by the newspaper *Vladivostok* in 1996, stated that from 1993 to 1995 almost one half million Chinese nationals had travelled to Primorsky Krai, but that only one-third of these had registered with the local authorities; the rest, claimed the report, had moved to other parts of the Russian Federation (Larin 1998: 106). However, the fact that the report could not be verified and the sheer impossibility to count all the illegal immigrants make these numbers highly unlikely. In addition, one wonders about the location where the allegedly hundreds of thousands of Chinese are actually living. Rumours abound of Chinese villages hidden from officialdom in the countryside, but no such villages have ever been detected (Humphrey 2002: 92). The largest known compact Chinese settlement in Primorsky Krai is located in Ussurisk, with a moderate population of around 2,000 (Alekseev 1999a: 2). Chinese settlements with populations numbering in the tens of thousands can be seen as modern urban myths or simply attributed to misinformation (Vitkovskaya 1999b: 2).

Proponents of the 'yellow peril' argument often cite the demographic imbalance between the southern districts of the Russian Far East – Primorsky Krai, Khabarovsky Krai, and Amurskaya Oblast' – and China's adjacent province of Heilongjiang. In the three Russian districts, the general population size is about 5 million, compared to 100 million across the border in China (Vitkovskaya 1999b: 2). The perceived threat of a Chinese demographic pressure is accentuated by unfavourable demographic developments in the Russian Federation (Larin 2012: 55). A falling fertility rate combined with increasing mortality has produced a significant decrease in Russia's population. From 1992 to 1998, Russia's population declined by approximately 1.4 million (Gerber 1999: 1). Out-migrations of ethnic Russians from northern and eastern regions of the Russian Federation have magnified the perception of a threatening population decline.

It is difficult to know whether this perceived threat is also real. There is hardly any reliable information concerning the size, composition, or behaviour of the Chinese population in Russia.[34] Population statistics, especially of immigrants, are often used by local elites to play political games with the central administration in Moscow and to manipulate public

---

[34] Official censuses are of little help either as they are able to count only a fragment of the actual numbers. According to the censuses, 3,476 Chinese nationals were resident in Primorsky Krai in 2002; and 4,005 in 2010. See Federal'naya Sluzhba Gosudarstvennoy Statistiki, 'Itogi vserossiyskoy perepisi naseleniya 2002 goda', http://www.perepis2002.ru/index.html?id=17, accessed 12 May 2006; and Federal'naya Sluzhba Gosudarstvennoy Statistiki, 'Naselenie naibolee mnogochislennikh natsional'nostei', http://www.gks.ru/free_doc/new_site/perepis2010/croc/Documents/Vol4/pub-04-14.pdf, accessed 13 April 2014.

opinion (Vitkovskaya 1999b: 2). The Carnegie Moscow Center estimates the number of Chinese migrants in the Russian Federation in the hundreds of thousands (Vitkovskaya 1999b: 1). Official estimates of Chinese arrivals number 1.5 million per year, but these numbers reflect entries rather than individuals. Shuttle traders, for example, enter the country multiple times during a single year. Compared to Chinese populations in other developed countries, the number of Chinese in Russia is relatively low. Vyacheslav Karlusov and Aleksandr Kudin estimated that the proportion of Chinese visitors in 2002 did not exceed 3.3 per cent of the total population of the Russian Far East (Karlusov and Kudin 2002: 81). But given the fact that during Soviet times there were virtually no Chinese in Russia, the sudden increase after the breakdown of the Soviet Union is perceived as a threatening fact.

Most of the Chinese nationals who enter Primorsky Krai visa-free on tourist permits are engaged in cross-border trade or local business (Larin 2012). Because of the informal character of that trade, it is difficult to separate visitors with business aspirations from visitors with purely touristic motives. Yet, one can safely presume that during the 1990s and the early 2000s that most of the Chinese visitors on tourist visas were actively engaged in trade. In 1994, roughly 40,000 Chinese nationals were registered by passport inspection and hotel registration as tourists in Primorsky Krai; in 2000, that number had already tripled to 150,000 (Bogaevskaya 2002: 19). Although the numbers of Chinese visitors entering Primorsky Krai on tourist visas rose gradually from 40,000 in 1994 to almost 80,000 in 1998, the numbers who failed to return dropped significantly from 15,000 in 1994 to below 300 in 1998 (Bogaevskaya 2002: 19).

After 2004 the use of tourist visas gradually fell as Chinese nationals shifted economically from shuttle to wholesale trade. The number of Chinese entering Primorsky Krai in the 2000s suggest a relatively stable annual in- and out-flow. In 2006, 218,200 Chinese nationals entered the Primorsky Krai, 77,000 of them as tourists (Larin 2012: 71).

In- and out-flow numbers of Chinese visitors give only an approximation of the actual numbers of Chinese citizens continually present in Primorsky Krai. For an absolute count I would follow here Viktor Larin who suggested that during the second half of the 1990s approximately 30,000-36,000 Chinese nationals resided in Primorsky Krai, among them 10,000-15,000 petty traders, 10,000-12,000 contract workers, and several hundred students and medium-scale businessmen (Larin 2012: 72). As a likely future trend, Chinese labour migration into the Russian Far East will probably diminish, as economic improvements in north-east China will employ the local workforce and Russia's ongoing economic crisis will make business less profitable (Repnikova and Balzer 2009: 35).

Contradicting public opinion, the economic activities of Chinese migrants have not generated major costs on Russian residents. The political scientist Mikhail Alekseev argued, 'that the economic activities of Chinese migrants in Primorye neither generate major economic benefits for, nor impose major costs on, Russian residents and governmental offices in nearly half of the 20 cities and borderline districts of Primorye' (Alekseev 1999b: 2). In some major cities, including Vladivostok, their presence has created economic benefits for local residents and government officials. In Ussurisk, for example, the Chinese trading centre has become one of the three major sources of revenue for the local government (Alekseev 2000: 2). In general, revenues from cross-border trade enhance the local tax base and provide the larger public with eagerly sought-after goods.[35] Underscoring my observations and interviews with long-time residents on the interaction between Chinese traders and Russian locals in Vladivostok and Ussurisk, Alekseev observed that, 'these interactions are cooperative by virtue of both mutual economic necessity (e.g. facing the same gangsters or the same rent-seeking official) and isolation of (rather small and dispersed) Chinese communities from the local Slavic population' (2000: 2).

The discrepancies between perceived and real threats cannot be understood as an isolated problem of the Russian Far East, but rather as part of far-ranging anti-migrant feelings in post-Soviet Russia (Sahedo 2012: 146). Xenophobia is a fairly constant trend in the history of Russia (Brooks 1992; Gudkov 1999; Rabinovich 1999). Some authors, however, have argued that post-Soviet xenophobia has more specific causes than mere continuity. For example, some have argued that anti-migrant feelings have surfaced because of social and economic crisis and loosening state control (Rancour-Lafferriere 2001). Others, such as Aleksey Malashenko (1999), have argued that because Russia lacks a liberal and democratic tradition there are no mechanisms to counteract the xenophobic dispositions arising with loosening state control. Another possibility is offered by Galina Vitkovskaya (1999a) who has used ethnographic observations and sociological surveys to trace anti-migrant feelings (*migrantofobiya*) back to the sharp drop of activity and frequency of inter-ethnic, inter-regional, and inter-cultural communications after the breakdown of the Soviet Union.

Nevertheless, the presence of the Chinese is perceived as a threat voiced in public polls. An opinion survey conducted in September 2000 by Mikhail Alekseev in cooperation with the Centre for the Study of Public

---

[35] Aleksandr Tkachev, 'Zhel'taya zavtra', *Zolotoy Rog*, 27 July 2004.

Opinion at the Vladivostok Institute of History, Ethnography, and Archaeology of the Russian Academy of Sciences shows that the scale of Chinese nationals in Primorsky Krai is significantly overestimated.[36] These perceptions are sometimes nurtured by rumours of China's territorial claims on certain parts of Primorsky Krai that date back to a border clash at Damanski Island on the Amur River in March 1969. In addition, a growing sense that Chinese traders are economically aggressive, reflected in other surveys, adds to the demographic fear of being overwhelmed by a wave of Chinese people (Alekseev 2000: 4).

Despite these negative perceptions, from the mid-2000s anti-Chinese media coverage in Primorsky Krai sharply dropped. This trend parallels the regional change of political elites. In 2001, Sergey Darkin replaced Yevgeniy Nazdratenko, who was known for his anti-Chinese bias, as governor. On the political level, economic incentives seem to override xenophobic sentiments, in part due to the recognition of the importance of growing economic and geopolitical ties to China. The notion of a 'yellow peril' is slowly being replaced in official discourse by references to a 'yellow future'. This new discourse re-examines the region's particular economic and geopolitical situation under a more constructive and positive light.

Ethnic Entrepreneurs – An Uzbek Case

'He just left for Magadan'.
– Erkin, age 24, Uzbek trader commenting on the disappearance of a fellow trader

In the following pages, I present a case study of Erkin, a labour migrant from Uzbekistan who owned a small stand at one of Vladivostok's central open-air markets. Over the course of several months I had the opportunity to share Erkin's life behind a market booth. I spent several days each week with him in the market, and occasionally sold his products by myself. This participatory observation introduced me not only to the everyday life of a market trader and his extensive social network, but also allowed me to have a glance at the more hidden aspects of Vladivostok's markets. The social embeddedness of his economic relations was a striking feature of Erkin's small business. An extended kinship network was central to his success as a

---

[36] Half of the interviewees estimated the percentage of Chinese in Primore to be between 10 per cent and 20 per cent, and projected an increase of up to 40 per cent in the next 5 to 10 years. A large proportion of respondents (55 per cent) believed that the Chinese pose a strong threat to Primorsky Krai (Alekseev 2001: 1-2).

foreign trader in Vladivostok. This case offers only a small glimpse into the world of the various trading minorities working in Vladivostok's open-air markets. Nevertheless, I think that this individual case has a model character and that the findings can be generalized and compared to a certain degree. Several comprehensive studies of open-air markets in the post-Soviet sphere, for instance Moscow (Yalçın-Heckmann 2014), Mongolia (Wheeler 2004; Pedersen 2007), Kyrgyzstan (Spector 2008) and Uzbekistan (Kaiser 1997), have equally highlighted how trade at these sites is embedded in informal networks and socio-cultural relationships.

Several factors contributed to the formation of social networks among migrant traders. First, networks form on a basis of cultural similarity, which simplifies communication and understanding. Second, the choice of co-workers, wholesale sellers, deliverers, and retail sellers from one's ethnic group or extended family is based on rational motives. Family members are a cheap workforce and family ties with the country of origin can be used as supply lines. Third, since trust is an important factor in money transfers and exchanges made in the informal economic sphere of the open-air market, migrant traders benefit from high levels of trust that can be secured through ethnic and family ties. Fourth, social sanctions for breach of trust are much easier to enforce in ethnic and family networks. Fifth, outside pressure is another factor in creating tight social networks among foreign traders in Vladivostok; such pressures include the complex bureaucratic procedures for foreign traders in Russia, discrimination in the workplace, xenophobia, and racially motivated attacks. Thus, kin and ethnic ties delineate a social blueprint for stability and trust among different groups in the uncertain and often unreliable space of the Russian transition economy.

Erkin came to Vladivostok in 2003. His case is a classical example of labour migration within the territory of the former Soviet Union. Erkin was born and raised in Asaka, a city of 60,000 in the Andijon Province of eastern Uzbekistan. The dire economic and political situation in contemporary Uzbekistan forced him, like many other young male Uzbeks, to find work in Russia.[37] Asked about the reason why he left his family to find work in Russia he explained to me, 'There is no work in my city, and [there are] very high taxes if you try to start your own business. The clan of the president [Islam Karimov] is very powerful. If you are not related to this clan you can

---

[37] Uzbeks and other Central Asians compose the latest immigration wave into the Russian Far East. They began to arrive at the end of the 1990s, and by the mid-2000s there were more than 700,000 Uzbeks working in Russia. The effects of migration on Uzbekistan's economy are substantial; migrants annually send back an estimated US$500 million. See IRIN, 'Uzbekistan: Focus on southern labour migration', UN Office for the Coordination of Humanitarian Affairs, http://www.irinnews.org/report.asp?ReportID=46009&SelectRegion= Central_Asia, accessed 16 May 2006.

hardly find any work. My oldest brother got lucky; he found a job as a driver for the local governor. He is the only one [of my 3 brothers] who stayed behind'. Russia was a natural choice for Erkin; he had kinship ties to family members who had successfully emigrated and started several businesses.

Erkin relied on a set of techniques and applied knowledge to guarantee his journey's success. First, knowledge of potential work possibilities was transferred back to him in Uzbekistan by relatives who had established small businesses in Russia during the late 1990s. Erkin's final decision to emigrate to Russia and his choice of potential profitable cities was based on his relatives' estimates of local economic situations. Second, his border crossing into Russia was facilitated with a forged immigration card. This is a mandatory document used in the registration of foreign nationals in Russia, but it is easily available in the black market of Uzbekistan's cities. For the actual journey to Russia, a two-day train ride to Novosibirsk, Erkin teamed up for safety and logistical reasons with several of his relatives. The group of travellers carried several hundred kilograms of merchandise into Russia; Erkin alone transported 200 kilograms of spices. In addition, some of the travellers had made the journey several times and were able to help Erkin in completing the necessary immigration documents. He stopped first in Novosibirsk (south-central Russia) where relatives had already established a small business. Finding that the local market was already saturated with traders, he continued until he reached Vladivostok, where his mother's brother ran several vegetable stands at Lugovaya Market. Kinship relations continued to play an important role for Erkin as he began and ran his business in Vladivostok. I will address the importance of kinship in strategies of ethnic entrepreneurs later in this chapter. First, I will sketch Erkin's business from an entrepreneurial point of view.

Erkin was a spice trader. A handwritten label praised his merchandise: *Spetsi iz Uzbekistana dlya vsekh blyud' – ochen vkusno!* (Spices from Uzbekistan for every dish – very tasty!). Erkin knew how to impress his customers. When he was about to sell one of his special spice mixes, he filled half of a paper cup with an already prepared mixture. The other half was mixed freshly in front of the customer. His spoon, scooping into a variety of colourful spices, danced over his assortment of seasonings. A first time customer normally bought the smallest quantity, a small paper cup for ten rubles. Regular customers often bought more. Erkin had several regular customers. The most popular seasoning was the one for *plov*, the national dish of Uzbekistan and also a well-known rice dish in Russian cuisine.

Erkin was not alone with his performing skills. One day I noticed a Russian woman who was selling cucumbers at a neighbouring stand for 25 rubles per kilogram. Her business did well. 'Cucumbers from Ussurisk', was her slogan to draw attention, and always the same question in response, 'Where are the cucumbers from? Are these ours?' 'They are not from China, these are ours, not Chinese, they are from Ussurisk', was her reassuring answer. Thus comforted, most of the shoppers were willing to buy. I purchased her last kilogram of the day. In the evening, her Azeri stall owner commented, slightly amused, on her sales strategy, 'Cucumbers from Ussurisk! That's the way to do it! She did not even lie'. The cucumbers were indeed from Ussurisk, but this town was also the location of the largest wholesale market for Chinese vegetables and fruits in Primorsky Krai. As Erkin shortly remarked, 'Of course, the cucumbers are from China, everything right now is from China, the Russians are just dumb'.

In the summer of 2004, Erkin ran a small stand in the south-eastern corner of Sportivnaya Market, selling a large variety of spices that he imported from Uzbekistan. His stand was at first a simple table, where he had arranged his spices in dozens of containers. Later during the year, he acquired a half-covered showcase, which protected his goods from gushing winds and whirling dust clouds. Erkin's booth was located between a vegetable trader from Azerbaijan and a seller from Tadzhikistan who specialized in dried fruits. Just across from Erkin's stand was a small improvised teahouse and cook shop that catered mainly to the Azeri traders of this section of the market. Older men met there regularly for tea, to play cards, and to share stories.

When I first met Erkin, he had a stand in Lugovaya Market. According to him, it was a more profitable place, mostly for the fact that his sales spot was located in a covered section of the market, which allowed him to trade even during the cold winter months. Erkin's older brother, Tolkin, had taken over this stand when he arrived in the spring of 2004. Already accustomed to Vladivostok's markets, Erkin moved to Sportivnaya to open another booth. Erkin's path was different from that of other Uzbek traders, but also demonstrated a general tendency for sellers to advance fairly quickly to other positions within the market structure. Most of the Uzbeks in the market work for a *khosyain* (stand proprietor), who supplies the produce in the morning and does the accounting with the seller in the evening. Many of the stand owners started as employees themselves. Artem, an Uzbek from Kyrgyzstan and a friend of Erkin, is one such new stand owner, though he does not yet have employees. He travels once a week to the *optovaya baza* (wholesale centre) in Ussurisk, 200 kilometres north of Vladivostok, to buy his supplies, mostly vegetables and greens, and runs the stall with his brother.

Plate 7. The author with an Uzbek spice trader, Sportivnaya Market, Vladivostok 2004.

During the summer months (June -September), many Uzbek traders returned to their home countries. The summer in Vladivostok was *mertvyy seson* (dead season) for the vegetable traders. During this time, most of the produce in the market came from local farms. The daily wage for a vegetable seller is five per cent of the day's turnover, normally between 200 and 300 rubles. Because Erkin owned his stand and merchandise he could make more; on good days he made up to 500 rubles in profit. He was his own *khosyain*, a fact he often stressed proudly.

Competition was high among the traders in this section of the market. At a neighbouring stand a Kyrgyz trader from Osh in the Fergana Valley complained to me, 'This is not a bazaar, this is just a chaotic street. The tomatoes cost here 25, over there 20, and at this place 18. In normal markets there is at least a standard price, like in Novosibirsk'. He used to have a fruit business in Novosibirsk. Grapes were his most profitable produce. On good days he had a turnover of almost US$1,000. Why did he come to Vladivostok? Artem's answer was typical for most of the Central Asian traders: 'Business is very bad in Kyrghyzstan right now, the people grow their own produce, there are no factories, and no jobs'.

Free space was scarce at the market, and demand was high. Consequently the prices for vacant sites rose. 'There are always people who are willing to pay a higher price for an open spot', summed up Erkin. An open booth in his section of the market cost 4,000 rubles; shipping containers cost 6,000 rubles each per month. Erkin's rental rate was 5,000 rubles a month. In addition to the stand fee, which he paid to the market administration, Erkin had a range of monthly fixed costs. He had to pay 500 rubles per month to an Uzbek racketeering group, an unavoidable fee, as he explained: 'You cannot do without a *krysha* (roof). Everybody has weapons here, the mafia looks after the order. Different mafia groups are active in the market, Russian, Uzbek, and Chinese, each collecting protection fees from their own [ethnic group]. The members of the Uzbek mafia are all sportsmen [*sportsmeny*], if you cross them …'. He finished the sentence with an unmistakable punching gesture of his fist. In addition to that protection fee, Erkin had to pay individual policemen who patrolled the market on a regular basis. Because he worked without the necessary permits, he had to bribe these policemen at the rate of 50 to 100 rubles per encounter.

Both Erkin and his stand neighbours often complained about the discrimination to which they were exposed on a daily basis in the form of police controls. The substantial fees of the numerous permits (work permit, residence permit, and sanitary inspection certificate) were the main reason some of the traders prefer to remain illegal. Even though Erkin was in possession of a valid entry visa to Russia, he lacked the essential *propusk* (entry permit) for Vladivostok. This document costs between 3,000 and 4,000 rubles on the black market, which is a substantial sum for a new open-air market trader. Work permits are also only granted to those with valid residence permits. According to Erkin's cost-benefit calculation the residence permit was not worth the money; rather, he opted to pay the occasional bribes, which could be a risky calculation, as the fines could quickly amount to several thousand rubles. In addition, during the time of my fieldwork, an informal three strike rule was in place such that if a person were caught three consecutive times without a valid residence permit, he was deported from Russia and banned from re-entering for five years. This threat made Erkin and his older brother decide to acquire a residence permit for their youngest sibling, Azizbek, who arrived in the summer of 2004 because Azizbek lacked the necessary Russian language skills and insider knowledge to deal adequately with police and bribes.

Their status as illegal migrant workers considerably reduced the brothers' freedom of movement. In general, they all tried to minimize their movement inside the city, mainly limiting their travel to and from their market workplaces. If the brothers had to travel longer distances, they usually preferred a taxi instead of public transportation because it reduced the chances of running into an unexpected police control.

The market administration, however, regularly supported the traders and informed them of imminent raids by the immigration police. One day I arrived late to the market and found half of the stands abandoned. I asked for the reason. Erkin explained, 'Today the police were checking work permits. Somebody from the market administration warned us yesterday. They are on our side, because they make a lot of money from us'. Occasionally, other security forces that operated in the market demanded their own share. For instance, Special Forces of the Interior Ministry (OMON) often backed up the local police on larger raids for illegal immigrants in Vladivostok's markets and therefore were also potential receivers of bribes. Personal relations with policemen or members of OMON were important assets for Erkin. Knowing a policeman and having bribed him successfully in the past meant he had established a rapport that made future encounters with that person predictable. Little gifts underscore these relationships. For instance, on one day an off-duty officer approached Erkin's stand. Erkin knew him from former encounters when he had been checking immigration documents and work permits. On this day, he was on a private mission. He needed spices for his weekend's shish kebab. Erkin prepared a large cup – for free, of course.

In addition to their high percentage of illegal migrant workers, open-air markets have other hidden dimensions. On a regular basis I could see mobile dealers scrutinizing the market to fence their goods, their main customers being the local traders looking for special resale deals. Young soldiers sell canned beef from poached army supplies, a policeman has two cartons of cigarettes to offer, two youngsters fence a German electric drill in its original casing, and others offer wrist watches and underpants. On the major roads surrounding the market, moneychangers wait on camping chairs or in cars to offer drive-by exchanges of American dollars, Russian rubles, and Chinese yuan. Vladivostok's open-air markets harbour a clandestine milieu that constitutes a market inside the market. This hidden level, a stratum under the visible surface of the market, is nested in the trader's relations among themselves and consists of different economic clusters that provide mostly for market traders. The services range from food catering and the above mentioned fencing of merchandise to the clandestine sale of forged immigration documents and residence permits. In addition, some of the traders are involved in the sale of bootlegged alcohol and illegal drugs.

Ethnic economies have been described as embedded economic relationships.[38] As already outlined above, Erkin was part of a larger

---

[38] The idea of socially and morally embedded economies traces back to the work of Polanyi (1944). Building on his work, other scholars have stressed and refined different aspects of economic embeddedness (Granovetter 1985; Portes and Sensenbrenner 1993).

network of kinsmen who had established several smaller businesses in Vladivostok's open-air markets (Figure 9). A closer look at his kin network reveals the importance of kinship ties in the organization and structure of economic activities, where the embeddedness in social networks creates bounded solidarity and facilitates reciprocity transactions based on enforceable trust (Portes and Sensenbrenner 1993: 1324).

Erkin's core family included his parents, four brothers, and five sisters. Among this group, Erkin was the first one to arrive and begin business in Vladivostok in 2003. His newly arrived older brother, Tolkin, was 28 years old when I met him in the spring of 2004. Before his arrival in Vladivostok, Tolkin had worked in a vegetable oil factory in the city of Andijon, Uzbekistan. As soon as his older brother arrived, Erkin was able to expand his business by opening a second stall in another market. Among Uzbek and Kyrgyz traders it was common to designate the oldest member of a (family) group as the *khoziain* (proprietor) of a stand. In the case of Erkin's family network in Vladivostok, Erkin's older brother Tolkin filled the position after his arrival. Azizbek, the youngest brother, was 21 years old when he arrived in the summer of 2004. Because Azizbek was relatively inexperienced and had only basic Russian language skills, Erkin trained him at his stand for a month before Azizbek was able to take over his business. The parents, the oldest brother, and the five sisters remained in Uzbekistan. Erkin's oldest sister's son arrived in the fall of 2004. Before Erkin's arrival, two of his mother's brothers were conducting business in the region. Mirkhomid, Erkin's 53-year-old uncle, was the first to open a spice stall in Lugovaya Market. His son had a similar business in the Pervaya Rechka food market, a small market located in the centre of Vladivostok. Sobirzhon, another uncle based out of Nakhodka, a major container port north of Vladivostok, was involved in the wholesale import trade and regularly supplied Erkin and his brothers on with the spices they needed from Uzbekistan.

In this exemplary case, close kinship ties structure the economic organization of an extended group of immigrant traders from Uzbekistan. Entrance into the market was facilitated through close-kin relationships. The first wave of immigrants of Erkin's family, namely his uncles, set up businesses in Vladivostok and provided job opportunities for newcomers. Once he was an already established trader, Erkin had a similar responsibility to provide work for his brothers. In his case, the immigrant family functions as an organizational base and resource pool (Sanders and Lee 1996: 246). This close cooperation based on kinship extends to the supply lines for the brother's businesses. The reliance on family members to supply goods and the utilization of family channels as a means of transport are a common characteristic of many ethnic trading communities (MacGaffey and Bazenguissa-Ganga 2000). Erkin received his supplies directly from Uzbekistan. Relatives also regularly sent him smaller amounts of merchandise as cargo and travelling family members (e.g. cousins) often transported larger quantities. Other traders I interviewed on the markets rely on similar kin networks for supply. For example, a trader from Tajikistan who sold dried fruits at Sportivnaya Market was regularly supplied by his brother who worked as a wholesale dealer of dried fruits from Tajikistan. This brother also owned five stands of his own and supplied local hospitals, barracks, and kindergartens with dried fruits for *kompot* (beverage made from dried fruits). These family-based supply lines represent direct trading circuits with a minimum number of involved persons, which helps to reduce the costs for middlemen. Resource mobilization is a decisive element for the success of ethnic enterprises. Outward linkages to co-ethnic suppliers can be advantageous because transactions can be made in the native language and co-ethnic wholesalers are usually more flexible on credit (Min 1988).

However, not all supply routes to the market traders are organized along these immediate lines. Most of the vegetables on sale in the market, for instance, are imported from China. The geographic proximity of industrial centres in China's northern provinces in association with an efficient infrastructure makes it relatively easy for Chinese traders to import large amounts of merchandise into the Russian Far East.[39] The commodity flow from China includes different ethnic networks and actors. For example, a regular sales circuit for vegetables originates at a Chinese agricultural farm that sells its produce to a Chinese middleman at one of the wholesale markets in Russia. A stand proprietor, often a trader from Central Asia or the Caucasus, buys produce at the wholesale market and then delivers it to his individual salespersons, often of Russian nationality, for retail sale. The individual actors participate here in different ethnic networks and at the same time interact with global commodity flows (Williams and Balaz 2005: 534).

Dealing with family members has several advantages in terms of business conduct. The strong personal ties present in kinship networks allow for delayed reciprocity (Sahlins 1965: 148-58). In addition, conducting business with family members is a safeguard against being cheated in an informal economic environment with few judicial safeguards. I follow here Claire Wallace's argument that emphasizes the importance of social capital

---

[39] Social networks additionally help to gather information about permits, laws, management practices, reliable suppliers, and promising business lines. The Chinese community in Moscow, for example, numbers between 20,000 and 25,000 individuals and has an extensive service system for its members that offer judicial help, financing, transport, and storage space (Vitkovskaya 1999b: 2).

as a strategy of ethnic entrepreneurs to secure economic returns and reduce the risk of business operations (Wallace et al. 1999: 752). Goods can be ordered without a formal contract, credits can be extended, and family members can be used as suppliers at no extra cost. The geographically dispersed kin networks facilitate international business ties. In this example, kinship is not centred on nuclear household groups, but rather organized along a network principle, a phenomenon Christine Ho described as 'the internationalization of the family' (Ho 1993: 34). Cooperation among immigrant traders is not confined to the extended family network. Family members are only the closest circle of a wider support network that can be potentially activated by trading minorities. Other support circles on which Erkin relied, for example, included fellow countrymen and other foreign traders in Vladivostok (Figure 6). Erkin often turned to a wider network of *zemlyaki* (fellow countrymen) to resolve problems that he had not experienced previously or that his immediate relatives were not able to solve. For instance, one of Erkin's acquaintances, whom he referred to as a *zemlyak*, worked as a lawyer in Vladivostok. Erkin contacted him one day when his passport was confiscated by the immigration police for a second time, and asked for help dealing with the court hearing. The widest association network to which Erkin could turn for support was the group of foreign traders with whom he shared a common market space. Numerous times I observed ad-hoc cooperation among traders from Central Asia and the Caucasus during immigration police raids in the market. The stands abandoned by illegal traders were temporarily managed by fellow traders who had escaped police scrutiny. In times of external threats, for instance an unexpected police raid, professional proximity as traders and the common status as a migrant worker created temporary group cohesion. On one occasion, one of Erkin's neighbouring traders was arrested by the police. His booth was suddenly deserted and a shopper asked for his whereabouts. Erkin, who ran the stand in his absence, answered with a twist of irony, 'He just left for Magadan'. During another police raid, while several of the Uzbek and Azeri traders fled their stands and disappeared in the maze of apartment blocks that surround the market, Erkin found refuge in one of the closed shop containers of an Azeri acquaintance.

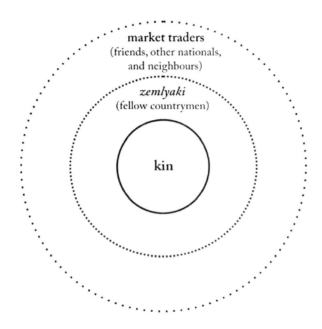

Figure 6. Affiliation among ethnic and non-ethnic traders in Vladivostok's open-air markets.

Informal networks at open-air markets function as a safety net in a high-risk environment. Kinship and ethnicity play a central role in the fabric of these networks. Olga Brednikova and Oleg Pachenkov, who conducted fieldwork in St. Petersburg among immigrant workers from the Caucasus, have isolated five factors that lead to the formation of tight ethnic networks among migrant traders: (1) simplicity, (2) rationality, (3) trust, (4) outside pressure, and (5) spatial proximity (Brednikova and Pachenkov 2002: 49-52). I will follow here their model by critically applying it to the presented case of the Uzbek brothers:

1. <u>Simplicity</u>. Erkin and his brothers did not cooperate with fellow Uzbeks just because of their ethnic similarity, but because it was easier to communicate in a common language. Cultural similarity helped them to understand each others' motives. Yet under certain circumstances, kinship obligations as well as binding and conflicting aspects of kin-cooperations can overrule the simplicity factor.
2. <u>Rationality</u>. The choice of co-workers, wholesale sellers, and retail sellers is based on a rational selection which

minimizes effort and at the same time maximizes profits. The economic ties among the three brothers and their maternal uncles were characterized by a high degree of cooperation and efficiency. The profits of the brother's business were collected in a common pool that covered their living expenses and was occasionally used to offset losses at one of their trading spots. However, kin solidarity is not necessarily a rational choice and free of conflicts.

3. <u>Trust</u>. Trust played an important role in the supply line of the brother's business and their day-to-day economic interactions. Shipments of merchandise from Uzbekistan, facilitated through family members, relied on confidence that the payment would be made without a formal contract. In addition, money transfers back to Uzbekistan were made with the help of family members or countrymen to whom the brothers entrusted part of their earnings.

4. <u>Outside pressure</u>. Complex and shifting bureaucratic procedures for immigrant workers in Russia, discrimination at the workplace, everyday xenophobia, racially motivated attacks, and frequent raids by the immigration police bring an outsider group close together.

5. <u>Spatial proximity</u>. Shared space at the market and spatial proximity on a day-to-day basis created close social relationships among individual traders that often transgressed ethnic boundaries. In the case of the Uzbek brothers, their kinship network was not only used for economic activities, but represented also the main social structure for organizing their everyday life, from shared living arrangements – Erkin lived with his brothers and two other Uzbeks in a three room apartment – to group travel from their apartment to the market.

To explain the rise of ethnic enterprises, Howard Aldrich relied on the notion that ethnic groups strategically adapt to the resources available in their environment.[40] In Aldrich's approach, structures of opportunity represent specific market conditions, which may favour certain ethnic enterprises. Traits or group characteristics depict the cultural dispositions of a given

---

[40] Howard Aldrich (1990) used a framework based on three dimensions to study ethnic enterprises: an ethnic group's access to opportunities and resources, specific cultural traits of that group, and emergent strategies as a reaction to the first two parameters. He argued that particular ethnic strategies emerge from the interaction of opportunities and group characteristics.

ethnic group, including the capacity to mobilize resources and to rely on social networks (Aldrich 1990: 114).

Given the fact that opportunity structures provide niches for potential entrepreneurs, the dominant market conditions are therefore of central importance to explain the prevalence of ethnic entrepreneurs in the Russian Far East. Ivan Light (1972) argued in his 'protected market hypothesis' that the initial market for ethnic entrepreneurs often originates in the ethnic community itself. In the case of trading minorities in Primorsky Krai, who almost without exception sell their goods to local Russians, this observation applies only partially. Only auxiliary services, like food catering, are rendered by a specific ethnic group to their own members. Yet other circumstances can lead to the rise of ethnic enterprises. Underserved or abandoned markets and markets with unstable or uncertain demand can create fertile ground for ethnic enterprises (Aldrich 1990: 114). The collapse of the Soviet-era consumer goods and agricultural industry in Primorsky Krai during the 1990s created such a vacuum in supplies. From 1990-97, the production of consumer goods dropped considerably in most of the districts of Primorsky Krai (Alekseev 1999a: 3). The local production of agricultural products (milk, eggs, meat, etc.) has also dropped dramatically since 1990. Chinese traders fill these gaps with imported goods from China. In addition, the decline in real wages in the Russian Far East forced most of the low-income population to buy the cheapest goods available. Prices in the Chinese markets average one-third less than those in local department stores or supermarkets. A Russian customer interviewed in Sportivnaya Market gave the following explanation for her choice of clothes made in China, 'You can buy cheap goods at the Chinese stands, and that is good, they helped us when we had a deficit. And they are good construction workers. You should see the buildings they have in China. Why can our construction workers not accomplish this?'.

Markets affected by instability and uncertainty present niches of opportunity for ethnic groups. Ethnic businesses thrive in an economic environment characterized by high risks and uncertain conditions. Their willingness to take higher risks makes them well suited for setting up businesses in an economic milieu abandoned by larger firms and the prevalence of unstable demand. The social embeddedness of immigrant traders in different circles of cohesion, from close kin networks to the temporary cooperation of immigrant traders, assists such traders to survive in the high-risk environment of the open-air markets' shadow economy. This is especially true for traders like Erkin, who worked as an illegal migrant worker without a valid residence or work permit.

Erkin was deported from Russia at the end of summer 2004. He had been caught for the third time by the police without a valid *propusk*. A stamp on the last page of his passport indicated that he had to leave the country within one month. In addition, he was banned from re-entering Russia for five years. Nevertheless, Erkin planned to return soon with the help of a simple ploy: in Uzbekistan he would apply for a new passport. Instead of his surname, it would show his patronym, and feature a slightly changed birth date. 'Everything is possible in Uzbekistan for money. If you have money, you have the power', clarified his brother Tolkin. Tolkin told me the rest of Erkin's plan: 'He will return in one or two months, although he has to find work at a different market, the police here now know him too well'. Tolkin, as the oldest of the three brothers in Russia, shouldered responsibility for the others, and he already had a plan. He dreamed of a new business on the island of Sakhalin, a place so far untouched by Uzbek spice merchants. One of his regular customers lived on Sakhalin. On his monthly trips to Vladivostok he always stopped by at the brothers' stalls to buy spices and seasonings. He had recommended that they start a business there and had promised to help them through his contacts. Tolkin planned to look into the situation and invest in a one or two month exploratory stay. Sakhalin, he thought, would be a good place for his returning brother to work.

Keith Hart has stressed the role and function of the informal economy as a source of economic dynamism and capital accumulation (Hart 2005: 9). The described ethnic entrepreneurs have found in Vladivostok's open-air markets an economic space that allows them to operate in the shadow of formal economic institutions. Indeed, the marginal geographic location of the Russian Far East especially offers a multitude of opportunities. L.E. Bliakher and L.A. Vasileva have argued that the Russian Far East has functioned historically as a 'land in reserve' (Bliakher and Vasileva 2010: 84). The status of the Russian Far East has thus been economically and politically structured by its relationship with Russia's political and economic centre (i.e. Moscow). In cyclical alterations, the Far East has experienced periods of state tutelage with increased material flows from the centre and phases of suspension when the region has been largely abandoned to its own devices. During the first 20 years of the post-Soviet period the region was in a state of suspension, when 'interregional space becomes invisible for the state' (ibid.: 90). This invisible economic space, what I have addressed as the shadow, has created a multitude of informal income opportunities for a range of actors, but has also divided the population into visible and invisible parts. The porosity of the post-Soviet border to China has even increased the shadow of economic solutions outside of state control, which is the topic of the next chapter.

Chapter 4
Eastern Porosity: Cross-Border Trade in the Russian Far East

Journey to Suifenhe, October 2004. It is still dawn as the coach leaves the bus terminal in the early morning. Located next to Vtoraya Rechka Market at the northern end of the city, the bus terminal is Vladivostok's long-distance transportation hub to various locations in Primorsky Krai and China. The coldness of a late October morning persists outside. The boardwalks are covered by a layer of ice from the snowfall of the preceding days. Vladivostok's suburbs pass by as the bus moves along the road that leaves the city towards the north. The bus windows are steamed up from inside and I am consumed by the effort to keep a patch clear to catch a glimpse of the passing urban landscape. Commuter traffic chokes the lanes of the incoming highways that wind through the outskirts of town. Multi-storey apartments line the road, their grey silhouettes contrasting with the lightening sky. Merry chatter fills the inside of the bus. Some of the passengers have already opened beers and begin discussing the trip that lies ahead. Most of my fellow travellers are *chelnoki* (lit. shuttle, i.e. tourist) traders. Our destination of Suifenhe, the prosperous border town in China's Heilongjiang Province, is just a day's trip away from Vladivostok. Almost exclusively women, the sojourners in the bus arrived this morning in little groups – each group with a person in charge overseeing the travel documents and customs clearance for five to ten women. The women will spend two or three days on their trip to Suifenhe, organized through a tourist company, to purchase merchandise, mostly clothes and shoes, and import it back to Russia.

After an hour, the wide floodplain of a peninsula that connects Vladivostok with the mainland begins to extend beyond the road. Waves of gushing wind roll through marshy meadows and patches of reed sway in a cold breeze. Snowdrifts from the first snowfall of the season nest in the hollows of the plain. Dacha colonies and small settlements separated by wide stretches of open farmland, forests, and swampland have replaced the city blocks and apartment complexes of Vladivostok. The landscape drifts by. North of here, on the frozen surface of Chanka Lake, Arsenyev once got lost and was almost killed in a fierce blizzard. Only the reeds, stacked to a warming shelter, saved the lives of the explorer and his native guide Dersu Uzala.

The kinetic of perception surprises me. When I glide through the cityscape of Vladivostok I am myself the vector, passing by. But now, riding in a bus outside of town, it is the surroundings that are in motion, everything is passing by. Calmness starts to grow in my head replacing the bustling noise of the city with silence.

After three hours we arrive in Pogranichnyy, 15 kilometres east of the Chinese border. Looking towards the west I catch a glimpse of the Laoye-Ling Mountains that separate Primorsky Krai from Heilongjiang Province. Rolling hills covered with a thin layer of snow gradually dissolve into the horizon. The inconspicuous border town with its 4,000 inhabitants lies tucked at the base of these hills. The wide boulevards are deserted. A cold down draught from the hills plays with leftover autumn leaves on the pavement. Long thin icicles hang in rows from the gabled roofs of wooden houses. The central bus station of Pogranichnyy is a rough concrete square. Dust mixes with the diesel fumes of buses. In an hourly rhythm, large coaches leave for China. Colourful motifs of Chinese dragons decorate the coaches, contrasting with the dusty grey pavement and buildings of the terminal. Chinese pop music sounds from inside. The terminal is a place of silent activity, a stage where the bustling cross-border trade between Russia and China pauses in its flow. It is a hub where commodities and border traders freeze in motion for a short while, waiting for transport. Large bundles of merchandise, each having the same format, are unloaded from buses and piled on the pavement in front of the terminal. Small groups of Russian women accompany these shipments. Sitting on their bundles they are seated close together to protect themselves from the cold wind. Next to the bus station and its small adjacent open-air market lies the train station. Freight cars loaded with timber destined for China line up for hundreds of metres on several tracks.

Plate 8. Last bus station before the Chinese border, Pogranichnyy 2004.

After an hour-long stop we continue our journey. The border is just minutes away. The driver stops the bus at the end of a line of trucks and buses filled with shuttle traders. The vehicles have to pass one by one through the Russian customs clearance. After an hour wait, it is our turn. We have to leave the bus and move individually with our personal luggage through customs. The customs office is a bleak, grey concrete block. Wind is pressing hard against the large windows that shiver from the strong gusts. I can feel the cold draught inside. A Russian inspector stares with boredom at the screen of an x-ray machine, and after checking our group he focuses again on his crossword puzzle. The inspector at passport control is more alert, slightly confused by my appearance. A German in the Russian-Chinese borderland is a rare occurrence. His eyes move from my passport to my face, then back again, several times. He double-checks my Russian visa. Then the stamp drops with a heavy thump. We board the bus again, which meanwhile passed through a separate clearance passage. On the other side of the lane, buses and trucks from China line up. Groups of *chelnoki* drag large bundles from the buses to the customs building.

We continue through no-man's-land. Tall watchtowers on the surrounding hillcrest rise above the brown forest. After several kilometres the road passes an enormous building site. About a dozen construction cranes, topped with the Chinese national flag, surround the foundation of the future cross-border trade complex of Suifenhe-Pogranichnyy. After we pass the 75 acres of steel and concrete groundwork we arrive at the Chinese border. As before on the Russian side, a similar customs procedure begins. In contrast to the Russian customs, everything on the Chinese side bears a touch of novelty: the uniforms of the customs officials glitter with golden epaulettes, the customs office is recently built, the floors are of shiny granite, and the waiting rooms are well heated. My group passes the inspections without any problems. Everybody seems to have experienced the procedures many times before. *Chelnoki* are seasoned sojourners of the borderland.

Shortly behind the border begins the city of Suifenhe. Only ten years ago, the city was a small village with only a few thousand inhabitants. In 2004, Suifenhe is a city of 200,000. As we approach the city I realize the scope of the Chinese modernization project in this region, which is mostly founded on the trading boom with Russia. Numerous high-rise apartments and office buildings surround the former town centre and sprawl into the surrounding forested hillsides, stripped of its leaves by the advanced fall. A Buddhist temple, erected on several terraces on an adjacent hill, seems detached from the rapidly grown city. The colossal statue of a chalk-white Buddha draped in an orange cape overlooks the city, his eyes patiently glaring into the blanket of smog hovering over the city's smokestacks. The bus drops us in the middle of town. My fellow travellers leave for their prearranged hotels. I follow a group to the Tao Juan Hotel, a favourite overnight destination for Russian shuttle traders.

Suifenhe's cityscape is dominated by steel and glass architecture. Large shopping centres flank the streets; the major ones surround the central square in the city's centre. Under the granite pavement of the plaza extends a two-storey underground shopping mall filled with hundreds of small stores. Most of the shop signs are bilingual in Chinese and Russian. Well-known Western brand names ornament the shopping fronts. The city is full of energy, a bustling trading hub thriving on the border with Russia. During the day, Russian shoppers stroll in small groups through the city, some of them carry heavy bags. Chinese helpers are abundant at the street corners, offering their service to guide or haul for a small fee.

In the evening, the lobby of the hotel fills with groups of *chelnoki* on their way out for dinner in town. I start a conversation with a woman in her early twenties, she calls herself a *pomogaika* (helper) because she works as a hired shuttle trader for a Russian import company. Kseniya arrived today with her sister and several aunts from a small town in the Russian border district. Tomorrow they will head back to Pogranichnyy, each loaded with 50 kilograms of merchandise for the wholesale dealer who pays her 200 rubles, plus the costs of the trip and overnight accommodation. Kseniya shows me her Russian passport. Dozens of Chinese immigration stamps fill the pages. A resident of Zharikovo, a small town in Pogranichnyy Rayon, approximately 60 kilometres away, Kseniya has been more than 50 times to Suifenhe, yet never before to Vladivostok. Many of her friends and relatives are involved in the shuttle trade with China. In the rural regions along the border to China, work as a shuttle trader represents one of the few income opportunities, especially for women. The high demand for cheap Chinese goods, sold in the open-air markets of the Russian Far East, has created a whole infrastructure of transporters, a fact well known to Kseniya, 'The Chinese markets in the region thrive on the backs of the helpers [*pomogaiki*]. We only do their work, but the others get rich. But what can I do, I need to make some living'. After our short conversation, she leaves for dinner with her relatives. I step outside into the evening.

Activity in the streets has slightly ebbed, although shops and department stores are still open. I pass by an opening ceremony for a new fur shopping centre. Flower bouquets surround a small speaker's platform. A red inflatable arch framed by dragon heads reaches over the large glass doors of the entrance. Above, golden letters spell '*Gorod Kozhi "Novii Vostok"*' (City of Pelts 'New East'). Seven storeys high, each floor is filled with dozens of small boutiques selling leather and fur clothes. The furs are imported from Russia, manufactured in China to coats, and then exported back to Russia. On a small stage, several Russian models in bikinis and fur coats freeze in the cold wind, waiting for their act. A DJ plays loud music; several speeches follow and then, firecrackers explode, baptizing the new mall.

Chelnoki – Weaving Shuttles

> 'You have to feel how a product is selling'.
> – Viktor, age 24, shuttle trader

The system of shuttle trade was originally based on the fact that, according to a federal resolution from 1 August 1996, merchandise up to the amount of 50 kilograms or US$1,000 can be imported duty-free into the Russian Federation.[41] This fact has far reaching implications and sustains a whole branch of informal traders, the *chelnoki*. A *chelnok* is a weaving shuttle, and its metaphorical extension to trade signifies the zigzag movements of shuttle traders across the border on a regular basis. The shuttle trade is by far not an

---

[41] In 2003 the law was changed to dissuade trade by emphasizing that the allowances were for 'tourists'. Under the new law, declared merchandise within the weight allowance must be accompanied personally across the border. In addition, the personal weight allowance for 'tourists' can be claimed only once per week. See Irina Skliarova, 'Konets chelnochnoy diplomatii', *Vladivostok*, 2 October 2002.

isolated phenomenon of the Russian Far East. It is applied in a wide-scale along the various borders of the Russian Federation.[42] Trader tourism in the post-Soviet sphere is mostly an effect of a collapsed local small-goods industry and the emphasized need for imported goods among local populations (Konstantinov 1996: 777). Essentially, two different classes of shuttle traders exist in Russia, *naemnye chelnoki* (hired shuttle traders) and *svobodnye chelnoki* (independent shuttle traders).[43]

The journeys of a hired shuttle trader start in most cases with a *turisticheskaya firma* (tourist company) that assembles the shuttle traders through word of mouth or newspaper advertisements. These tourist companies normally assemble groups between 20 and 40 people who are sent to China to receive cargo in increments of the personal 50 kilogram allowance. In this way, wholesale dealers import large quantities of merchandise from China essentially tax free.[44] The tourist company provides bus transportation, arranges hotel accommodation, and deals with the necessary border formalities.[45]

All major towns in Primorsky Krai have several tourist companies that facilitate shopping tours to Heilongjiang Province, mainly the cities of Suifenhe and Harbin. Primorsky Krai has five border crossings to China (see Map 4). The city of Ussurisk, 100 kilometres north of Vladivostok, is the main centre for shuttle traders in Primorsky Krai. Ussurisk's central location in the region and its relative proximity to China, only two hours by bus to Suifenhe, made it the centre of cross-border trade between China and Russia in Primorsky Krai. Two border crossings are usually accessed from Ussurisk. One, the border crossing at Pogranichnyy, is a combined railroad and road border crossing; the other at Pokrovka, features solely a road connection.

---

[42] According to different counts, the total numbers of shuttle traders in Russia ranges between four and six million. Up to 10,000 shuttle traders operate in Primorsky Krai on a regular basis. See Viktor Serdyuk, 'Chelnoki ostanutsya bez pomogaek, a zaodno i bez raboty', *Vladivostok*, 19 July 2002. In 1999, 209,300 Russian tourists crossed across the border from Primorsky Krai to China (Barannik 2002: 48).

[43] In colloquial language, hired shuttle traders are referred to as *pomogaiki* (helpers) or sometimes as *kemely* (camels).

[44] A full bus of 30-40 people is able to import 1,500- 2,000 kilograms per trip. The Russian customs office estimates the daily loss of import taxes from shuttle trade in the Russian Far East to be as high as US$700,000. See Vasiliy Avchenko, 'Kombinator iz Suifen'khe, ili Imperiya podnebesnoy khitrosti', *Vladivostok*, 13 August 2003.

[45] Tourist companies are able to provide visa-free tours according to an agreement signed by Russia and China in February 2000.

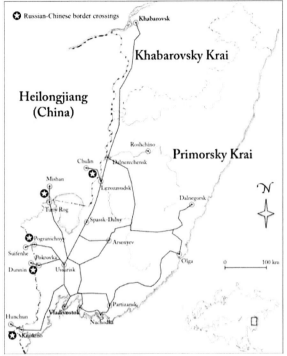

Map 4. International border crossings in Primorsky Krai.

Upon arrival in Suifenhe, a group of shuttle traders checks into a hotel. They usually arrive after lunch and the details of the cargo hand-over are discussed with an organizer at dinner. The next morning, the group is handed the cargo in packages of 20, 30, or 50 kilograms for the *optovik* (wholesale dealer) in Russia. Occasionally, the cargo has already been loaded onto the bus. When the group arrives back in Russia the cargo is handed to the wholesale dealer and the shuttle traders receive their wage, which normally ranges between 100 and 400 rubles. The wholesale dealer plays a central role in the system. He or she organizes the cargo, hires the tour company to select the traders and organize the trip, and redistributes the merchandise after its arrival in Russia.

Primorsky Krai is an important transit location for commodities originating in China and functions as a commodity hub for the territory of the whole Russian Far East. Wholesale dealers based in Primorsky Krai deliver goods to marginal locations such as Sakhalin Island, the Kurile Islands, or Chukotka, where the retail prices are almost twice as high as in Primorsky Krai. The widespread use of hired shuttle traders reduces transport costs and bypasses import taxes. Almost all of the merchandise imported with the help of *chelnoki* is destined for sale in open-air markets or the recently established boutiques in shopping centres.

A *svobodnyy chelnok* (independent shuttle trader) works independently of tourist companies. An independent trader usually holds a multi-entry Chinese visa, valid for either six months or one year. The journey is self-organized and the trader invests his own capital in the goods he buys in China. Although the profit margin is higher compared to the hired shuttle traders who merely receive a wage, more self-initiative and larger investments are required. Another hurdle consists in finding a wholesale trader to buy the merchandise once it is imported. For independent shuttle traders, social networks based on kin and acquaintances are therefore crucial to success. Often, two or three helpers (usually from within the trader's networks) are employed to increase the amount of imported goods, thus increasing the profit. Traders also use their networks to place their merchandise for sale. The enlargement of trading operations can include a whole set of social relations to sellers, buyers, and custom officers (Humphrey 2002: 77).

Plate 9. Pre-packed packages ready for shuttle transport, Suifenhe, China 2004.

I learned much about the shuttle trade from Viktor, a 24-year-old native of Ussurisk. Viktor has a university degree in Japanese language and had taught part time as a language instructor at the Vladivostok University. As a student he worked for two years as a shuttle trader; first he was a hired trader and then later he became an independent *chelnok*. Not able to survive on the meagre income from this job, he had recently switched to better paying work as a salesman for a large dealership which imports car tires from Japan. On several occasions we had conversations on his former profession as a shuttle trader. He always stressed the importance of social networking: 'It is very difficult for an independent shuttle trader to sell merchandise to wholesale dealers in the market if you are unknown. You need connections [*svyazi*] and acquaintance [*znakomstvo*] with the right people. If you are unknown in the business, nobody trusts you and wants to deal with you. It is like in every other business in Russia, connections are the most important thing'.

Hotels in Harbin or Suifenhe where the groups of shuttle traders are accommodated play an important role as social nodes for independent shuttle traders who want to contact potential Russian or Chinese wholesale dealers. Experience and a wide network of personal relationships are important for the long-term success of an independent shuttle trader. Independent *chelnoki* who lack the necessary connections are often forced to sell directly to stand owners in Russian open-air markets, which bears considerable economic risks in terms of securing the sale of one's merchandise. For instance, one of my informants who made the transition from work as a hired *chelnok* to independent shuttle trade was once left with 100 pairs of shoes that he could not sell for an economically viable price. Another way for independent shuttle traders to sell their merchandise is to independently own one or several market stands or boutiques. Still, the economic risks remain elevated, if the scale of trade is high, as one's own capital is invested.

The work as an independent shuttle trader demands a range of different skills. Beyond social networking abilities, intimate knowledge of current and future fashion trends is indispensable for the success of an independent business operation. Viktor explained this specific knowledge:

> What kind of goods the *chelnoki* bring to the market very much depends on the season and on fashion trends. Fashion constantly changes. For instance, new shoes are already out of fashion after two months, replaced by new models. The same applies to leather goods. The Chinese who trade in the markets in China dictate more or less the fashion. For instance, they say, now this is the new product, absolutely new fashion. They also look at the amount that Russian buyers are purchasing and so see what is currently fashionable. Television commercials play also an important role. For instance, people see on television an Adidas commercial for a new pair of sneakers. The Chinese are very good in copying that specific model and people are looking out for it. Of course it is not the real model, just a copy. When the people see that model, they think, 'Oh, I have

seen that on television, I want that shoe'. My father had a market stand in Ussurisk. He first went to China [for merchandise] and went later on to Turkey. He knew exactly which fashion is good and which does not sell. You have to feel how a product is selling.

The *chelnoki* system provides various possibilities for the participants who show a skilful use of insider knowledge and personal relationships. Viktor mentioned the case of his cousin:

> My cousin first worked as a hired *chelnok*, and then he acquired a visa [for China] and began to work on his own. But first you have to work under a company, as a hired *chelnok*, in order to understand the business and the market, to see everything with your own eyes. Then, if you have acquainted yourself with Chinese dealers, know where to find the cheap goods, found out the best way to bring the merchandise to Russia, and collected enough experience, you may do it on your own. The same applies to the Russian counterparts. Every time the bus stops at the border for a couple of hours, people go and eat and begin to talk to each other. This is where you meet with other *chelnoki* and it is the time to work on connections. After all these experiences it is easier to work on your own.

Such a career trajectory is exemplified by a female entrepreneur I interviewed in 2002. The woman had started her career in the early 1990s as a simple hired shuttle trader, crossing the border to China on a regular basis. Later she invested her profit by working as an independent shuttle trader, adding trips to southern Chinese cities and Korea, thus increasing her profit margin. Now she imports used cars from Japan.

This economic biography of a former hired shuttle trader is not exceptional. The system of shuttle trade follows a simple logic of capital accumulation, investment, and expanding knowledge of the market. Successful entrepreneurship creates vertical economic mobility for the participants. Capital and knowledge, acquired through work as a hired *chelnok* for a company, can be invested into an independent business. The increase of venture capital is usually accompanied by spatial expansion, which means more distant and profitable destinations are visited. A common step of an independent *chelnok* based out of Primorsky Krai, for example, is to expand his shuttle sojourns from Suifenhe to Harbin. Harbin is slightly further from the border, but it is the provincial capital and merchandise of higher quality is available. Other destinations are even more profitable, but require higher investments to cover the costs of travel and transportation. Some experienced shuttle traders with the necessary capital travel as far as Beijing, Japan, Korea, and Turkey.

The increase of venture capital and spatial expansion lead to new forms of cooperation among individual shuttle traders. As a first step, independent *chelnoki* include close friends or family members in their business. Thus, resources can be pooled to increase the amount of the purchase in addition to the extra weight allowance that comes with each member of a small shuttle trader group.[46] A next possible step is to increase the group size even more by employing several shuttle traders who buy goods on behalf of an independent trader. At this point the circle closes and the independent *chelnok* turns into a wholesale trader who uses hired shuttle traders to import merchandise on a larger scale.

Layered into the grey economy of the shuttle trade is yet another commercial activity, which is also based on the lower commodity prices in China. The smuggling of vodka from China into Russia, the *vodichnyy biznes* (vodka business), presents an extra income for some of the hired shuttle traders to supplement their relatively low pay.[47] Two different ways of smuggling vodka into Russia on a small scale are usually employed. One way is to tape vodka that is sold in flexible plastic bags to the body underneath a layer of clothing. An experienced smuggler can tape up to ten bags on his body without raising too much suspicion at the customs inspection. The other way is to use the ventilation shafts of the buses which usually have room to hide up to two cases of vodka, approximately 40 bottles. To conduct this side business successfully, shuttle traders need to acquire a specific knowledge: which bus drivers are willing to partake in the smuggling, where cheap vodka is sold in China, and where to sell the contraband in Russia. The vodka is usually sold in open-air markets by traders who offer it to known clients.

In these cases, the crossing of a single shuttle trader can integrate different forms of legal and illegal conduct – a *chelnok* is legally importing merchandise into the country but at the same time smuggling illegal contraband. This blending of legal and illegal spheres is exactly what characterizes cross-border trade in many instances. Cross-border trade consists of multi-layered routes, where the legal blends with the illegal in a single transportation channel.[48]

---

[46] The pooling of money is especially common among traders who import used cars from Japan.

[47] Vodka is sold in China for approximately half the Russian price; traders net a profit of approximately 20 rubles per smuggled bottle. The legal quantity for import is two bottles.

[48] Carolyn Nordstrom described cross-border as 'entangled roads' because of the ways in which the formal and the legal mix with the non-formal and the illicit in one channel (Nordstrom 2004: 93).

The system of shuttle trade is a highly flexible and adaptable form of small-scale cross-border trade that regularly reacts to changing border jurisdiction. Developments during the mid-2000s fundamentally changed the conditions for cross-border trade between China and Russia. The laws of 1996 and 2003 have already been mentioned; conditions have continually changed in the subsequent decade. In the fall of 2005, 15 of Primorsky Krai's largest tourist companies that had facilitated shuttle trade between China and Russia were legally banned from organizing visa-free tours. In February 2006, Russia enacted a new federal import law which limited individual persons to importing 35 kilograms per month.[49] In 2010, the customs union between Russia, Belarus, and Kazakhstan led to yet another profound change, as the previous baggage allowance was raised to 50kg/US$2,000 and all limits governing the frequency of border crossings were removed. This law, originally meant to benefit the three countries, had also a substantial impact on Chinese-Russian border trade. Generally speaking, shuttle trade in Russia has transformed over the years from a trade strategy that was born out of the necessities that resulted from the collapsed Soviet economic system towards a form of advantageous trade (Stammler-Gossman 2011: 234). In addition, touristic motives play an increasing role, as traders combine the potential economic advantages of a cross-border sojourn with the amenities of a brief but enjoyable stay in the neighbouring country.

This shift from necessity to advantageous trade that is combined with touristic interest is reflected in a new generation of shuttle traders and tour operators. In 2012, I had a conversation with a Russian tourist group leader from Vladivostok in her hotel in Suifenhe. Surrounded by the pre-packaged bags of her customers and her bed covered with receipts and notes, she was busy preparing her group's departure to the border crossing later that day. In her mid-fifties, Olga had started her business as a *turisticheskiy rukovoditel'* (tourist group leader) after six months of vocational training at the beginning of 2000. Since then, she had been organizing *ekonom tury* (economic tours) for Russian shopping tourists, mostly from Vladivostok. Her usual group size ranges from 5 to 15 persons who generally stay for 3 days and 2 nights in Suifenhe. After an initial meeting at the Vladivostok bus station, Olga helps her tourist clients to cross the border, arranges hotel rooms, and helps to locate specific commodities. As she stressed, the majority of her clients take the journey mostly for personal shopping and recreation (for example, food, fishing, drinking, and Chinese massages), as the prices for those services are still much cheaper in China compared to Russia. To help her

---

[49] Aleksandr Ognevskiy, 'Bagazh na tamozhennom formate', *Vladivostok*, 17 February 2006.

enterprise succeed in China and to accommodate her clients' specific shopping needs, Olga works closely with a Chinese middleman who acts as a facilitator on the ground, and with whom she operates a storage warehouse in town. Despite the new import laws that have liberalized the amount of allowed goods and frequency of border-crossings, increased visa fees have hampered independent work as a shuttle trader. By offering organized tourist trips to China she is able to facilitate visa-free travel for Russians to Suifenhe for an affordable price. Creative adaptations and solutions to frequently changing customs regulations is key for her business success, as she stressed on several occasions: 'We have very smart lawyers and lawmakers in Russia who constantly think about new laws that affect the cross-border trade and we always have to react and find a way around those laws'.

Plate 10. Russian 'tourists' in Suifenhe, China 2012.

The sentiment of trading against the state or circumventing legal regulations surfaces repeatedly in conversations that other researchers have had with shuttle traders along Russia's borders. For instance, Natalia Ryzhova argued based on her research among shuttle traders in the twin border towns of Blagoveshchensk (Russia) and Heihe (China) that these forms of informal strategies lead to trans-local market consolidations against the state (Ryzhova 2008). The everyday trans-border (economic) contacts between these two cities have created forms of informal trans-locality independent of state interactions. Anna Stammler-Gossman, encountered a similar 'beat-the-system' approach in her work along the Russian-Finish border, as one of her informants expressed elegantly: 'Do not violate the law, but know the ways to avoid it' (Stammler-Gossman 2011: 241).

Informal Cross-Border Trade

> 'For one can go across the border naked but not without one's skin; for, unlike clothes, one cannot get a new skin'.
> – Karl Kraus, *Half-Truths*

The opening of the Russian-Chinese border and the numerous crossings that have been enabled since the collapse of the Soviet Union has transformed the face of the Russian Far East as an economic, national, and geopolitical borderland. Citizens and traders in the region are invariably affected by cross-border flows of people and commodities as increased commodity flows and labour migration, especially from China, have created both economic challenges and opportunities for the local population.

Cross-border trade is a two-way flow. The trade between Russia and China includes both Russian and Chinese citizens. Although I have only mentioned Russian shuttle traders in the preceding section, Chinese are equally involved in the trade.[50] Embedded in the overall exchange relations between the two countries, the shuttle trade represents only one aspect of Chinese-Russian cross-border trade. As the border is used for commercial purposes on many levels, including both legal and illegal economic activities, licit and illicit conduct is blurred, and the border economies are characterized by their constant oscillation between the formal and the informal.

Borders divide, but they also bring people and commodities into contact and create opportunities to forge networks of cross-border cooperation. Scholars of borderlands have invoked various images of passageways to better understand the flows of commodities and people through the bottlenecks of border crossings. In the early twentieth century, Georg Simmel evoked the image of a bridge and door that mark boundaries by separating and connecting them at the same time (Simmel 1997 [1909]). This rather static image, however, has only limited value when applied to contemporary borderlands that are often in perpetual flux in regard to their

---

[50] The actual number of Chinese shuttle traders is difficult to estimate. Like the Russian traders, most Chinese nationals who work as shuttle traders enter Primorsky Krai on a tourist visa or make use of the visa-free travel regime for tourist groups. In 2001, 154,500 Chinese tourists were registered as visiting Primorsky Krai (Barannik 2002: 44).

permeability for certain goods or people. To adequately address the waxing and waning of border permeability through time, Hastings Donnan and Dieter Haller proposed the image of a zipper that is 'never completely open or closed when seen over the long term' (Donnan and Haller 2000: 13). In this chapter, I have found it useful to adopt the metaphor of a 'programme' that 'let[s] certain people and things through, while keeping others out' (Delaplace 2012: 4).

The Russian-Chinese borderland is a constantly changing programme through which local entrepreneurs skilfully engage the state. In what follows below, I focus on how small-scale cross-border traders have evolved various informal economic practices to cope with the border programme on a regular basis. Dwelling on Delaplace's image, I focus on the subversive economic practices that evolved as a reaction to a specific border programme.

The relationship between traders and the border provides a lens for better understanding how the state is perceived by actors on its periphery. The Russian Far East has been an outlying borderland throughout its history; in this respect it is similar to other peripheral localities of Russia. Cycles of decentralization and recentralization have shaped the region's relationship between local elites, inhabitants of the borderland, and the state's power centre (Gorenburg 2010; Libmann 2010). Phases of 'state tutelage' characterized by increased material inflow into the region have alternated with periods of 'suspension' when the region had been essentially abandoned by the state (Bliakher and Vasileva 2010). Since the collapse of the Soviet Union, the Far East has been in such a state of suspension and the informal economy has grown substantially. With President Putin's so-called strengthening of the power vertical, Russia has sought to recapture its influence over its eastern borderland. This effort at recentralization has been only partially successful in curtailing the region's burgeoning informal economy.

Small-scale informal cross-border trade can be seen as a particular set of trading practices that are levied against the state. Smuggling, as the state often terms such informal trade, involves the 'clandestine' importation or exportation of goods from one jurisdiction to another. The transported goods may be explicitly prohibited, and the carriers may seek to evade custom duties (Deflem and Henry-Turrer 2000: 473). Price disparities between markets and differential custom duties are normally seen as determining the likelihood of smuggling. However, cultural differences in consumption and specific ecological conditions play an equally important role. This is especially true on the Russian-Chinese border where certain species of flora and fauna that flourish in Russia are in high demand in China.[51] Whatever the motivation to undertake it, smuggling is defined always by the tax regime of a specific nation-state, and rarely by those who actively transport the goods. 'Smuggled' goods, whether or not their trade is prohibited, are never taxed. Thus, 'smuggling' should not be understood merely as a reaction or adaptation to any particular border regime, but as a generally subversive practice against the state and its tax regime (Karras 2009).

The trader's perspective that the penalization of small-scale cross-border trade is 'unnatural' smuggling was described by none other than Adam Smith. Smith, who was appointed in 1778 to the post of Commissioner of Customs for the United States, addressed the problem plainly: 'The hope of evading such taxes by smuggling, gives frequent occasion to forfeitures and other penalties, which entirely ruin the smuggler; a person who, though no doubt highly blameable for violating the laws of his country, is frequently incapable of violating those of natural justice, and would have been, in every respect, an excellent citizen, had not the laws of his country made that a crime which nature never meant to be so' (Smith 2001: 460).

When seen as a response to unnatural legislation, where the 'laws of a country' are juxtaposed to the 'laws of natural justice', basic perceptions of the state are at stake. Certain informal economic practices, especially those aimed at avoiding import taxes, are not necessarily seen as illicit by its practitioners or other members of society. The emic perspective of the smuggler often fundamentally differs from the legal viewpoint of state institutions and their agents (Abraham and van Schendel 2005: 4). The difference between what traders think should be legal and what the state decrees as legal, thus illuminates the very relation of citizens to their own state.

To draw attention to the frequently 'unnatural' programme of borders for those who live near them is not to say that borders represent merely a symbolic exercise of state power. Rather, borders are social constructs with symbolic values. And, they are also very material places, in which commodities, bodies, and ecological systems are brought together and mutually transformed.[52]

---

[51] Wild ginseng (*Panax ginseng*), Siberian or Amur tiger (*Panthera tigris altaica*), brown bear (*Ursus arctos horribilis*), Himalayan black bear (*Ursus torquatus*), and sea cucumber (*Apostichopus japonicus*) are the major poached species in Primorsky Krai that are in high demand in China as culinary and medicinal ingredients.

[52] Eeva Berglund's study on the Finnish-Russian border demonstrates how ecological processes interlink with social ties. As Finnish logging companies entering Russian Karelia, the materiality of the border forest creates social links fostered by environmentalists across the border (Berglund 2000).

The Russian borderland in the Far East is a multi-layered cultural zone that entangles people and commodities in specific networks and blurs the very border between them. Borders have different grades of permeability that can fluctuate and change through time, depending on the category of goods or people that move across. Border permeability is a function of state control, yet in the case of the Russian Far East, it is difficult to assess the actual capacity for control that the Russian state can muster. On the one hand, the border with China is a tightly controlled, well-demarcated military and state border with thousands of kilometres of fortified barbed wire fences and watchtowers eyeing each other across a barren strip of no-man's-land. On the other hand, endemic corruption in the Russian border guards and a limited visa-free travel regime for Russian and Chinese tourists has transformed the border into a rather porous demarcation line for both people and commodities. Though the border is porous, its existence accentuates local differences, particularly those influenced by the state, on each side. Despite the fragmented and fluid nature of modern-day global commerce and commodity flows, shuttle traders are part of a process of territorialization, rooted in the specific geography of the border zone, what Donna Flynn addresses as 'deep placement' (1997: 312).

In addition to focusing on the effects of the border, I also attend to the larger dynamics of the 'borderland milieu'.[53] Borderlands have special characteristics and functions (Anderson 1996). Economic practices thriving in a border region are based on border crossings and commodity flows from one country into the other. The concept of borderland helps to spatially resituate legal and illegal commodity flows by focusing on local actors who constitute a borderland society and profit from the peculiar characteristics of the border (van Schendel 2005: 44). Ecological processes, commodity flows, and social networks intertwine in a borderland.

Border spaces represent contact zones. The temporary halt of commodities, border crossers, and border commuters at border checkpoints creates necessities of social networking. For instance, *chelnoki* regularly make connections with fellow professionals at these points where their journey is inevitably interrupted for several hours at a time. This momentary stasis also presents a privileged point of observance for the anthropologist, who tries to get a hold of the elusive character of transnational commodity flows and cross-border trade.[54]

---

[53] Oskar Martinez (1994) described a 'borderland milieu' as being shaped by transnationalism, political and social separateness, ethnic and international conflict, and accommodation.

[54] Willem van Schendel has proposed five perspectives on illegal flows that can be gained by closely analyzing the borderland and its actors: (1) the perspective of transporters of illicit

Plate 11. Custom control zone, Vladivostok harbour 2004.

What is the border? Where does it begin and where does it end? This might be a naive question, given the fact that state borders are clearly demarcated entities, authoritatively inscribed in the landscape, and ultimately defined on maps. Yet under closer scrutiny the question becomes relevant. Robert Alvarez and Gorge Collier have shown in their ethnographic study of long-haul truck drivers from Mexico that the concept of borderland expands well into the hinterland of a country. In the case of Mexican truck drivers, even Los Angeles, California falls along of the border between Mexico and the United States (Alvarez and Collier 1994: 607). Based on her work in Central Asia, Madeleine Reeves followed a similar logic by addressing the overlapping structures of the new international borders as 'chessboards' rather than lines (Reeves 2007; 2014).

The expansion of the border concept can similarly be applied to the Russian Far East. Where is the borderland in the Russian Far East? Along the fences separating the two nation-states? In the woods of the Sikhote-Alin mountain range where Russian poachers meet with their Chinese

---

goods, (2) the intermingling of legal and illegal flows, (3) social networking around the border, (4) local perspectives on illegal flows, and (5) everyday negotiation of territoriality and transnationality (van Schendel 2005: 47-49).

middlemen? Or amidst the thousands of Chinese-dominated market stands in Russian cities? As I have shown in the proceeding chapter, cultural borders are constantly erected inside the cities, exemplified by the ethnically divided topography of street markets and niche economies monopolized by different ethnic groups.

Poaching Economies

> 'I like fish and I like bear's paw, but if I have to choose between them, I will let go of the fish and take the bear's paw'.
> – Mencius, 372-289 BC

Various illicit economies flourish along the borders of the Russian Far East (see Map 5). For instance, the export of scrap metal has become a lucrative business for port cities with large loading facilities, like Vladivostok and Nakhodka. The high demand for steel in the Asian market, especially in China, has increased substantially the prices of raw materials. During the 1990s and early 2000s Vladivostok's fishing harbour was turned into a large interim storage facility for scrap metal from Siberia and the Russian Far East. The metal came from abandoned Soviet industrial complexes that were scoured by scrap metal collectors and from ships of the former Soviet navy and Pacific fishing fleets.

During the 1990s, Vladivostok also turned into Russia's hub for the import of used Japanese cars. Vladivostok's proximity to Japan, its large port facilities, and the existing railway linkage to central Russia made for an almost ideal setting. The large supply of used cars in Japan satisfied the rising demand for affordable cars in post-Soviet Russia. Japan's strict automobile inspection laws led to a dynamic market with a high turnover of relatively new cars, attracting international car brokers in large numbers to the used-vehicle auction sites.[55] Although the trade in used vehicles is mostly a legitimate business, it nevertheless presented organized crime syndicates with a variety of opportunities for illegal transactions. Cars could be smuggled into Russia on board cargo liners, thus avoiding import taxes and increasing profit margins; and stolen cars endowed with new titles could be sold on the legal used car market. According to Japan's national police agency, illegal trade with Russia in 2001 was responsible for the theft of 63,000 cars with a total estimated value of up to US$2 billion (Kattoulas

---

[55] Russian nationals bidding at these auctions represent only a part of the international used car dealer community. Approximately half of the international dealers are from Pakistan, Bangladesh and Sri Lanka. See Tomoko Otake, 'Foreigners dominate used-vehicle export trade in Japan', *The Japan Times*, 3 June 2004.

2002: 50). These numbers point to the large scale of this illegal market and the possible profits for those involved. Primorye's Interior Ministry notes that the smuggling of stolen cars constitutes one of the most lucrative income bases for organized crime groups in the region.[56]

Maritime resources represent yet another important illicit income for organized crime groups in the Russian Far East. Complex schemes of poaching and document fraud involve Russian fishermen, customs officials, and importers from Japan (one of the main destinations for Russia's maritime resources).[57] The comparison of the registered catch in Russia with the numbers of marine products entering annually the Japanese market is indirect evidence for the large scope of poaching in North Pacific waters. For instance, in 2004, the total crab harvest in the Far Eastern sea basin was registered at 2,050 tons according to Japanese customs data, but the import of crab into Hokkaido during the same period amounted to 27,600 tons.[58] Economic losses from illegal catches of Kamchatka, blue, and Mintai crabs in the Russian Far East are estimated at more than US$750 million per year.[59]

Two main methods, essentially a combination of poaching and smuggling, are used by Russian poachers. One method is based on a scheme where a ship without the mandatory quotas or licenses uses faked documents to import their illegal catch to Japan or other Asian countries. The second method is to surpass the allowed quota and to transfer the excess catch to a foreign trawler on the high seas. The so-called Flying Dutchmen (i.e. Russian ships calling at foreign ports, mainly Pusan and Hokkaido) play a key role in the illegal harvest of maritime resources in the Far East (Williams 2003: 713). Sailing under Russian flag, these ships are allowed to harvest marine resources in the Exclusive Economic Zone which stretches 200 nautical miles from Russia's territorial waters, without going through normal customs clearance. The poaching operations are highly organized criminal activities, often involving several ships, the cover of official companies, and the complicity of custom officials (Vaisman 2001: 66-67).

---

[56] Sukharenko, A.H. 'Kontrabanda ugnannykh iaponskikh avtomobilei na Dal'nii Vostok', Vladivostokskiy Tsentr Issledovaniya Organizovannoy Prestupnosti, electronic document, http://crime.vl.ru/docs/stats/stat_70.htm, accessed 21 March 2006.
[57] Boris Reznik, 'Mafiya i More', *Izvestiya*, 21 October 1997.
[58] 'Brakonery bez barerov', *Vladivostok*, 9 Novemebr 2005.
[59] 'Far Eastern Fishing', *Russian Regional Report* 11, 7 (19 March 2006).

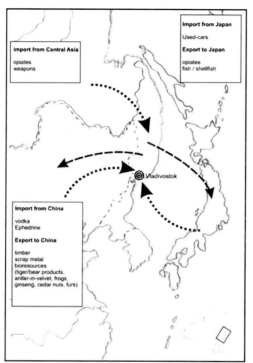
Map 5. Illegal cross-border flows in and out of Primorsky Krai.

Timber, especially hardwoods, is an equally important export of Primorsky Krai. Since the 2000s, Chinese companies have invested substantial amounts of money in the local timber industry for harvest and export rights. One of the largest multinational pulp companies, the Chinese based Asia Pulp & Paper (APP), signed a one billion dollar contract in 2004 to harvest timber and construct processing facilities in Primorsky Krai.[60] Yet approximately 70 per cent of the timber export from Primorsky Krai to China is considered to be illegal contraband.[61] In total, some 9.2 million cubic metres of timber are exported illegally each year from Russia to China.[62] Illegal timber trade is often conducted by organized crime groups, often in cooperation with customs officials. Through various schemes the crime groups establish

---

[60] Yevgeniya Gavriliuk, 'Kitaytsy vyrubyat dal'nevostochnye lesa', *Zolotoy Rog*, 20 June 2004.
[61] Ernest Filippovskiy, 'Tamozhnaya sgovorilas' s militsiey perekryt' kanaly kontrabandy lesa', *Kommersant*, 18 September 2004.
[62] Vladivostokskiy Tsentr Issledovaniya Organizovannoy Prestupnosti, 'Organizovannaya prestupnost' na Dal'nem Vostoke, obzor pressy 2005', http://crime.vl.ru/docs/obzor/obzor_2005.htm, p. 59, accessed 19 June 2006.

fictitious companies to receive official export permissions, and then use these to disguise their illegal exports.[63]

During the early 2000s, Vladivostok also became an important reloading point and export hub for heroin from Central Asia. With the closure of Iran's border to Afghanistan in 1998, opium and its derivates are increasingly shipped through Central Asia and Russia to reach the European and East Asian markets. Vladivostok mainly functions as a conduit for the import of heroin into Japan. Regular freight routes between Japan and the Russian Far East present profound opportunities for smugglers to hide their contraband in conventional shipments to Japanese ports. On the receiving end, Vladivostok and the Russian Far East are subject to the import of ephedrine from China. Ephedrine pills are transformed in simple local laboratories into the meta-amphetamine ephedron (*moolka* or *marsifal* in Russian slang) which enjoys a rising popularity among Russian drug-users.

Hunting and gathering of endangered species and the illegal harvest of plants contribute to a burgeoning shadow economy in Primorsky Krai. Several species are of interest for poachers and smugglers (see Table 2, Appendix). Driven by Chinese culinary and medicinal demand, main export commodities include ginseng, bear gallbladder, tiger bones, bear paws, and musk deer glands.

Among the coastal maritime fauna, *trepang* (sea cucumber) is of exceptional high demand in China. As outlined in chapter 2, the harvest of sea cucumbers in Primorsky Krai has a long history that dates back at least to the nineteenth century, when Chinese seasonal workers combed the Golden Horn Bay for the valuable animal. Pollution and over-harvesting has since led to a depletion of the stocks in the bay's surroundings. Nevertheless, several areas to the north-east of Vladivostok still harbour sea cucumber populations. Nowadays, the poaching of sea cucumbers is almost exclusively in Russian hands. The economic collapse of the small-scale fishing industry in many coastal villages of Primorsky Krai left few solutions for the working population, and many people turned to poaching as a survival strategy. Organized in individual boat brigades of four to five men equipped with aqualungs and outboard engines, the poachers systematically search the seafloor for the sea cucumbers that live in depths of up to 150 metres. A strict division of labour controls the work of the poachers. Two divers are in

---

[63] Corruption and complicity with smugglers is especially high in the customs department. For instance, in the summer of 2004 a trial was opened against the head of the customs inspection of Gordekovo (Pogranichnyy). Ruslan Bashko was accused of facilitating in 2003 the tax-free import of merchandise (pork, fur clothing, and shoes) from China into Russia with a total value of approximately US$300,000. See Aleksey Chernyshev, 'Kontrabandniy kanal napravili v sud: Nachaln'nik tamozhni obvinyaetsya v postavkakh promtovarov iz Kitaya', *Kommersant*, 1 July 2004.

the water, one steers the boat, and the remaining one or two use binoculars and radios to scan the beach for game wardens. On land, several people organize the processing of the delicate animal. Local children are often employed as additional lookouts to warn the poachers of approaching wildlife inspectors.

Trepang harvest is a dangerous business. In addition to the surprise inspections of game wardens who confiscate boats and equipment and arrest members of poaching brigades, the diving itself constitutes a dangerous activity. Due to over-harvesting, the sea cucumbers have to be retrieved from increasingly deeper waters, which bears a consequently higher risk for the divers. Accidents are common, as seen in the regular wash-ups of bodies and diving equipment after every spring thaw. Even in the remote bays and coves at the foot of the Sikhote-Alin mountain range over-harvesting has taken its toll. During the mid-1990s, the daily harvest of a brigade could reach up to 1,200 sea cucumbers. In 2001 the catch had dropped to 400-500.[64]

Organized crime groups from Nakhodka and Bolshoy Kamen are allegedly controlling the trade in sea cucumbers in Primorsky Krai. Each poaching brigade has to pay weekly dues of US$100-250 to these protection rackets.[65] The groups operate simultaneously as middlemen between the poachers and the Chinese wholesale dealers who organize the transport and smuggling to China. Because of high competition and depleted sea cucumber populations, the catching areas have consequently moved to northwards as far as Sakhalin and the Kuril Islands. As economic pressure builds, some of the poachers have already left for a more profitable business, such as the harvest of sea urchin roe for export to Japan.

During the Soviet period, the mountainous regions of the Russian Far East, especially the Sikhote-Alin mountain range, were economically important for commercial trapping and hunting of fur-bearing animals. The international Soviet fur trade was conducted exclusively through the St. Petersburg (then Leningrad) auction house. This monopoly has disappeared since the beginning of the 1990s as the Chinese market became one of the main destinations for illegally harvested furs from the Russian Far East, especially furs of squirrel, Siberian weasel, raccoon, lynx, and otter. Chinese buyers became popular as they did not asked for hunting licenses and paid right away. The acquisition of furs developed over time. During the early post-Soviet years, Chinese entrepreneurs bought furs from middlemen or directly from the hunters. Subsequently, Russian citizens were more involved and Chinese buyers merely organized the process and secured the acquisition of the furs at a minimal distance from the border. By the 2000s,

---

[64] Aleksandr Mal'tsev, 'Brakonery', *Vladivostok*, 20 July 2001.
[65] Ibid.

Chinese buyers were increasingly organizing the trade from a safe distance through Russian middlemen and Chinese partners (*predstaviteli*) in Russian trading companies. Chinese buyers regularly advance credits to middlemen to buy furs and are known to give credits to hunters for several seasons in advance. The modes of the (illegal) transport of furs include maritime connections to China, South Korea, Hong Kong, Taiwan, and Japan; routes by train and road connect to China. Small shipments are normally hidden in secret compartments on busses, trains, or ships, while larger consignments are layered in bulk shipments of timber or scrap metal. During the fall and winter, processed furs and manufactured fur cloaks flow back from China into Russia. Yet fur trapping and hunting has become less profitable over the years and most of the hunters have diversified by gathering ginseng, ferns, and other wild plants, and hunting deer and other animals that are not used for fur.

Several other species of terrestrial fauna are also in high demand by Chinese wholesale dealers. The Amur tiger is mostly valued for its skin and bones. Almost extinct during the mid-twentieth century, the rare cat is regularly stalked by poachers in the forest of the Sikhote-Alin, who extract the precious parts for sale to Chinese middlemen. In China, tiger bones are used for aphrodisiacs and medicinal products, and liquor based on tiger bones is a valuable wedding gift for the groom.[66]

Poachers, who are often only interested in certain parts of the animals, also endanger brown bears and the rare Asiatic black bear. Gall bladder, as a source of medicinal bile, is used in traditional Chinese medicine for a number of purposes (Mills, Simba and Ishihara 1995). In addition, bear paws have been regarded as a delicacy in Chinese cuisine ever since Mencius, a follower of Confucianism, extolled it as a most precious food item in 300 BCE.[67] The young, blood-rich antlers-in-velvet (*panty*) of Manchurian deer are also used as medicinal ingredients and are frequently delivered by poachers to Chinese traders. Frogs too - valued in China for their fat - are harvested by rural Russians for a price of up to ten rubles per frog.[68]

---

[66] Japan also has a small market for medicinal and alcoholic products based on tiger bones. See 'Japanese Market Survey of Products Containing Tiger Parts and Derivatives', TRAFFIC East Asia – Japan, 15 February 1999, http://www.traffic.org/publications/summaries/tigersurvey.html, accessed 12 June 2006.

[67] Mencius wrote, 'I like fish and I like bear's paw, but if I have to choose between them, I will let go of the fish and take the bear's paw. I like life and I like Rightness. But if I have to choose between them I will let go of life and take Rightness'. Charles Muller, trans., 'Mencius (selections)', 6A:10. Tōyō Gakuen University, http://www.hm.tyg.jp/~acmuller/contao/mencius.htm, accessed 5 June 2006.

[68] Viktor Debelov, 'Lyagushki puteshestvuyut v Kitay i dazhe na Ukrainu', *Vladivostok*, 2 June 1999.

Chinese wholesale traders regularly buy a variety of plant and animal species from the villages of the Sikhote-Alin Mountains. Buying prices vary, but can sustain a successful harvester with a profitable income. Table 3 illustrates the prices that a Chinese trader was willing to pay in 2004 in Roshchino, the former Chinese village of Kartun on the Iman (Bolshaya Ussurka) River.

The volume of contraband these middlemen traders turnover is far from small. In the spring of 2004, a police raid in Vladivostok discovered a cache of more than 5,000 kilograms of deer antlers in several containers of a storage area located near an open-air market in the city centre.[69] During another raid by local customs inspection, an equally staggering amount of animal parts was located in a truck at the border station of Poltavka. Owned by the Chinese company Kamaz, the confiscated truckload included 768 bear paws, 1,660 squirrel pelts, 1,600 sable furs, 2,180 black squirrel hides, 388 kilograms of dried sea cucumber, 49 kilograms of frog fat, and 64 reindeer penises, among other things.[70]

Table 3: Average prices for poached animals and plants paid by Chinese wholesale buyers to Russian sellers in Roshchino, Primorsky Krai

Item	Price in rubles per unit (28 R = US$1, 2004)
Cedar nuts	20-50 R/ kg (shelled)
	100-120 R/ bag (approx. 30 kg, with shells)
Snake	100 R/ metre
Frogs	5-10 R/ frog
Gland of musk-deer	200 R/ gram
Bear paw	5,000 R/ kg
Ginseng	240 R/ gram
Pelts: Mink Black squirrel Siberian polecat	1000 R/ pelt 500 R/ pelt 500 R/ pelt

One of the most highly priced items on the black market for bio-resources in Primorsky Krai is the ginseng root. Large-scale agricultural farms in China, Korea, and the United States produce the root for the international medicinal market, but wild ginseng is more highly valued and commands a higher price. The mountainous, deciduous forests of Primorsky Krai offer ideal

---

[69] Andrey Goriainov, 'Kitaytsev vsyali za roga', *Vladivostok*, 17 March 2004.
[70] Vladivostokskiy Tsentr Issledovaniya Organizovannoy Prestupnosti, 'Organizovannaya prestupnost' na Dal'nem Vostoke, obzor pressy 2004', 68-69, http://crime.vl.ru/docs/obzor/obzor_2004.htm, accessed 20 June 2006.

conditions for the growth of these rare roots.[71] The best ginseng harvest season is in August and September when the plant is clearly visible by its drove of red berries. Ginseng harvested in the mountainous interior (*ulikhins'kiy zhen'shen'*) is the most valuable from Primorsky Krai, while that harvested along the coast is normally valued at 20 per cent less. Yet prices vary widely, depending on the age and anthropomorphic resemblance of the root; large and old ginseng roots fetch the highest prices.[72] An average root sells for US$200, but the upper price range is at several thousand dollars for a single root.

Plate 12. Wild ginseng from Primorsky Krai for sale in Heilongjiang Province, China 2012.

---

[71] The locations of patches of ginseng roots in the forests are strictly guarded secrets, and stories abound in rural folklore about hidden ginseng plots deep inside the forest. Some stories are true. For instance, the father of an interviewee kept several ginseng roots as a form of retirement savings in a remote and hidden garden plot; on several occasions I was told of ginseng farmers who shot trespassers on their plots.

[72] The anthropomorphic appearance of a ginseng root has major influence on its value. A good human-like form represents a powerful spirit, thus signifies more potency. The Chinese word for ginseng is composed of two characters, *ren shen* (human ginseng), thus underscoring its human-like qualities. Sea cucumber, on the other hand, is *hai shen* (sea ginseng). I thank Harald Sorg for this insight.

Cedar nuts present a seasonal income opportunity for rural areas. During the fall, cedar nut collectors swarm out into the cedar woods of Primorsky Krai to collect the cones and extract the nuts. Groups that go for weeks on a gathering spree erect base camps in the forest where they extract the nuts from the cones and shells; weekend collectors carry portable graters and screens. For several Sunday evenings during early fall, cedar nut collectors with heavy bags stand in line at the train stations near the gathering grounds. Their faces and hands are blackened by resin and the train platforms are covered with nut shells. Many children are among the gatherers. The dirty and strenuous work is prosperous. Chinese buyers pay 20-50 rubles per kilogram of shelled nuts.[73] The prices rise during the winter months to 100 rubles. Experienced collectors are thus able to earn US$1,000-2,000 per season. Almost the complete annual harvest in Primorsky Krai is exported to China, where cedar nut oil is appreciated for its nutritional value and therapeutic purposes.

In Primorsky Krai, conflicting images exist of what role the border population play in the trade between China and Russia. One image portrays shuttle traders and poachers as mere unintentional helpers of Chinese middlemen who exploit the national resources for personal gain.[74] A second image presents poachers are stigmatized predatory exploiters of Russian resources and as wilful accomplices of foreign entrepreneurs. A third, apologetic image, recognizes the illegal nature of poaching and the depletion of endangered species, but insists on the importance of the economic benefits for the local population; poaching provides a needed and 'secure' cash income in a debilitated economic environment.

For many residents in rural areas poaching presents an economic survival strategy. As a local poacher explained, 'If you find a good root [of ginseng], you might not have to go hunting the whole season anymore. I have to pay 20,000 rubles for the education of my daughter. If I go to the taiga, dig up a root and sell it to the Chinese everything is taken care [of]' (cited in Dronova and Shestakov 2005: 54). A similar situation applies to the population living in the provinces of Primorsky Krai along the border to China. Excluded from the economic boom of the late 1990s, which was mainly profitable for urban centres like Vladivostok, a mostly rural population found eagerly needed employment in the grey economic sector of the shuttle trade.

---

[73] Tatyana Kurochkina, 'Narod shishkuet', *Zolotoy Rog*, 10 October 2004.

[74] In an article on resource exploitation, a journalist in Vladivostok angrily commented on the role of his fellow countrymen, 'We, like usual, play the role of stupid resource suppliers [*tupykh postavshchikov syr'ya*]'. See Aleksandr Losev, 'Orekhovyy pozhar', *Vladivostok*, 11 November 1998.

Small Business, Big Business: The Moral Economy of Contraband

> 'After the collapse of the Soviet Union life opened like a harmonica, yet somehow it all contracted again'.
>
> – Igor, age 51, cross-border trader

The illegal export of bio-resources to China is not the only international trade that heavily relies on informal networks. Other Asian Pacific countries equally participate in the flourishing informal cross-border trade with Russia that followed the breakdown of the Soviet Union. Japan, as mentioned above, is the largest car importer into the Russian Far East. The city of Vladivostok has one of the highest rates of personal car ownership per capita in the Russian Federation; almost all of the cars one sees in the streets are Japanese. Japanese cars enter the Russian Far East mainly through three ports, Nakhodka, Vostochnii, and Vladivostok. In Vladivostok, Russian car ferries from Japan regularly dock at the port's arrival and departure building downtown.

The *morskoy vokzal* (maritime port) is an important hub for Japanese imports. Shuttle trade from Japan passes through this port, along with the cars, and sailors and passengers are visibly involved. A long line of passengers wait to pass customs clearance. On a large scale at the end of the gangway, customs inspectors check the weight of personally imported goods. The primary goods that make up this shuttle trade - car tires, hoods, and spare parts, computers, television sets, and other electronic equipment – all make their way through customs.

In the following pages, however, I shift attention specifically to car importation. Mini-buses, small trucks, and cars are stacked on and below the decks of arriving ferries. Large cranes heave them on to waiting rail wagons. Customs inspection happens on the pier, where the car's registration numbers are double-checked with the import papers. The import of used cars from Japan presents a profitable income for several groups and businesses in Primorsky Krai, often on the brink of legality.

Vladivostok, Green Corner, August 2012. On a hilltop, above the city's power plant, high-rise buildings, and green patches of city parks, sits Vladivostok's famous used car market. Locals refer to the open-air market as Zelenyy Ugol (Green Corner), an allusion to the city district's name and its location along the densely wooded outskirts of town. In the distance below, glaring summer light reflects off the Golden Horn Bay, where Vladivostok's commercial port and city centre are situated. Green Corner used to be the largest used car market in Russia. Founded in 1993, it had reached its heyday by the turn of the twenty-first century, when the market's large and affordable selection of used Japanese cars attracted customers from all over Siberia and the Russian Far East.

In 2009, the Russian government substantially increased the import tariffs on foreign cars. As part of its recentralization strategy, the new tariffs were meant to expand the demand for domestic car production. As a result, the once burgeoning market of Green Corner has been significantly impacted.[75] During its golden days, Green Corner was a city inside the city: cafés, insurance brokers, hair salons, lawyers' offices, stores, and numerous kiosks supported the infrastructural backbone of a regional car market. Despite its economic recession, the market still presents an impressive labyrinth of thousands of cars parked in long rows inside of individual fenced-off plots that hug the hilly terrain on different levels.

Plate 13. Green Corner used car market, Vladivostok 2012.

Almost exclusively *yaponomarki* (Japanese makes) the cars are in excellent condition, and generally not more than five years old. During a clear and sunny day, the hoods of the latest models are opened, exposing the gleaming and spotless engines to the sun, while car lot helpers constantly wash and

---

[75] The market's notoriety and its economic predicament after the tariff increase was even the topic of a diplomatic cable from the United States embassy in Vladivostok that was later made public by Wikileaks (see http://www.cablegatesearch.net/cable.php?id= 09VLADIVOSTOK61, accessed July 2012).

wax the shining bodies. A constant stream of mostly male customers flows in and out along the market's central road, spilling into the individual lots for a stroll through this unique open-air shopping arcade. In between, colourful umbrellas and the open beds of small trucks mark the location of street vendors selling a range of Japanese products such as whiskey, cigarettes, and toiletries that are imported free of duty by Russian sailors on their regular sojourns.

On a foggy day, when large drops condense on the polished surfaces and drip off the windshields, the car rows disappear in the drifting mist that blows over the bleak hilltops, and the traders huddle in the lots' guard sheds, warming themselves with steaming plastic cups of coffee. Often shrouded in dripping mist, the market is also a place of foggy business practices that point beyond the actual market and connect a range of economic actors and practices in a variety of business schemes that often border on or go beyond the legal. In addition to the proffered duty-free Japanese consumer goods that come in with the regular maritime car shipments, the large demand for used cars has created a multitude of small businesses that specifically cater to owners and buyers of Japanese cars, from mechanics and insurance brokers to tuning specialists and spare parts resellers.

Complex trade circuits and elaborate schemes are employed to navigate the border and to react to ever-changing import laws. As an immediate reaction to the increased import tariffs that eliminated the profits on a legally imported used car, new avoidance schemes surfaced. One specific form is the practice of cutting the cars in half before import. Half cars can be declared as spare parts, a trick which substantially reduces the import tax. Once in Russia, the parts are reassembled and the cars are given new titles before they legally re-enter the market. This practice supports a range of underground mechanics whose shops are hidden in the city's numerous back alleys and corners.

To further explore the informal trans-border economies between Russia and China, I focus on yet another business that grew with the expanding used car market. As approximately 90 per cent of the local car owners drive a Japanese car, the demand for spare parts is accordingly high. This spawned a range of suppliers who specialize in counterfeit Japanese car parts made in China that cost two to ten times less than the originals from Japan.

Anton operates such an import and resale business that specializes in parts and accessories for Japanese sports cars. The parts are all made in China and legally classify as counterfeits. His little store on the second floor of a car repair shop close to the Green Corner market is a meeting place for car enthusiasts who exchange stories and advice, as they browse through the assortment of parts displayed in open cardboard boxes and on several shelves in Anton's overcrowded sales room. Anton currently employs four people, but thinks about expanding because he has been using his profits to enlarge his warehouse stock. 'I am not just a reseller', he clarifies, because he integrates the whole supply and resale chain within his business. He also stresses the importance of receiving feedback from his customers: 'If a guy tells me I need this specific product, I sit down with him and listen to his specific needs. If [there are] already three requests [for] a similar item, I produce a sample. Either I take a pre-existing part or construct [it] myself, and ship it to my manufacturers in China'. Anton relies on a network of about 20 suppliers, all small factories in mainland China and Taiwan.

Anton imports up to 3,000 kilograms per month in merchandise from China. Compared to three years ago, when all of his goods were shipped across the border with the help of shuttle traders, he now mostly relies on Russian or Chinese trucking companies that operate in a grey zone of informal wholesale imports. These companies see to it that no import taxes are added, and the transfer is made without documents or contracts. Nevertheless, for items with counterfeit logos, Anton still prefers the service of shuttle traders who carry the parts without their boxes; meanwhile, he ships the boxes with the imprinted logos separately from the actual goods. Anton pays his suppliers in China either with bank-to-bank transfers, or sends Russian rubles in cash with *chelnoki* across the border to Suifenhe where it is exchanged into Chinese currency and forwarded to the respective supplier. Due the constant crossing of commodities and money from one currency zone to the other, his profit margins are closely tied to the current exchange rate of the US Dollar.

Anton claims that his entrepreneurial success is dependent on his ability to find manufacturers in China that offer cheap yet high quality products. Personal contacts, forged through multiple visits to the factories, are fundamental to his business success. In addition, for his business conduct in China he significantly relies on a Chinese middleman in Suifenhe, who arranges shipments from China and helps out with local paperwork and contacts. Trust and honesty is paramount in his business relationships, as no documents are normally issued for the transactions:

> The whole shuttle trade business is built upon honesty, absolute honesty. The first time you steal, you are kicked out of the market. The Chinese all know each other and the moment you take what is not yours the Chinese are instantly alerted and no one will deal with you after that. You can shut your business down. Plus they tell the customs that you are a shyster [*zhulik*] and you will start having

problems with the customs. The whole system is built upon trust and honesty.

From a legal perspective, Anton imports and sells *kontrafakty* (counterfeits), however the border between the fake and the real product is blurred, especially when dealing with products of an almost identical quality as the original. The degree of counterfeiture depends to a large degree on how the part is labelled. Most of the car parts he sells are true counterfeits because they are identical copies of Japanese originals, but not all; some differ slightly but bear the original logo, some bear no logo, and some even bear Anton's own brand name. Although Anton is keenly aware of the illegal character of his business in terms of its legal aspect of importing and selling counterfeit products, he personally sees his business as thoroughly licit and morally justifiable.

Anton's position recalls the fine distinction between illicit and illegal activities that have been made repeatedly by researchers of the informal (see van Schendel 2005: 17ff.; Bruns, Miggelbrink and Mueller 2011: 665). A state's definition of illegal activities frequently contradicts the perception of people who are involved in informal economic activities. This is especially true for small-scale cross-border traders and smugglers, who deal in legal goods, yet use illegal channels to transport goods across the border. In those cases, the trader's own economic activities are seen as a legitimate way to conduct business in an environment that is otherwise perceived as too constraining or cumbersome. To understand this perception thoroughly, it is important to consider the specific relationship of these informal economic practices to the state and its institutions (Bruns and Miggelbrink 2011: 16). Current approaches developed inside the framework of New Institutional Economics that focus on transaction costs and principal agent relations are helpful to explain the prevalence of informal solutions (Egbert 2006).

In conversations with cross-border traders at the Russian-Chinese border a particular perception of the state regularly surfaced that was directly related to the higher transactions costs associated with legal and formal cross-border modes of transport. Transaction costs in these cases are not only counted in monetary value, but rather include time as a crucial variable. Traders like Anton weight the unreliability and unpredictability of official import channels against the practicability of informal solutions:

> *Chelnoki* exist because there is no other way. Dealing with them is fast and easy. I would like to import goods legally, in their original packages, so that everything is correct. But I do not have this possibility. I would lose money. I do not like all these bags here, I would prefer to have my goods all in neat cardboard boxes, but I have no alternative. If I would know that a truck from China would

take a week to get here, I would not even think of using the *chelnoki*. But I do not know how many days it will take. It could be 5, 7, 30, or 40 days. If there are no rules, you have to make up your own. If the government is not able to create the conditions to make a living, we are going to cheat the government. What other option do we have?

Time is here of crucial value for the cross-border trader, even if the informal solution sometimes entails higher financial costs. Chronic mistrust in state institutions dominates the perception of formal transport channels, as Anton explained:

If normal laws would exist, nobody would need this business. It is not cheaper for me that way. I would prefer to have my goods delivered by truck, legally. Although nobody wants to have to do with the state – it is a different world. This is one reason why I do not want to work clean [*belyy*]. Get rid of this nonsense. I say, organize the market in a normal way, transparent, understandable, then nobody needs any more the *chelnoki*, there would not be any more contraband.

The pronounced mistrust in state institutions, especially the unpredictability and corruption of customs officials appeared as a recurring theme in several conversations that I had with small-scale cross-border traders during my research. Igor, who runs a small furniture business in Vladivostok used to regularly import fabrics for his furniture from China through legal channels. Yet, mostly due to recurring problems with custom officials, he now increasingly relies on informal cross-border channels:

I pay 100 rubles per kilogram to a Chinese shipping company to get my goods across the border, from Suifenhe to Vladivostok. That is more than the official tariff, but I do not want to deal with the border authorities. Not because I ship illegal goods, but I am so fed up with the hassle that you face if you use the normal channels. For example, they can tell you that your weight was not 1,000 kilograms, but 1,003 kilograms. That means you are dealing in contraband, you have to pay a fine, or you need a special certificate for this commodity, which is only available in Moscow.

This attitude and peculiar perception of the state and its institutions is not only limited to the customs agency, but rather extends to the general condition of a greatly centralized state and the particular relation between Moscow and Russia's peripheral regions, as Igor elaborated further in our conversation:

After the collapse of the Soviet Union life opened like a harmonica, yet somehow it all contracted again. A couple of years ago, we still laughed at it, but now it has become unbearable. At every point of my business I have to pay bribes, sometimes more hidden, and sometimes just plain cash in an envelope. A couple of years ago everybody talked about the 'yellow peril'. Chinese and other migrant workers were seen as the enemy. Nowadays there is only one enemy: Moscow!

Moscow is not the only perceived antagonist of small-scale traders in Primorsky Krai. The state is not necessarily the only entity that holds regulatory power and controls access in a borderland. Along many international borders the regulatory authority in a borderland is contested by non-state actors, in the form of merchant elites, rebel groups, or corrupt officials, who reconstitute state power on their own accord (Roitman 2005: 165). This is likewise the case along the Russian-Chinese border, where a few large and politically well-connected private companies control access to trans-border and regional networks. As a result, small-scale traders are confronted on a regular basis with these companies' attempts to monopolize certain transportation channels. Large shipping companies regularly try to sideline and push smaller traders out of the lucrative cross-border business.

For example, Andrey is the owner of a small shipping company that specializes in the transportation of vegetables and other perishable goods from China into Russia. His small fleet of six refrigerator trucks has been recently forced out of the business by three large Russian shipping companies (one each from Ussurisk, Vladivostok, and Khabarovsk), which put pressure on his Chinese partners who now refuse to cooperate with Andrey's business. Yet, these monopolization efforts are in a constant flux as border laws and local powers change frequently. For instance, since the opening of the Russian-Chinese border during the late 1980s, private travel across the border was strictly limited to bus transport, which gave local, long-distance bus companies a quasi monopoly on cross-border passenger transport. However, the recent opening of the Russian-Chinese border to private cars in the fall of 2012 broke the monopoly of the local bus companies. This change is paramount for small-scale traders like Andrey, to whom it gives a slight shimmer of hope. As he put it, 'The local powers have understood that they eventually have to yield to the people. In the end, people want choice. If you only have one mode of transportation [long-distance busses] there is no choice. People want to choose their own mode of transport to cross the border'.

The 'pluralization of regulatory authority' (Roitman 2005: 165) at the Russian-Chinese border does not include only private actors in the form of trading elites, but also extends to individual state actors who profit from their official position for private gain. The collusion between organized crime groups and corrupt officials inside state institutions, and especially inside the customs office, is a chronic problem in post-Soviet Russia (see Wedel 2001; Holmes 2008). Due to its international ports and gateway position in the Far East, Vladivostok, and Primorsky Krai with it, has evolved as a hotbed of state-actor complicity in illegal trade since the mid-1990s. The participation of state officials in large-scale smuggling operations is an open secret and part of the everyday knowledge of cross-border traders. Border entrepreneurs like Anton are acutely aware of the practical difference between petty smuggling and the large-scale smuggling that is protected by corrupt officials.

In another conversation, Anton referred to a large-scale smuggling operation centred on the Tri Kita (Three Whales) furniture-shopping complex in Moscow that was uncovered in 2000. The smuggling operation had been protected by high-ranking state officials:

> Related with the Three Whales scandal, wagons and whole train loads full of stuff moved through our customs in Nakhodka to Cherkisovskiy Market in Moscow. This was a big case, but it was closed and nobody was convicted. So apparently you can smuggle on this scale without being bothered. You can import 20 containers full of Adidas sneakers, but you are not allowed to import a single bag of them. You know why? Because the people from Moscow do not earn anything from the small-scale smuggling here.

Despite a high profile investigation by the customs inspection, which implicated senior FSB (Federal Security Bureau) officials, the investigation into the Three Whales was eventually halted, pending charges were dismissed, and the customs officials who led the investigation were charged with abuse of office.[76]

A similar case of large-scale smuggling that involved senior FSB personnel and local politicians was also centred on the Primorsky port of Nakhodka, the major commodity entry point into the Russian Far East. As in the Three Whales case, the actual persons who were tried in court were not the alleged corrupt officials, but rather the officials who led the investigation. In this case, the victim was the Far Eastern Customs Directorate Chief, General Ernest Bakhshetsyan, who had been tasked, ironically enough, to strengthen his office's fight against smuggling and corruption and to increase tariff revenues.[77] He was ultimately convicted on charges of abuse of office by a Vladivostok court and sentenced to five years in prison in 2007.

---

[76] Elena Kiseleva, 'Kit i mech: FSB popalas' na kontrabande', *Kommersant*, 14 September 2006.

[77] Artem Iyutenkov, 'Eto prosto Nakhodka, ili put' kontrabandistov', *Novaya Gazeta*, 24 November 2010.

Cross-border hubs like the port of Nakhodka offer ample opportunities for state and non-state actors to contest the regulatory authority of the state. Igor the furniture merchant explained it in this way: 'Everything could be imported through Nakhodka before the closure of that channel – everything besides guns and drugs, which were their [FSB] own business. For US$7,000 per container, no questions [were] asked. The pipeline was closed in 2007, now only small holes remain. Back then they were dealing in billions, not millions [of dollars]'. Smuggling activities that are protected by officials have the inherent advantage over those that are not protected. Legal structures, in the form of fake paperwork and customs receipts, can be used to mask illegal actions. Organized crime groups, often in cooperation with customs officials, establish fictitious companies to receive official export permissions, which are then used to disguise the illegal exports. At this point, petty smuggling, as an economic activity against the state, becomes transformed into large-scale smuggling that exists in collusion with and is even undertaken by the state.

The Anti-Programme: Middlemen, Ties, and Tactics of Informal Cross-Border Trade

Anthropological case studies on trader tourism, involving the movement of sellers and buyers into neighbouring countries under the guise of tourism, reflect the important role of borders and border zones in the fields of production, trade, and consumption (Hannerz 1996; Hann and Beller-Hann 1998). Trader tourism has become an essential part of the economies of the post-Soviet successor states by mainly supplying the open-air markets with an array of goods. Vladivostok and the Russian Far East are no exceptions. To a certain degree, these informal economies that flourish in the borderlands have subverted the hegemony of the state and its territorial integrity. Informal economic activities at a state's borders 'threaten to subvert state institutions by compromising the ability of these institutions to control their self-defined territory' (Donnan and Wilson 1999: 88). That is, shuttle trade and smuggling escape state control and subvert the state's claim to control trade through and with its monopoly on taxation. These crimes against the state (see Price 1974), also expose the state's weakness and 'the complicity of state agents in many cross-border activities' (Donnan and Wilson 1999: 105).

A border can be used as a resource on many levels and by a range of actors, from small-scale traders to well-connected individuals inside state institutions. In the Russian-Chinese borderland informality plays a central role. It is used to increase the profits made by individual traders and as a strategy for ensuring easier, more predictable, and less restricted commodity flows. In the absence of trust in state institutions, specifically the customs office, informal solutions are considered more practical and more reliable. This is especially true for the small-scale traders of Primorsky Krai, who seek informal solutions for commodity flows outside of state control by relying on their own cross-border networks. Investigating the reality of smuggling networks not only sheds light on the specific social and economic mechanisms of the trade, but rather exposes a particular relationship of individuals to the state and its institutions. The crafty anti-programme of smuggling operations, which subverts the border regime on a regular basis, demonstrates not only the decidedly creative and practical solutions of cross-border traders, but moreover exposes the rather ambiguous relationship of borderlanders to their own state.

Far from being passive players in the borderland, shuttle traders and other border entrepreneurs negotiate different roles and strategies. Small-scale entrepreneurs interact with different social and ethnic groups, transgressing group boundaries on a regular basis (Konstantinov, Kressel and Thuen 1998: 736). Cases of informal cross-border trade in different regions of the world have underscored similar notions of highly agile economic actors in borderlands. The 'practice of flexible sojourning' in cross-border trade is a creative and strategic way for border residents of different social backgrounds to use the potential of a border in an active and dynamic way (Lin and Tse 2005: 889).

Borders are discriminatory devices that can be open and closed at the same time, permeable or impervious for certain people and commodities. Technological approaches to borders stress the fact that a border itself can be seen as a technique, operating as a discriminatory programme (Delaplace 2012: 4). The material dimension of a border, its physical demarcation line, barbed wire fences, strips of no-man's-land, checkpoints and customs booths, as well as the applied jurisdiction of the customs code constitute the complex border assemblage that decides on and regulates the permeability for specific people and commodities.

Yet, every programme is inherently faulty, possesses weak points and backdoors, or -conveyed in the language of computer programming - is intrinsically open to exploits. Cross-border traders and smugglers understand and use these exploits to their own advantage, subverting the ever-changing border programme through loopholes and backdoors. Their informal trading practices constitute the anti-programme to the border apparatus' master code. Following de Certeau's distinction between strategies and tactics in the practices of everyday life one can argue that a nation-state creates the power relationships of a border space in the form of a strategy, thus postulating a place under state control, while cross-border traders use their own countertactics to manipulate this particular space (Round, Williams and Rodgers 2008: 173).

What are the features of these anti-programmes or countertactics? What makes them successful despite the constant efforts of nation-states to exert control over their crucial entrances and exits? The foregoing ethnographic examples from the Russian-Chinese borderland present vital answers to these questions. Structurally speaking, the practices of small-scale traders in the Russian Far East constitute trade circuits that incorporate several people in an economic network in which commodities and money flow in various directions. Middlemen play a crucial role in these networks that cross national, ethnic, and language divides on a regular basis. These middlemen represent important nodes in the cross-border commodity flows as they facilitate contacts between different economic actors on both sides of the border. As important mediators and facilitators of the borderland, their services are crucial on different levels in the trade circuits of informal cross-border trade between Russia and China.

In Russia, Chinese middlemen play a key role as buyers of poached bio-resources from the local population or as brokers of Chinese migrant workers in Primorsky Krai's timber industry. By the same token, Russian middlemen help Chinese entrepreneurs to secure market space in open-air markets or department stores by acting as 'straw men' or nominal 'owners' to circumvent the legal obstacles that prevent Chinese business ownership. Russian middlemen also support Chinese investors acquiring companies, especially in the timber sector in the Russia Far East. For Russian small-scale cross-border entrepreneurs, Chinese *pomogaiki* (helpers) facilitate trade and business connections in China, while Russian middlemen act as tour operators, offer visa services, specialize in informal cross-border money transfers, or facilitate business contacts in China for the occasional shopping tourist. All the aforementioned, interviewed small-scale traders rely heavily on the services of these middlemen in China with whom they often have established long-term friendships and partnerships. For instance, Anton's car parts import business would be unthinkable without the help of a Chinese facilitator who arranges business contacts and manages money transfers for him. Equally important is the role of the Chinese partner of Olga, the tour operator; the Chinese partner helps Olga's tour groups locate the merchandise they seek and manages Olga's warehouse.

Informal economies in the Russian Far East and the different actors involved at certain points of the commodity flow can form complex commodity chains. Producers, traders, transporters, middleman, and consumers are interconnected through commodity flows as well as money transfers. Different grades of complexity can be distinguished. Janet MacGaffey and Rémy Bazenguissa-Ganga differentiated in their study on African informal traders in Paris between simple and complex sales circuits according to the number of involved actors, or what they called 'roles' (MacGaffey and Bazenguissa-Ganga 2000: 74). Complex sales circuits involve more than three roles or combine different circuits with each other. The work of an independent shuttle trader along the Russian-Chinese border represents a simple sales circuit (see Figure 7 C). Without the help of a transporter, that is a tour company, the *chelnok* acquires merchandise in China, imports it to Russia, and either sells it to a wholesale dealer or organizes the retail sale on his own. Hired shuttle traders, on the other hand, are employed by a middleman tour company which organizes the transport and border formalities (see Figure 7 B). Although the work of a hired *chelnok* is simpler than that of an independent trader, the actual sales circuit is more complex because it includes a minimum of four actors (i.e. buyer, seller, tour company, and *chelnok*). Even more complex is the sales circuit involved in the smuggling of *trepang* (see Figure 7 A). A poacher brigade sells to a middleman, who resells to a wholesale dealer, who hires smugglers to transport the merchandise to China for subsequent retail sale.

Higher complexity within a sales circuit also means a more intricate money flow. A simple, but very effective underground banking system has therefore evolved. Known under its Chinese name *hui kuan* (to remit sums of money) or *fei chien* (flying money), the remittance system is regularly used by Chinese traders to transfer money back and forth from China to their countries of operation.[78] The system works in a simple way. A wholesale dealer in Vladivostok who wants to buy a shipment of shoes from China pays the cost of the shipment and some fees to a broker in Russia; the broker transfers the money to a partner in China; the designated receiving party in China then picks up the money from the Russian broker's Chinese partner. Chinese-owned tour companies often facilitate these money transfers. The term 'flying money' is actually a misnomer, because no money actually crosses the border. The transfer between the Russian and Chinese brokers is made only on account. The money broker in Russia owes his Chinese partner the sum in question, but the debt is cancelled through reciprocal transfers. In another transaction, a dealer in China will pay the Chinese broker for a shipment of *trepang* from the Russian Far East. In this case, the payment is destined for the Russian broker and subsequently the Russian suppliers. But

---

[78] The Chinese remittance system is structurally identical to the *hawala* system, which is widely used in the Arabic world as an underground banking system (Naylor 2002: 196-246). In 2002, an estimated amount of US$200 million was transferred from China to the Russian Far East, mostly through underground remittance systems (Lindter 2005).

the cash does not move; the Russian broker simply uses the money he was paid for the shoe shipment to pay the *trepang* suppliers. Subsequent money remittances from both sides counterbalance each other and occasionally the books are entirely balanced. Financial records are kept to a minimum, the communication consisting merely of phone calls, e-mails, and encoded notes. This transaction system hardly leaves any paper trail and anonymity for all participants is guaranteed, which makes it an almost ideal transnational remittance system for both legal and illegal border transfers.

A. *Trepang* smuggling

B. Hired shuttle trade

C. Independent shuttle trade

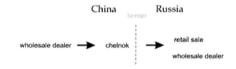

Figure 7. Cross-border trade circuits.

Equal tactics are used in the world of illegal timber exports.[79] Due to the substantially higher export tax on round wood, illegally harvested timber is

---

[79] Hardwoods are an important export of Primorsky Krai, and Chinese companies have invested substantial amounts over the last years in the local timber industry for harvest and export rights. Nevertheless, illegal logging and grey export is endemic in the timber industry. Approximately 70 per cent of the timber export from Primorsky Krai to China is considered to be illegal contraband. See Ernest Filiippovskii, 'Tamozhnaya sgovorilas' s', op. cit.

cut into rough boards in local sawmills to declare them as already processed wood for customs purposes. Shuttle traders use the tactics of weight distribution between passengers, under-invoicing, or the spreading of similar items in different bags to retain the masquerade of a single tourist on a personal journey.

Changing border and customs laws require from traders continuous creative adaptations on the ground. The specific features of the trade evolve out of the necessity to circumvent the border regime and the requirement to organize business ventures outside of formal rules and mechanisms. Multi-layered routes, commodity disintegration, and strong social ties based on trust are all part of a set of tactics that has shown extreme flexibility and resilience to an ever-changing border programme and the physical constraints of a controlled border zone. The fluid social and economic mechanisms that are part of the informal cross-border trade are highly adaptable and have revealed their persistence through time. The strong reliance on middlemen is a specific part of cross-border trade that not only crosses a national border, but also transgresses significant cultural and language barriers on a regular basis. In the featured cases, long-term personal relationships to Chinese brokers are essential for the success of Russian small-scale border entrepreneurs. In the absence of a legal framework that is able to enforce contracts, trust plays a paramount role in securing business arrangements outside of state laws. Trust is created through time by repeated transactions that are successful and beneficial for both sides. Together, these features compose an anti-programme to the monopoly of the border apparatus, enabling and structurally supporting a cross-border trade against the state.

Chapter 5
'The Harder the Rain the Tighter the Roof': Organized Crime Networks in the Russian Far East

Komsomolsk-na-Amure, 10 November 2004. The dense snowfall of the night has covered the city with a fine powdery layer of snow. The white shroud of winter has fallen. The black Volga taxi pushes sluggishly through the snowstorm. 'There will be many accidents today', the driver notes briefly while he takes the right turn to the old graveyard. Matching the colour of his car, he is dressed in black. The roads are slippery. We keep silent, as we leave the outskirts of town behind us. First we pass the local steel plant; then, only for a moment, the contours of the cooling towers of the city's heating plant appear out of the white swirl. The snowstorm increases its intensity, as dense clouds of spindrift roll toward us. By now, the road is completely covered with snow. Suddenly, the Volga goes slightly off its lane. Gnawing on his lips, the driver wrestles to control the heavy car. The worn-out windshield wipers scratch a monotonous beat.

Komsomolsk-na-Amure, an industrial city of 300,000 at the lower reaches of the Amur River, was for decades the home of one of Russia's notorious underworld authorities. Known under his criminal nickname Dzhem, he had been recognized among his peers as the exclusive *krestniy otets* (godfather) of the Russian Far East. Indeed, he ranked high in the all-Russian underworld pantheon populated by famous godfathers such as Yaponchik (Vyacheslav Ivan'kov), Taivanchik (Alimzhan Takhtakhunov), and Silvester (Sergey Timove'ev).

After 30 minutes, the taxi driver and I arrive at the old graveyard of Komsomolsk-na-Amure. 'I'll be back in half an hour', I explain to the taxi driver; then step out of the car. The door slams shut. Only a few cars are standing on the parking lot next to the graveyard. The graveyard expands between several small hills that are dotted with patches of birch trees. Avoiding the main entrance of the graveyard, I jump over a little fence. The narrow paths between the graves are covered in knee-deep snow. Looking for a suitable way to navigate between the graves, I end up on a little hill overlooking the graveyard. A monumental grave has been placed on the open crest for a young man who died in 2003 at age 29. Sergey Aleksandrovich Lepeshkin had been found dead in his prison cell in Khabarovsk, hanged by his own shoelaces. He was well known to the local underworld under his alias Lepeskha, and was one of the city's youngest criminal authorities. He had been 'crowned' by Dzhem, the godfather himself, as a true *vor v zakone*, a thief professing the code, an aristocrat in Russia's traditional criminal underworld, and a member of Dzehm's powerful organization.[80] Russian gangsters often die young.

Plate 14. Dzehm's grave, Komsomolsk-na-Amure 2004.

A dark grey marble headstone in the middle of a polished tomb-like grave inset in the ground is situated next to an oversized Orthodox cross. The headstone reaches out into the whirly white sky. The image of the deceased is engraved into the headstone, larger than life and exceedingly clear. A beaten trail runs down the hill. Fresh tracks lead through the snow down the trail. I follow them. A couple of yards behind a bend at the foot of the hill another grave appears. It is even larger than the one on the top. This is

---

[80] Moskovskaya Khel'sinkskaya Gruppa, 'Politicheskie i drugie ubiystva, sovershennye agentam vlastey', http://www.g.ru/publications/3DE13AA, accessed 29 November 2005.

Dzhem's final resting place, the tomb of the famous godfather. His larger-than-life image, a beefy face on a hefty body in a suit, is engraved on the black, polished headstone. Dzhem had died in federal prison 2001, just a month after his arrest. The circumstances of his death were mysterious and still fuel rumours and numerous conspiracy theories. The official version of his death is plain: cardiac arrest. I remember the words of my friend Viktor, who had led me to the tomb for the first time a couple of days earlier, 'He was a real *vor*, he had spent half of his life in prison, and that is where he finally died'. He missed his fiftieth birthday by only two weeks.

Dzhem was born Yevgeniy Petrovich Vasin on 10 November 1951 in Borzia, in the Chitinskaya Oblast' of southern Siberia. Soon after his birth, his family moved to Komsomolsk-na-Amure, which became the place where he prospered. At the age of 14, he was arrested for hooliganism, a common charge during the Soviet period under which all kinds of different 'anti-social' behaviours were subsumed. During the 1970s, Dzhem was coach of the local football club of Komsomolsk-na-Amure. His plan to advance his team to the next higher league failed. Instead, the team members, under his guidance, branched out into forms of extortion, such as extracting money from small-scale informal traders. Extortion in the Soviet Union during that time was still in its infancy, nevertheless Dzhem's group managed to monopolize all business in Komsomolsk-na-Amure by violently pushing out other criminal groups (Razinkin 1998: 2).

Succeeding arrests followed on charges of hostage-taking, robbery, and murder. Serving various prison terms, Dzhem moved through the prison camps of the Far East, where he was introduced to the criminal subculture of the Soviet penal system, and where he made the acquaintance of several high-ranking criminals. In 1985, he received his *kreshchenie* (baptism) as a *vor v zakone* by Datiko Pavlovich Tsikhelashviliy (Dato Tashkentskii), a close friend to the legendary Russian godfather Yaponchik.[81]

It was during the 1980s that Dzhem established an alliance of *vory v zakone* under his leadership in the Russian Far East (Nomokonov 1998). Dzhem's prison sentences totalled almost twenty years of incarceration and made him a respectable person, a true authority in the world of thieves. Before Dzhem's time, the Russian Far East had been of little appeal to organized crime groups in the Soviet Union. Due to its peripheral location as a borderland, it was a heavily controlled region with a high number of border guards and other members of the security services. In addition, Vladivostok was a closed city, the border to China was essentially closed, and the

---

[81] Vladimir Novikov, 'Yablochnyy Dzhem', *Ezhednevnye Novosti*, 2 November 2001.

comparatively low population did not present an ideal environment for illegal economic activities.

Yet Dzhem was on his home ground in the Russian Far East, and perestroika suddenly opened a wide variety of economic opportunities. Compared to his predecessors, the *zakonniki* (honourable thieves) of the camp system, Dzhem was increasingly involved in a diversity of businesses in various economic sectors: gambling-houses, gas stations, car parks and dealerships, fisheries, shipping companies, precious metals, and oil.[82] The coastal zone of the Russian Far East presented a profitable environment both logistically and in terms of available resources.[83] Based out of Komsomolsk-na-Amure, Dzhem's group, Dal'nevostochnyy Obshchak (the Far Eastern Obshchak), became a leading and far reaching organized crime group in the Russian Far East. Despite the group's new economic orientations, its structure incorporated the hierarchical system of *polozhentsy*, regional appointees who act like governors on behalf of the leading *vor*. With the help of those appointees, Dzhem's organization controlled large parts of the underground economy in a territory encompassing three regions of the Russian Federation (Amurskaya Oblast', Khabarovsky Krai, and Primorsky Krai). Regional centres of the group's wide-ranging illegal activities were in Khabarovsk and Komsomolsk-na-Amure.

Released from prison again in the early 1990s, he officially worked as a supplier for the cooperative Druzhba in Komsomolsk-na-Amure. Dzhem's influence in the city and the region grew substantially during the mid-1990s, culminating in his takeover of the Far Eastern Obshchak, a conglomerate of traditional crime groups with a common fund or treasury. As the shadow ruler of Komsomolsk-na-Amure, Dzhem cultivated the image of a provider of law and order in his town. His business practices openly challenged both the local security organs and competing criminals. On a local television broadcast in 2000, he proudly announced, 'This is my *krai* (region), and I want order here'.[84]

The 10 November 2004, would have been Dzhem's fifty-third birthday. This is the reason I have come to the cemetery. Fresh snow covers the old flower arrangements on Dzhem's grave and the marble table and benches adjacent to the grave. In Russia, the living celebrate and honour the

---

[82] Ibid.

[83] Especially the oil- and gas-rich shelf off the coast of Sakhalin was of central interest for organized crime groups in the 1990s and the stage for a turf war between Dzhem's group and a local authority nicknamed Lopukh (Aleksandr Tiukavin) over the influence of the nascent oil- and gas industry. See Nikolay Khlebnikov, 'Konets Ery Dzhema', *Interpol Ekspress* 21 (November 2001).

[84] Galina Mironova, 'Ugolovnik, ob'yavliavshiy sebya pervym nomerom v Primor'ye, umer v Khabarovskom SIZO', *Komsomol'skaia Pravda*, 25 October 2001.

deceased at their graves. Next to Dzhem's monument, and part of the same complex, is the grave of Aleksandr Anatol'evich Volkov (Volkov), another authority from Russia's Far Eastern illustrious criminal underworld. Suddenly, my contemplations are interrupted. A small group of people approaches the tomb. I attempt to project indifference and start heading down the trail toward them. Without uttering a word, the group of men in well-tailored black winter coats passes by. Some of them carry red roses. After a short while, I stop in my tracks and hide behind a gravestone framed by two birch trees. The procession stops in silence in front of Dzhem's grave. Some of the men remove the freshly fallen snow from the graveside. Their heads are lowered.

A legendary funeral is an excellent beginning for a sustainable myth. Dzhem's funeral three years before had been a nationally televised event. More than 2,000 people had attended the memorial service, stretching the logistical abilities of Dzhem's organization to the limits. The director of the regional crime fighting unit of the Interior Ministry estimated that more than 50 leaders of Russia's criminal world attended the funeral.[85] Guests came from the entire territory of the former Soviet Union – Ukraine, Georgia, Azerbaijan, Armenia, and the Central Asian republics – an echo of the widespread nature of Russia's traditional crime networks. All hotels and boarding houses in Komsomolsk-na-Amure and vicinity were booked well in advance. Because Komsomolsk has no national airport, most of the guests had to fly into Khabarovsk, and had to be driven in vehicles for the last stretch of 350 kilometres. To make matters worse for the organizers, one of the more important guests, the Georgian *vor v zakone* Revas Tsitseshvili, also known as Tsitsa, died of a heart attack during his flight from Moscow to Khabarovsk, raising even more questions about the state's involvement in Dzhem's death.[86]

In order to keep more distance from the group, I now retreat into the graveyard. My movements are frantic and one of my feet gets caught in a root underneath the snow. I slip and fall between two graves. The snow feels like cold dry powder as it creeps up my sleeves. I curse myself, stumble back on my feet, pad the snow off my coat, and disappear into the maze of hundreds of regular graves. Only few of them have actual gravestones. Most are decorated with a simple wooden or metal cross, some front the communist star. These small graves, surrounded by little fences, bear little resemblance to the monumental tombs of the godfathers.

---

[85] Irina Petrakova, 'U kriminal'nykh avtoritetov epidemiya infarktov', *Gazeta.ru*, 27 October 2001, http://www.gazeta.ru/2001/10/26/ukriminaljny.shtml, accessed July 2006.
[86] Oleg Zhunusov, 'Vor v zakone umer po puti na pokhorony kollegi', *Izvestiya*, 26 October 2001.

During his last years, Dzhem had successfully cultivated the public image of an ordinary businessman with a benevolent spirit. In 1996, he founded the charitable foundation Sostradanie (Compassion) in Komsomolsk-na-Amure with subdivisions in Khabarovsk, Birobidzhan, and on the Sakhalin Island.[87] Supporters of this social charity included former inmates, writers, former police officers, university teachers, and several *vory v zakone*. In addition, Dzhem had set up recreational camps for orphans on two islands of the Amur River. One camp on the island of Malaikina, which is close to Komsomolsk-na-Amure, is called 'Dzhem's Island' by some of the locals. The other camp is on the island of Lesnoy, which is located in Amurskaya Oblast', and is popularly called '*tabor*' (a traditional gypsy encampment).[88]

There was one incident that shattered Dzhem's image as a guarantor of stability and order in Komsomolsk-na-Amure, the incident that ultimately led to his sudden death. In the early evening on 22 February 2001, the café Charodeika, a popular spot among the town's youth, was firebombed. Several assailants set the wood and the plastic of the interior on fire, turning the café into a crematorium. Eight died, twenty were wounded, some of them severely. Most of the victims were girls in their late teens.[89] The city was in shock. The firebomb attack had been the first documented 'terror act' in Komsomolsk-na-Amure, a city that, so far, had been spared by the gangland shootouts characteristic of so many Russian cities in the mid-1990s. The city's inhabitants were outraged; parents and school children demonstrated, demanding decisive action from the local authorities.

The owner of the afflicted café was the businessman Eduard Zaitsev. Zaitsev was a member of the local city parliament and the director of the company Vtormet, specialized in scrap metal recycling. He had invested his profits in several cafés and restaurants. Rumours spread fast: Zaitsev had been reluctant to cooperate with Dzhem's organization and had refused to pay the protection fees. Instead, he had collaborated with a minor crime group with contacts to the local police, facilitating an alternative protection contract for his business.[90] The public perceived the attack on the café as a sheer power demonstration of Komsomolsk's shadow lord. Soon after the incident, four young men directly involved in the firebombing were arrested. Yet the authorities did not stop here. Seven months after the attack on the

---

[87] Irina Petrakova, 'U kriminal'nykh avtoritetov epidemia infarktov', op. cit.
[88] Oleg Zhunusov, 'Vor v zakone umer po puti na pokhorony kollegi', op. cit.
[89] Galina Mironova, 'Ugolovnik, ob'yavliavshiy sebya', op. cit.
[90] Sergey Minigazov, 'Ubit' Drakona', *Molodoy Dal'nevostochnik* 15, 11 April 2001.

café, Dzhem was detained. This was a high profile case. Russia's general prosecutor himself had sanctioned the arrest.[91]

I return twenty minutes later to Dzhem's tomb, which lies now abandoned, the marble table freed of snow. Several bundles of red roses had been placed on the gravestone. Some of the petals had fallen off, scattered on the snow like fresh drops of blood. Suddenly, while I am taking some pictures of the tomb, two men approach me quick and determined. I hastily retreat through deep snow. One of the men follows me uphill. Again, I try to appear casual, scrutinizing some random gravestones. 'Did you get lost?' suddenly asks a voice right next to me. I startle and look up into a smirking face. My friend had warned me of the tomb's guardians, all members of the thieves' brotherhood. One of their duties is to safeguard the tomb against potential grave robbers. A large amount of gold had been buried with the godfather. 'I am looking for my relative's grave', I reply dumbfounded. To my surprise and relief, the answer satisfies his prying. He turns around and disappears between the graves. Relieved, I walk towards the exit of the graveyard. Another guardian is already waiting for me. He is not grinning. His left cheek is swollen. A large fur hat sits firmly on his bulky head. He comes straight to the point: 'Why were you taking pictures of the tomb?' 'Just because', is my unresourceful answer. This does not satisfy him at all. 'Hey brothers, come over here, we have a guest'. He waves to a group of young men standing between two metal sheds next to the entrance portal. It takes only a moment and I am surrounded. Emotionless eyes stare me down. Everybody is wearing a similar looking large fur hat. One seems to be the leader of the group. He steps forward and plants himself in front of me starting the interrogation: what are you doing here, why do you take pictures, where are you from, where do you live? I am taken by surprise; my excuses are more than pathetic. Yet, my unstudied naivety seems to be disarming. The spokesman tones down his inquisitive voice and asks me for my address in town. I show my hotel's check-in card. He studies it intensely, memorizing my name and room number. 'How much longer are you going to be in town?' 'At least a week', I lie, though I was already planning to leave by tomorrow. My answer seems to satisfy him. He thinks for a moment, nods without really looking at me, and then hands me back my card. The circle of towering fur hats parts. I slip away. Picking up my pace, I can hear the leader ask one of his crewmembers what pictures I was actually taking. I do not wait for an answer and head swiftly to my waiting taxi, slip into the seat, and close the door. The engine roars and the departing car gusts

---

[91] Galina Mironova, 'Ugolovnik, ob'yavliavshiy sebya', op. cit.

up a cloud of snow. In silence we ride back to town. It is still snowing heavily.

The Thieves Professing the Code

'Vor v Zakone: Particularly dangerous, in their environment authoritative and committed career criminal'.
– Encyclopaedia of the Russian Interior Ministry (MVD)

The concept of *vor v zakone* (pl. *vory v zakone*) is central to understanding the history and genesis of organized crime in Russia. The phrase literally means 'thief in law', but a looser translation of 'a thief professing the code' is more accurate (see Serio and Razinkin 1995). In the following pages, I use interchangeably the shorter forms *vor(y)* or thief(-ves), though these professional and highly organized thieves are not to be confused with petty criminals. The beginnings of the *vory* and their professional code can be traced back to the late 1920s and early 1930s. During this time, Stalin's purges filled the numerous prison and work camps of the Soviet Union with an endless stream of political prisoners and common criminals alike, creating a world of its own, detached and secluded from the rest of Soviet society. Informal structures and hierarchies soon emerged inside the prison camps.

The fraternity of the *vory v zakone* was paramount in shaping the social structure inside the Soviet penal system. Situated at the top of the prisons' social hierarchy, the *vory* constituted a criminal aristocracy that ruled supreme in the individual camps. They acted as organizers of criminal activities, as arbitrators in struggles between individuals or groups, and as the ultimate informal judicial institution inside the prison walls. The thieves' world was a social institution with its own internal cohesion and ethical code. Central to this code was the notion of rejecting one's own kinship ties in order to join the criminal fraternity. In addition, based on an ethic of non-compliance with the Soviet state, the *vory* systematically refused to work for or cooperate with the camps' authorities. An unwritten codex, the *vorovskoy zakon* (thieves' law), sketched the outlines and rules of conduct of this alternative social frame and informal network (Serio and Razinkin 1995: 79-80).

The *vory* created extra-state entities inside the Gulag system, 'a state inside the state, a structure inside a structure' (Kabo 1990: 110). Through extortion, they levied taxes from fellow prisoners who were not part of the criminal elite (Razgon 1997: 185). As mediators and judges, they created an alternative judicial system inside the prison and work camps to uphold the internal order. The *vory v zakone* held annual *skhody* (conferences), which served as meetings and courts at the same time, to mediate disputes, plan future criminal activities, and debate on the admission of new members (Chaldize 1977: 45). The incorporation of novices into the inner circle of the thieves' world was marked by an initiation ritual referred to alternately as *koronatsiya* (coronation) or *kreshchenie* (baptism). A new aspiring member, a *patsan* (lad), had first to prove himself to have the right qualities of being a potential *vor*; he must have defied camp discipline for a prolonged time and partaken in the thieves' regime of controlling other prisoners (Varese 2001: 147). With references from several established *vory* and by unanimous decision, the *patsan* was finally admitted to the coronation ritual where he had to deliver an oath of adherence to the thieves' code. In the course of the ritual, he shed his former name and acquired a new *klichka* (nickname). Nicknaming was an essential part of the ritual, as Dimitrii Likhachev, a prisoner during the construction of the Belomorsko-Baltiiskii canal in the 1930s, observed, 'The adoption of a nickname is a necessary act of transition to the *vory*'s sphere (it amounts to a peculiar "taking of monastic vows")' (cited in Varese 2001: 150).

The camp authorities were well aware of this power structure inside the penal system and used it as a tool to control the rising number of political prisoners in the 1930s and 1940s. The dichotomy of political prisoners and criminals was partially created and enforced by the camp authorities.[92] From 1937-45 the camp administration used the professional criminals, who often had privileged access to camp resources, as a check on fellow prisoners (Applebaum 2003: 283). The official power in the prison camp zones used the thieves as a tool to establish and maintain internal order, thus recognizing in the thieves' internal camp structure an equivalent of their own goals, that is order, discipline, hierarchy, and structure (Kabo 1990: 110).

The situation changed fundamentally after the Second World War when the camps' population swelled rapidly. Conscripts who were pressed into the army during the war were returned to the prisons, Soviet soldiers and officers captured by the enemy were deported to the camps on their return, and arrested members of nationalist movements in the Baltic republics and Ukraine began to fill the ranks of the penal colonies (Varese 1998: 527). The *vory* saw the returning convict-soldiers as traitors or *suki* (bitches) who had transgressed the informal law of non-cooperation with state by taking up arms on behalf of the Soviet Union (Serio and Razinkin 1995: 74). At this point, most of the returning prisoners and newcomers were trained in and accustomed to the use of violence, and the thieves' authority was not taken for granted anymore. Violent clashes spread through the

---

[92] Ordinary criminals as well as the thieves professing the code were seen as *sotsialno-blizkii* (socially close), unlike the political prisoners, who were seen as *sotsialno-opasnyi* (socially dangerous) (Applebaum 2003: 282-83).

whole prison system leaving hundreds of casualties behind. The so-called *such'ya voyna* (bitches' war) lasted from 1948-53. By the end of the 1950s, the society of the thieves professing the code had almost vanished (Varese 1998: 526). It took two decades to recover.

I would like to focus here on the informal structure of this criminal subculture and the symbolic markers used to signify the internal social stratification. Memoirs of imprisoned dissidents open the view on a complex and symbolically charged prison culture enclosed in the numerous labour camps of the Gulag system. Varlam Shalamov, an articulate eye-witness of the internal prison culture, was arrested in 1937 and spent the following 17 years in prison camps in the Kolyma region of north-eastern Siberia. As a political prisoner, Shalamov was at the bottom of the prison's hierarchy, banned from work and at the mercy of the thieves who treated the 'politicals' and their possessions as their personal property. His descriptions offer a small glimpse of the thieves' changing insignias and dress codes:

> In the twenties the thieves wore trade school caps; still earlier, the military officer's cap was in fashion. In the forties, during the winter, they wore peakless leather caps, folded down the tops of their felt boots, and wore a cross around the neck. The cross was usually smooth but if an artist was around, he was forced to use a needle to paint it with the most diverse subjects: a heart, cards, a crucifixion, a naked woman (Shalamov 1982: 108-09).

Distinct body gestures and postures underscored the peculiar habitus of the *vory*. Georgii Feldgun, a prisoner of the camps in the 1940s, described their distinctive walk: 'with small steps, legs held slightly apart' (cited in Applebaum 2003: 287). In addition to dress codes and body techniques, tattoos played an important role in the prison's subculture. Insignias of social position were applied to the prisoner's bodies, signifying the rank of individuals, their deeds, and highpoints of their criminal biography (Plutser-Sarno 2003: 27). In the form of a criminal vita inscribed forever on the body of the convict, these tattoos were symbolic representations of a thief's reputation. For instance, the eight-pointed star, often applied to the front part of the shoulder, was the sign for a professional *vor* (Samoilov 1990: 102). In addition, prison tattoos were used to stigmatize social deviance inside the informal structure. Trespassers of the thieves' code were often marked with forcibly applied tattoos or finger amputations.

The prison camp system itself was subject to change, mirror imaging the changes of the post-war Soviet Union. Lev Razgon, a journalist, author, and one of the founding members of the human rights organization Memorial, was sent to the camps twice, in 1938 and 1951. During his second sentence, which lasted until Stalin's death in 1953, he noted the significant changes that had spread through the camp system after the Second World War:

> The post-war criminals differed from the older generation in their extremism. What happened to the good old criminal occupations of swindlers, pickpockets, frauds and con men? The post-war criminals were cold-blooded killers, vicious rapists and organized robbers. That was not the only distinguishing mark of the new generation, however. Now they were split up into castes and communities, each with its own iron discipline, with many rules and customs, and if any of these were infringed the punishment was harsh: at best the individual was expelled from that group and at worst, he was killed. The most widespread criminal community of this kind in the camp were the "honorable thieves" [*zakonniki*].[93] To be more "honorable" meant: going out each day with the rest but only performing the semblance of work; not working for the administration, even as cook or hospital orderly; never having any but the most murderous hostile relations with the "ratters" (i.e. those who in criminal terminology had ceased to be "honorable" and begun to work for the camp administration); and to submit wholly and unconditionally to the criminal "leaders" and unswervingly carry out their orders (Razgon 1997: 184-85).

Lev Samoilov, an archaeologist and author, spent one and one-half years in a prison camp near Leningrad at the beginning of the 1980s and documented the internal social structure of the prison's population and its criminal subculture (*ugolovnaya subkul'tura*) in a meticulous account (Samoilov 1990). Samoilov observed and distinguished three different 'castes' (*kasty* or *masti*) as the basic building blocks of a hierarchical society with strict boundaries (see Figure 8).[94] At the top of the hierarchy were the *vory v zakone*. Following the *vorovskoy zakon*, they represented the 'aristocratic' elite of the prison system; they exercised the system's legislative, judicative, and executive powers. Through the *vorovskoi sud chesti* (thieves' honour court), they had the right and the power to sanction any transgressors of the

---

[93] In Russian the word *zakonniki* derives from the word *zakon* (law), thus signifying persons who are following the (thieves') law.

[94] *Mast'* (pl. *masti*) is the Russian word for a suit of cards. *Chodit' v mast'* means to follow suit; in the thieves' argot it means 'to hold suit' (i.e. to control a community of thieves). Card symbols play an important role in prison folklore and tattoo art. Different 'suits' demarcate different classes inside the prison hierarchy, and belonging is often expressed through tattoos. The 'black suits' (i.e. clubs and spades), are associated with the *vory v zakone*. The 'red suits' mark socially inferior persons, often through forcibly applied tattoos. For example, diamonds, known as *kummovskaya mast'* (chummy suit) stigmatize the bearer as a *stukach*, a stool pigeon or informer to the prison authorities (Plutser-Sarno 2003: 41-47).

thieves' law. The second caste, which included most of the prison's population, was composed of the *muzhiki* (men) or *fraer* (guys). These were the commoners of the penal system who worked for the prison authorities and the *vory* at the same time. In the lowest caste were the *chushki* (piglets) or *obizhenniki* (the offended), forced to perform the lowest duties, from cleaning to being passive homosexual partners. An informal dress code underwrote these social hierarchies. The *vory* wore black dyed prison uniforms, the *muzhiki* the standard-issue blue prison uniforms, and the *chushki* plain, grey robes. In addition, the hierarchy was underscored by spatial and nutritional segregation. The *vory* ate the best food and were placed at the best seats, while the *chushki* stood in the corner and ate the leftovers (Samoilov 1990: 98-99). Yet, the 'caste' borders were not impenetrable. Vertical movements could occur in both directions, upward in form of promotion into the ranks of *vory* or downwards in form of reprisal, which was a serious punishment (Kabo 1990: 110-11).

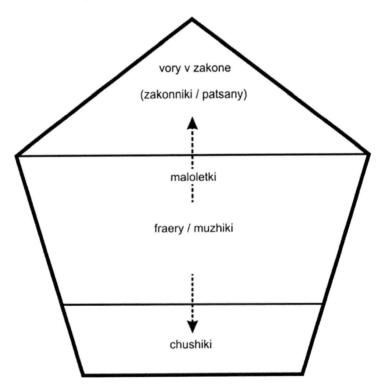

Figure 8. Social organization inside the prison camps.

The society of the *vory v zakone* was a criminal fraternity of independently operating groups of equal standing bound by a common value system and ethical code. Theoretically, the society of the *vory* was an egalitarian fraternity, although in practice older and more established individuals, the *pakhany* (gang leaders), had more authority (Varese 1998: 517). Compared to the Italian mafia, where initiation rituals mark the entrance of novices into the lowest ranks, the *vory* ritual of coronation was only reserved for the highest members of the fraternity. As in the Italian case, future members were under the scrutiny of senior members who judged the worthiness of the novice according to the organizations' standards for an 'honourable' criminal. Similar to Italian mafia initiation rituals entry into the ranks of *vory* is marked by a rite of passage signifying the beginning of a new life as part of the brotherhood: the candidate is presented to a group of established *vory* as a worthwhile member and swears an oath of allegiance to the values and rules of the fraternity. This step was irreversible. Trespassers face dire consequences:

> The life of the 'honorable thieves' [*zakonniki*] in the camp were surrounded by rules of behavior that were observed with almost religious fervor. If a criminal was 'honorable' and then broke the rules he had no alternative but to 'run for the dead zone'. This was a ploughed and raked strip of land between the high fence and a low barrier of barbed wire ... From there, after some time' they would be put in a transport to another camp in the same system. They could no longer remain where they were, since they had been declared outside the law [...] (Razgon 1997: 185).

The internal prison camp hierarchy of the thieves was like a mirror image of the prison camp administration and society at large (Samoilov 1989: 155). Vladimir Kabo, a prisoner from 1949 to 1954, points to the hierarchical similarities between Stalinism and the system of the *vory*. Aspiring future thieves (*maloletki*) were a social reflection of members of the communist youth organization (*komsomoltsy*), and the betrayers (*syki*) of the thieves' code had their counterpart in Stalin's *vragi naroda*, the enemies of the people (Kabo 1990: 110).[95] On the other hand the stratification and stigmatization were not solely confined inside the camp system. The prison camp culture had diffused into everyday culture by sheer numbers. Between 1950 and 1980, millions of people went through the Soviet prison system, bringing back a criminal subculture and language into society at large (see Galler and Marquess 1972). The society of the *vory v zakone* was a product of the Soviet penal system, yet extended well beyond the walls and barbed

---

[95] Membership rituals and forms of social marking are also reminiscent of those described for the Soviet army (see Bannikov 2002).

wire fences of the so-called Gulag Archipelago. Although individual *vory* were often serving life sentences or were frequently rearrested, they nevertheless could establish a far reaching network of criminals bound by the thieves' code. Regular rotations of prisoners in the camp system helped to spread the network throughout the Soviet Union. Outside the camps the *vory* had organized a network of mutual aid for their imprisoned fellows and freshly released convicts, which also provided financial support to relatives of imprisoned *vory*. These networks were at the same time a platform for the recruitment of new members and the organization of criminal activities outside the camp. A communal monetary fund, the *obshchaya kassa* or *obshchak*, provided the necessary means of support and was used to bribe officials inside and outside the camps (Serio and Razinkin 1995: 81-82). The fund was under the control of a *vor v zakone*, who at the same time was able to draw his authority and capacity to act from it, sustained by the joint profits of the groups' criminal activities and contributions of individual members.

The gradual dismantling of the Gulag system after Stalin's death substantially eroded the power base of the *vory*. Although almost extinguished during the 'bitches' war' of the 1950s the society of the *vory v zakone* seemed to have weathered out the pressure of internal and external forces. In the late 1980s, the number of *vory* began to rise significantly compared to the post-war period. Data extrapolated from police reports show a significant rise in the number of *vory* after the break-up of the Soviet Union and a subsequent drop towards the late 1990s. In 1999, the Russian Interior Ministry estimated that there were 387 active *vory* in the Russian Federation and 800 in the Commonwealth of Independent States (CIS) (Varese 2001: 167-68). The estimated ethnic composition of the society of the *vory v zakone* in the Russian Federation during the early 1990s was 33.1 per cent Russians; 31.6 per cent Georgians; 8.2 per cent Armenians; 5.2 per cent Azeri; 21.9 per cent others (including Uzbeks, Ukrainians, Kazakhs, and Abkhazi) (Serio and Razinkin 1995: 83).

Parallel to the *vory v zakone*, another set of organized criminal activity flourished in the Soviet Union that was based on the misappropriation of state allocated resources and their redirection into illegal production. In the Soviet Union the term *mafia* referred to 'occupationally specific corruption' (e.g. the fishing, fruit, vegetable, hotel, or transportation mafia) that diverted goods from certain sectors of the industry into a black market (Naylor 2002: 38). Shortages of consumer goods provided many opportunities for illegal business activities, especially in the beginning of the 1970s when the centralized economy of the Soviet Union was increasingly incapable of satisfying the growing demand for consumer goods among the population (Frisby 1998: 33). Excessive bureaucratic power and a flourishing black market led to the growth of these specific informal structures in the Soviet Union (Anderson 1995: 345). Bribes and widespread corruption were endemic in the Soviet bureaucratic system and close cooperation between black market entrepreneurs and party officials guaranteed partial immunity from state prosecution (Grossman 1977: 32). The cooperation between actors in the shadow economy and party officials demarcated an important turning point in the scope of criminal activities. The separation between state and criminal underground, exemplified in the thieves' anti-state ethos, became increasingly blurred (Finckenauer and Voronin 2001: 6). Starting in the 1960s, criminals, black marketeers and party bureaucrats began to cooperate. Criminal activities, illegal economic practices, and high level patronage became increasingly intertwined.[96] According to Patricia Rawlinson, organized crime in Russia developed from a stance of opposition to an increasingly assimilative position, with a growing active component that penetrated the state structures (Rawlinson 1997: 29). A symbiotic relationship of organized crime networks with state structures led to a sudden increase of economic crime that was slowly consuming its host.

At this point it is important to stress the difficulty to clearly separate different forms of organized crime that existed during the Soviet Union. This becomes even truer for the following post-Soviet years, where traditional views of the *vory* erode and various strands of organized crime coexist and blend into each other. The criminal categories discussed in the following pages are therefore rather ideal types and should reflect on the heterogeneity of organized crime in contemporary Russia.

The 1980s marked a turning point in the nature of organized crime in the Soviet Union. In addition to the burgeoning group of black marketeers, the introduction of market-oriented cooperatives had created a new class of entrepreneurs who increasingly became targets of extortion rings. Illegal entrepreneurs and black marketeers were easy prey for criminals who exploited the inability of those entrepreneurs to contact legitimate structures for protection (Rawlinson 1997: 45). Organized crime evolved into a predatory institution. In addition, the war in Afghanistan and the decade-long involvement of the Soviet military led to an influx of drugs, such as heroin and cannabis, which formed a new substantial economic base for already established criminal groups. With the official dissolution of the Soviet Union, these groups were well poised to bloom in the volatile economic and political environment of the new Russia.

---

[96] The Okean investigation at the end of the 1970s uncovered a far flung patronage network of regional party leaders and indicted party officials up to the rank of ministers. This 'Sochi-Krasnodar party mafia', diverted fish delicacies from a chain of state stores to illegal international export (Vaksberg 1991: 5-17).

Violent Entrepreneurs

> 'The harder the rain, the tighter the roof has to be'.
> – Kirill, age 24, used car dealer

A leading argument attributes the dominance of organized crime in post-Soviet Russia to the imperfect transition to a market economy that resulted in the conversion of over 100,000 former state commercial entities into the hands of private ownership by the end of 1996 (Varese 2001: 17). This transformation and the assets and resources freed from state control presented a rising group of businessmen with astonishing possibilities and equally impressive profit margins. What started as privatization turned into 'grabification' (Grant 1999: 214). In this process, a unique group of entrepreneurs emerged who traded in protection. Privatization encompassed not only the economic sphere, but also affected the very foundation of state power. During the transition phase after the breakdown of the Soviet Union, the state's monopoly on violence was significantly eroded and made room for alternative protectors.

To characterize the economic and political transformations of the Soviet Union I follow the approach of Mark Beisinger and Crawford Young who understand 'state crisis as a set of dysfunctional syndromes rather than as a category' (Beisinger and Young 2002: 11). Symptoms of this flawed transformation were plenty in post-Soviet Russia. The confusion in the law and tax system between federal and regional degrees led to a complex, often contradictory, and extremely restrictive system of taxation. The 1999 index of economic freedom published by the Heritage Foundation listed Russia as 'mostly unfree' ranking it as 106 of 160 countries (Johnson et al.: 1999). Corruption reigned at all levels of government, in part as a continuation of the old system of informal contacts and personal networks used during the Soviet Union to access restricted goods in a malfunctioning planned economy.[97] A rapid increase in registered crimes by almost 200 per cent (1985-95) and a soaring homicide rate (30 per 100,000 in 1995)[98]; shows the far-reaching effects of Russia's transition on the whole society (Varese 2001: 19-21).

---

[97] Transparency International annually rates countries on a perception-based corruption index with a scale of 1-10; the lower the score the higher the level of perceived corruption. In 2001, Russia ranked 2.3, placing it at 81 of 91 countries. See Transparency International, 'Corruption Perceptions Index 2001', http://www.transparency.org/policy_and_research/surveys_indices/cpi/20011997), accessed 4 April 2004.
[98] Comparative homicide rates were 80 for Colombia, 19 in Brazil, 8.6 in the United States, and 1 in the United Kingdom.

Widespread corruption in the state organs undermined the security of private property on a large scale. The sale of natural resources, asset stripping, and the creation of large new monopolies characterized the early stages of transition. In 1988, a newly implemented law gave cooperatives the right to make independent decisions and privately engage in foreign trade. Managers of state oil companies were then able to buy oil from their enterprises privately at a fixed rate and sell it abroad through the newly established cooperatives.[99] Asset stripping depleted formerly state owned enterprises of their valuable resources.[100] During this phase, the state failed to adequately secure common property rights, and alternative forms of protection of private property were demanded.

Large-scale privatization measures were accompanied by privatization and compartmentalization of state powers. Major rearrangements of state security organs, especially the KGB, and a significant reduction in security personnel – 20,000 officers were dismissed between 1991 and 1992 from the KGB alone – flooded the nascent market of protection with thousands of suddenly unemployed individuals who were highly skilled in the use of violence. As a reaction to this new reality a federal law was implemented that legalized private protection agencies and led to the creation of new entities.[101] Supplementing these agencies was an order issued by the Interior Ministry in 1998 to allow policemen to provide private security services for commercial organizations.[102] By 1998, the 10,800 existing private security agencies in Russia had absorbed nearly 50,000 former officers of state security agencies and law enforcement organs (Volkov 1999: 3). Former military expertise or work experience in the security organs was a valuable asset for the protection agencies, not only in terms of the personnel's proficiency in the use of violence, but also in respect to potential contacts and access to restricted information that these individuals brought to their new jobs. Thus, former KGB senior officials became the heads of various

---

[99] Given the asymmetric price structure between the national economy and international markets – in 1992 the Russian price for oil was one percent of the world market – these dealings reaped extreme profit margins (Varese 2001: 33-34).

[100] In asset stripping, a person or group bought a former state company and then sold its products below market price to subsidiary companies. The revenues were then transferred to subordinated closed joint-stock companies under the control of hand-picked directors who guaranteed a backflow of the profits.

[101] The law 'On private detective and protection activity' adopted on 22 March 1992 created three different types of security companies: private detective agencies (*chastnye detektivnye agenstva*), private security services (*chastnye sluzhby bezopasnosti*), and private protection companies (*chastnye okhranye predpriyatiya*) (Volkov 2002a: 87).

[102] For instance, in 1991 the Union of Veterans of Afghanistan formed a joint venture with the Moscow police to facilitate protection services for private companies (Varese 2001: 59-60).

private security services. For instance, Argus, the biggest provider of private security in Moscow and a special partner for telecommunication firms, was headed by Yuri Levitski, a former commander of *vympel* (a KGB anti-terrorist unit) (Kryshtanovskaya 1995: 95). Namakom, a private security and consulting company was managed by Ivanovich Drozhov, the former head of KGB Department S, the branch that handled so-called illegals (undercover agents working abroad without diplomatic cover) who were involved with international terrorists and militant Palestinian groups (Knight 1996: 58). Major companies even internalized protection on a large scale. Gazprom, the biggest natural gas company in Russia contracted the services of a 20,000 employee private protection company headed by former KGB colonel Viktor Marushchenko (Varese 2001: 61). According to the executive director of the Association of Russian Banks on Security Questions, by 1995 half of the managers of independent security services consisted of former KGB employees, the other half came from the Interior Ministry and military (Knight 1996: 57). In addition, the ongoing war in Chechnya and the weakening of state control over a vast arsenal of weapons from Soviet times presented a constant supply of arms for these agencies (Frisby 1998: 31).

The field of private protection in Russia is a grey area where the boundary between legal and illegal activities is rather vague. Private protection presents business opportunities for state- sanctioned protection agencies, but also for non-formal actors. The economic transition phase in post-Soviet Russia, characterized by the appearance of numerous open-air markets and newly founded small private businesses, created an ideal setting for a new class of predatory criminals. Thousands of small racketeering groups formed in the early 1990s extorted protection money from the new class of private entrepreneurs. The members of these gangs were young, the majority having a background in martial arts or bodybuilding, and were organized according to neighbourhoods or city districts. The sports clubs and fitness centres of former state enterprises made for perfect recruiting grounds (Volkov 2002b: 100). These groups of street racketeers were named *sportsmeny* (sportsmen) or *kachki* (iron pumpers) due to their physical prowess and conspicuously worn tracksuits. During the early 1990s, *sportsmeny* became a visible feature of almost every open-air market in Russia. Similar to the officially sanctioned protection agencies these 'violent entrepreneurs' carried out multiple functions in the emerging market economy. As Vadim Volkov noted, 'They intimidated, protected, gathered information, settled disputes, gave guarantees, enforced contracts, and taxed' (2000: 709).

The general term for the protection services offered by these groups is *krysha* (roof). Originally a term from the professional vocabulary of the intelligence community, meaning the cover for a spy, the term has come to designate the service package to a client to protect him physically and minimize his business risks.[103] Volume and guarantees of these services depend on the client's requests, or as one of my informants phrased it, 'The harder the rain, the tighter the roof has to be'. The rain serves here as a metaphor in a criminal and corrupt business environment where companies are exposed to a variety of penetrating and often damaging outside influences. Services offered by protection agencies varies, and can include providing security guards, protecting clients from other racketeers, safeguarding business deals, and gathering information on competitors. A *banditskaya krysha* (bandit roof) is needed for 'special' needs, like recovering bad debts and delayed payments, or effective muscle against competitors. This kind of roof is facilitated through crime groups that deal in the execution of illegal activities.[104] The demand for dispute resolution and trusted mediators is especially high in the underworld, considering the fact that 'the greatest fear of a criminal is being cheated by another criminal' (Varese 2001: 5). On the other hand, policemen and other employees of state security agencies offer their own 'roofs' for protection against criminal gangs. Usually, a strict division of territorial influence is observed that separates the different protection spheres from each other (Shlapentokh 1996: 402).

These 'violence-managing agencies' successfully understood how to convert potential violence into a marketable service (Volkov 1999). In that respect, crime groups in post-Soviet Russia are an example of the capitalist logic of supply and demand, satisfying the demand for alternative sources of protection. The violent environment in Russia and the high level of distrust in state organizations, especially in the police and municipal offices created a dilemma for individual entrepreneurs with few solutions. Entrepreneurs could either recourse enter unmediated and personalized barter relations with those who threatened their enterprises, or they could pay violence-managing agencies to undertake the work for them. The new space of the market economy created the backdrop for new forms of organized crime in the post-Soviet period. As Katherine Verdery eloquently argued, 'mafia is a symbol for what happens when the visible hand of the state is being replaced by the invisible hand of the market' (1996: 219). The virtuous 'invisible hand' of

---

[103] For Nancy Ries, the term *krysha* represented a 'key cultural referent' to understand the post-Soviet economic sphere (2002: 309). Caroline Humphrey traced the essence of the racket back to the patronage structures during Soviet times, when political protection was paramount for the economic and political survival of the elites (1999: 209-12).

[104] In contrast, a 'red roof' (*krasnaya krysha*) is a protection arrangement facilitated through state security agencies, e.g. police.

the market, predicted by the Western advisors to bring Russia to a collective economic optimum, turned into an 'invisible fist'.

At the end of the 1990s, one could observe in Russia a consolidation of crime groups towards regular enterprises, and the integration of violence-managing agencies into the formal business world. In addition, self-destructive methods of competition, which peaked in large-scale gang wars of 1992-95, were replaced by targeted assassinations of individual gang leaders (Volkov 2002c: 91). A new capitalist-oriented pragmatic rationality took root among organized crime syndicates in Russia. The large sums of capital accumulated in the years directly after the disintegration of the Soviet economy were invested in the formal economy. By the end of the 1990s, Vadim Radaev's interview data collected from entrepreneurs and managers in 1997-98 indicated that, 'the opposition of business and criminality is shifting towards integration' (1999: 2). Within a decade, the use of violence had been integrated as a 'standard' element of economic relations and the basic practice of racketeering was replaced by more sustainable forms of control over enterprises. Organized crime groups re-organized their activities to influence the new emerging market, and were transformed in the process. Speaking at least for those groups, the invisible hand of the market has left its imprint.

Testimonies

> 'Non so che significa [I do not know what that means]'.
> – Amoroso Mini, Italian mafioso, cited in Henner Hess, *Mafia & Mafiosi: Origin, Power and Myth*

The first time I stumbled across the topic of organized crime in the Russian Far East was during the preparations for my first field visit to Vladivostok. Researching Chinese migration into Primorsky Krai and related media reactions in online editions of local newspapers, I was puzzled by the great numbers of contract killings of businessmen and underworld figures that were mentioned in the media outlets. Gangland related shootings in Moscow and central Russia were a common news item during the 1990s. By 2000, the situation had normalized. Not so in Vladivostok. Several important underworld figures had been killed in the early 2000s, some of them quite openly in front of hotels or restaurants. Not one month had passed without the assassination of several entrepreneurs.[105]

---

[105] Vitaliy Nomokonov, law professor in Vladivostok and head of the Vladivostok Centre for the Study of Organized Crime, estimated that Primorsky Krai had approximately 30 contract killings in 2002 (2003: 7).

In 2004, during fieldwork in Vladivostok, I encountered the presence of organized crime as a frequently recurring subject of everyday talk. The identity of important gang leaders and their economic activities were often well known and the subject of an open discourse in public as well in the media. Nancy Ries encountered a similar phenomenon during her fieldwork in Russia, when details and stories about mafia and criminal personalities turned out to be 'normal features of the daily landscape, of conversation, of humor, and of popular culture' (2002: 309). Wherever it occurs, talk about organized crime is saturated with rumours. Following up on these discussions, I entered a murky world of anecdotal evidence where factuality drowns in the grey zone of conspiracy theories, slander, rumours, gossip, and anecdotes. Rumours are ambiguous, multivocal, and yet take on symbolic quality in their actualization of abstract concepts or distanced events. At the same time, gossip and rumours also present a way for individuals to debate their everyday world, a narrative form to make sense of an opaque social reality (Haviland 1977; Heilmann 1978). Talk on organized crime is no exception. As indicated above, Katherine Verdery has drawn attention to the fact that organized crime in the former Soviet Union is at the same time a 'real Mafia' and a symbolic or 'conceptual' phenomenon, subject to a lively public discourse that tries to make sense of a rapid socio-economic change (Verdery 1996: 219).

Conducting fieldwork in the major central open-air markets of Vladivostok and specifically behind the booth of a family of Uzbek traders exposed me almost daily to numerous conversations about the hidden economy and its individual actors. I also saw much evidence of organized crime activities. In open-air markets, organized crime becomes visible on a very basic and formative level. Large-scale rackets and the extortion of protection fees are a common phenomenon at almost all of Russia's open-air markets. In contrast to popular imagery, extortion can be a very quiet and subtle activity, a silent transaction void of any violent form. The transactions, the collection of protection fees, become visible in swift encounters between stand owner and racketeer – a recognizing nod, casual small talk, and a quick passing of the weekly protection sum. The known group affiliation of a racketeer is common knowledge among the traders, which is of course part of the system. In the market, I found myself in a world of openly shared secret knowledge, subtle gestures, hushed words, and transient ruble notes. I used the rumours and encounters of the markets to begin my enquiry into the structures of organized crime in the Russian Far East.

The method through which I approach the topic of organized crime in Vladivostok and the way I try to uncover, at least partially, its subtle structures is a synthesis of different types of sources: participant observation, interviews, newspaper articles, and secondary literature. I draw from a range of sources to address the multiple perspectives on organized crime. Formal analysis and local discourse do not contradict here; they rather reflect unique positions that are informed by different experiences.

Despite its public surface, organized crime research in Russia presents a more hidden field if compared to the Italian case. Analytic literature on organized crime in Russia is a relatively new phenomenon. No large anti-mafia trials have been conducted in Russia, comparable to the so-called maxi-trials in Italy during the 1980s which greatly enhanced the field of Italian Mafia Studies. The Italian trials led to numerous testimonies of high ranking turncoats, the *pentiti*, and were able to penetrate, at least partially, the wall of silence that had surrounded Sicilian and Calabrian mafia groups for many years. These testimonies allowed for an intimate study of the Mafia's inner workings and structure (e.g. Arlacchi 1995; Paoli 2003; Schneider and Schneider 2003).

I began by trying to connect the recurring topics and emerging patterns in the rumours and gossip that I heard in the street about known gangsters and crime groups to information in the archives of the local print media. A crucial information source was the database and compiled press digests of the Vladivostok Centre for the Study of Organized Crime.[106] In the course of my research, structures and connections between individual crime figures and big business emerged. From this knowledge base I developed specific questions, which I brought back to 'expert' informants – market sellers, officials working in the local administration, journalists, and friends with loose connections to Vladivostok's underworld – for clarification. Graphic representations of possible crime networks turned out to be a useful methodological tool to discuss and check my data with informants who had an intimate knowledge on the development of organized crime structures in the region.

During my research, various perspectives surfaced in respect to the nature of organized crime in the Russian Far East. These sometimes contradictory perspectives show the heterogeneity of organized crime and represent at the same time differing evaluations of those structures. To get at this heterogeneity of perspective, it is essential to let different voices speak.

---

[106] The Vladivostok Center for the Study of Organized Crime (Vladivostokskiy Tsentr Issledovaniya Organizovannoy Prestupnosti), hereafter VTsIOP in text and references, is part of the School of Law at the Far East State University (Yuridicheskiy Institut DVGTU). The centre is partially financed by TraCCC (Transnational Crime and Corruption Center) and is one of several related centres in Russia and other countries. At the time of research, TraCCC was headquartered at American University, but it has more recently moved to George Mason University. Vladivostok homepage: http://www.crime.vl.ru.

Organized crime is an elusive subject. In addition to the epistemological grey zone of rumours and anecdotal evidence, emic and etic perspectives clash in the evaluation of illegal conduct.

Formal analysis and local discourse are not contradictory here; they rather reflect unique positions that are informed by different experiences. I draw from a range of sources (interviews, newspaper articles, and secondary literature) to address multiple perspectives on organized crime as well as to distinguish different forms. Both Nancy Ries and Caroline Humphrey have hinted convincingly in their work at the existence of a number of conceptual as well as real mafias in contemporary Russia (Humphrey 1999; Ries 2002).

To explore and analyze the development of organized crime networks in the Russian Far East in this chapter, I will: 1) point out some epistemological problems that are central to organized crime research when dealing with various testimonies of high ranking crime figures; 2) explore the evolution of organized crime networks in Vladivostok from the late 1980s by focusing on several important groups and analyzing their economic activities; 3) incorporate the case studies from Vladivostok into the larger theoretical debate on organized crime and the Mafia. I will start with an example from the formative period of organized crime in the Russian Far East to illustrate some of the methodological problems.

Koval

Researchers from VTsIOP place the appearance of the first organized crime groups in Primorsky Krai during the 1970s and 1980s.[107] The active criminal groups during this period came to be known among prosecutors and police as the *tretaya smena* (nightshift). Despite its status as a closed city, the underground economy of Vladivostok's port and nightlife made for a wide range of criminal opportunities. Main sources of income were robbery, racketeering, blackmailing of informal traders, and the trading of imported foreign goods. Anatoliy Kovalev (Koval) and Leonid Ivlev (Kaban) emerged during that time as the primary leaders of Vladivostok's underworld. It is difficult to evaluate the extent of Koval's and Kaban's control and the magnitude of their involvement in illegal activities. The perspective of law enforcement agencies differs here substantially from the self-reflection of the involved persons. For example, Koval gave an interview to a local newspaper in 1996, in which he responded to the journalist's questions of his involvement in organized crime during the 1970s and 1980s:

---

[107] VTsIOP, 'Khronika organizovannoy prestupnosti (obzor pressy 1997-2002)', http://www.crime.vl.ru/docs/obzor/obzor_dv.htm, p. 2, accessed 23 February 2006.

> I am a native inhabitant of Vladivostok, born and raised in Morgorod [city district], in a family without a father. My mother was often on business trips and from early on in my youth I was on my own. Like a lot of my peers I went to the dances. Today one hardly remembers how popular the dances where back then. The youngsters met at the small House of Culture, farther down at the restaurant Okean, in the big House of Culture, and in front of the submarine [monument]. We did not drink and smoke back then. There were fights at every dance. Back then a strong division along city districts came into being. [...] During that time we were acquainted with and associated with everybody. We knew each other well and therefore could freely go to the other districts of town. The original group was composed of famous people, whom the city knows very well, for example, my friends Victor Alekseenko and Sasha Kostenko. We three were not only born during the same year, we are also of the same zodiac sign, the Ram [...] There were not any of these groups back then. There were companions [*tovarichshi*] who were close to each other. I do not see anything bad in that [...] Of course, during that time some connections started, but not in a criminal sense. It is true, though, that when the street markets [*barakholki*] where the sailors sold imported jeans appeared, we collected the goods from them and gave them only the money they were worth. That means we didn't get into profiteering. You can even say that we played the role of the OBKhSS [Department for the Fight against Misappropriation of Socialist Property].[108]

Koval's view of the formative period of organized crime in Vladivostok and his own involvements differ considerably from the view held by specialists in law enforcement. What criminologists recognize as the formation of an early organized crime syndicate was according to Koval only a group of close friends who were determined to fight for respect in a town divided by street gangs and who were justly participating in an evolving shadow economy. Questions on systematic control over the underground economy and personal concentration of power were brushed away by Koval with a similar argument, 'I never controlled any territory. I just have a group of determined friends, who each do their own work and none is connected to criminal activities'.[109]

---

[108] D. Kashirin, 'Anatoliy Kovalev: Tret'ey smeny nikogda ne bylo', *Zolotoy Rog*, 27 August 1996.

[109] D. Kashirin, 'Anatoliy Kovalev: Ya chestnyy biznesmen i rabotayu, kak vse', *Zolotoy Rog*, 3 September 1996.

Plate 15. Koval's grave, Vladivostok 2004.

Koval's emic perspective, including his demonstrated naiveté and innocence, are not an uncommon phenomenon encountered in organized crime research, especially in dealing with first-hand accounts of persons who are accused of being leading crime figures. Even if trials often defy their flaunted innocence, the accused often take recourse in cultural codes to legitimate their behaviour and identity (Paoli 2003: 97). The longing for respect, obligations to friends, and altruistic motives are at the centre of these public self-legitimization strategies. Paolo Campo, a Sicilian *capomafia* on trial in 1986 defended himself along the following lines:

> I declare myself innocent of the crime of delinquent and mafia association, meaning that I have never committed crimes, nor have I associated with others to this end. I must say, however, that I was born and will die a Mafioso, if by *mafia* one means, as I do, to do good to one's neighbor, to give something to those in need, to find work for the unemployed, to bring help to those who are in a difficult situation [cited in Paoli 2003: 97].

As part of Campo's defensive argument, he ascribed a different meaning to a common term. Koval too took such a strategy when responding to some questions asked to him in the same interview previously cited. For example, when asked about his reputation as a protector, as a facilitator of 'roofs' in Vladivostok's underworld, Koval responded: 'I do not understand this word ['roof']. In this case, I have my money invested; I work with those people as a team [*v upriazhke*], but the officers from the UOP [Organized Crime Directorate] present this as if I would be a 'roof' for them. What kind of 'roof' are we talking about? Yes, I build myself a name, I know people, with whom I was together at the dances, that's all'.[110]

The reinterpretation of one's own activities in the light of lawful conduct is a common spin. It becomes a matter of perspective where truth ends and deliberate deceit begins. Even the Russian Far East's famous *vor* Dzhem exemplifies this argumentative strategy with his interpretation of a thief professing the code, '*Vor v zakone* would be called that person who could judge rightfully and settle disputes without spilling blood. That is what I was actually doing in prison'.[111] Notions of friendship and brotherhood underscore the casual character of informal relationships; the *vor* appears as a peaceful mediator. Asked about his affiliation to fellow inmates, often hardened criminals serving multi-year sentences, Dzhem responded in reference to their concurring interests, 'These are just people I befriended, with whom I associated. We are like-minded people; you might say we are brotherly comrades [*bratva*]. And we are a lot, not only a hundred, but we are not bandits, as the police think'.[112]

Official views on organized crime and legal categories rarely match the personal accounts of involved persons. The instrumental use of specific terms is part of the particular language used by law enforcement officials and the judicial system alike (Solan and Tiersma 2005). In addition, designated judicial terms can pass into a popular sphere, where they might be used for different purposes. Koval's own view of the term 'nightshift' exemplifies this process:

> The notorious "nightshift" was invented during that time by the former head of the Regional Criminal Investigation Department, the police colonel Babicheviy, with whom I found myself later together in the holding cell. [...] The "nightshift" never existed, it was invented for the officials [*dlya galochki*], for the reports to Moscow. Although, the definition was used by the youngsters to strengthen their authority among their fellows, that is why they started to say: "I'm with the nightshift". That's all.[113]

---

[110] Ibid.
[111] 'Ya khochu chto u menya zdes' byl poryadok', *Kommersant*, 5 October 2001.
[112] Ibid.
[113] D. Kashirin, 'Anatoliy Kovalev: Ya chestnyy biznesmen', op. cit.

Is this just a linguistic strategy of a former criminal redefining his involvement in illegal activities, or an actual mismatch of a judicial signifier and the reality of the signified? Again, a comparison with Italian cases underscores the contradictory dilemma of etic ascription and emic self-depiction.

In the Italian case, high-ranking members of mafia groups often dispute the very existence of 'mafia'. It is true that the term *mafia* has a literary origin. It probably made its first appearance in Italy in a theatre play staged by Giuseppe Rizzotto and Gaspare Mosca in 1863, titled *I mafiusi de la Vicaria*. The play's *mafiusi* were a group of prisoners who defined themselves as 'men of respect' (Schneider and Schneider 2003: 32).

In 1984, Tommaso Buscetta, a main player in the Sicilian mafia group Cosa Nostra and a key witness in a maxi-trial, turned the term's literary invention to his own defence. 'The word mafia', he said, 'is a literary creation, while the true Mafiosi are simply called men of honor. Each of them belongs to a *borgata* [neighborhood] and he is a member of a family [...] as a whole this association is called Cosa Nostra' (cited in Paoli 2003: 24). In their own language, mafiosi see themselves as *uomini d'onore*, men of honour. The Calabrian mafia is referred to as the Ndrangheta (Society of Men of Honour), and the Sicilian Cosa Nostra translates as 'Our Cause'. Still, the term 'mafia' is widely used in Italy, a popular consent exists on its meaning, and nobody would neglect its existence on pure linguistic terms. The contradictory statements of known mafiosi and law enforcement agencies about the nature of the former's activities are part of a larger problem in determining the boundaries of organized crime and its relation to society.[114]

Natasha

I first met Natasha at one of Vladivostok's markets. She was working as a vendor for a vegetable and fruit trader from Baku. She had just arrived from Komsomolsk-na-Amure, her hometown for many years. Born in a gypsy *tabor* outside of Odessa, she had moved at the age of five with her Russian father, a boat captain on the Amur River, to Komsomolsk-na-Amure. Since separating from her husband two years previously, her life had spiralled downwards to the brink of despair. She had never before worked in a market. In Komsomolsk-na-Amure she had worked as a wholesale dealer for leather

---

[114] Thomas Hauschild (2006) has traced differing views of the Italian mafia in the sociological and anthropological literatures. He finds that scholars too are divided by two main perspectives: (1) the mafia is seen as a constructive member of society, a folk structure of mediators and helpful patrons serving the common people; or (2) the mafia is seen as a criminal network of violent entrepreneurs and predators, undermining society.

and fur clothing, making an average of US$100 per day. With no other job prospects and cut off from her former husband's network she now works as a vegetable seller for a meagre 200 rubles (US$8) per day. Although she had escaped from an unbearable marriage, she also had lost any material support from her estranged husband. Her economic and social network had been cut. Yet she remembered other days. Her husband had been a close acquaintance of Dzhem. It was a prosperous connection, ripe with benefits, and full of social warmth:

> During the summer we sometimes went to an island on the river. People call it Thief's Island [*vorovskoi ostrov*; i.e. Malaikina Island]. It was Dzhem's island where he invited people who were close to him; it was like a retreat for the *vory*. We always had such a good time there, joking, sitting around the fire, having good food. He [Dzhem] was a very nice man. He liked children, placed them on horses, let them ride. When my son was six, he put him up for sparring against a distant cousin of his. My son still remembers that day. He had won his first fight.

Natasha saw social proximity to the godfather as benefitting families rather than placing them in danger. As she explained, 'I am glad that my brother's son has found a job with the thieves. The families who are close to them always prosper. The family members have good jobs, there is always enough food, and they live a secure life'.

In the summer of 1997, Special Forces (SOBR) raided the island. Operation Lager rounded up 49 people between the ages of 12 and 22, some of them former inmates.[115] Alcohol and drugs were seized in the former Soviet touristic centre Lesnaia Skazka (Forest Fairy Tale) on Dzhem's island, a multi-building complex that included cottages and sport fields. Boris Reznik, member of the Russian Duma and a journalist, researched the story for the daily newspaper *Izvestiya*. He concluded that the summer camp for juveniles and former convicts, run by Dzhem's charitable foundation Sostradanie, functioned as a rigid training site for the next generation of thieves.[116] Dzhem's perspective on the camp's purpose, presented in the same article, was quite different. For him, it was a recreational and sports centre for orphans and ex-convicts who had no other place to turn. 'There is discipline in the camp, order [*poryadok*]. In seven years there was not one accident, not one fight [...] We, the boys from the Dzemgi neighbourhood, had always been the most determined, the most courageous. We could stand

---

[115] Similar summer camps for juveniles run by *vory* have been discovered on Sakhalin. See Konstantin Getmanskiy, 'Pionerlager usilennogo rezhima', *Izvestiya*, 29 July 2004.

[116] Boris Reznik, 'Ostrov Dzhema', *Izvestiya*, 11 July 1997.

on our own feet. This is what we teach to the youth, we educate [*vospityvaem*] them for Russia'.[117]

The prosecutor's office did not press any charges, but closed the camp for sanitary reasons. Dzhem filed a complaint in court denouncing the journalist for addressing him in the article as a *vor v zakone* and demanded a rectification in the newspaper. Reznik agreed, on one condition: Dzhem should announce in front of television cameras that *vory* do not exist. Dzhem never complied.

Everything had changed in the city after the unforgettable explosion in the café Charodeika and the later arrest of Dzhem. One of Natasha's friends had died in the Charodeika, another friend's face was disfigured beyond recognition by the fire. She still walks the street, Natasha said, the prelude to Dzhem's death gruesomely inscribed on her face. What remained of Dzhem's death was a conspicuous tomb, memories of his lavish funeral, and Natasha's own memories of a better time:

> No president is buried like that. They came from all over Russia. From the graveyard's entrance the row of parked cars and SUVs stretched for more than five kilometres. Helicopters of the major television channels circled in the air above. All the visitors were fed well at the funeral and everything was conducted in a very cultivated [*kul'turnyy*] manner. [...] When Dzhem was the ruler of Komsomolsk, it was a safe city. I could walk the streets at night with all my jewellery, nothing would happen to me. While Dzhem was in charge we had no drug users [*narkomany*] on the streets, it was completely safe in the city.

A funeral worthy of a statesman and the perception of his protecting hand extended over the city elevates Dzhem into the ranks of post-Soviet mythology, a realm where the protecting hand of godfathers disguises the invisible fist of organized crime. Depicted as a benevolent protector, Dzhem is seen as a vital factor in guaranteeing the social order in a lawless time. The *Kommersant* journalist Sergey Dyupin captured similar notions while interviewing members of Dzhem's organization during the welcoming ceremony for the funeral in the Hotel Voskhod in Komsomolsk-na-Amure:

> Thanks to Petrovich [Dzhem], we do not have chaos [*bespredel'*] here in town [...] this is a thief's [*vorvskiy*] town, not a bandit's [*banditskiy*] one [...] If they steal your wallet out of your pocket, this is normal, you cannot say anything against that. But if they beat you with a baseball bat and steal your fur hat, that's already chaos. We had these things happening in our town. When Petrovich took

---

[117] Ibid.

command we caught all this fowl [*polovili dich'*]. Up to this day everything was quiet. You could walk drunk and in socks through the whole town at night, with a golden chain around your neck, your wallet in your hand and nobody would touch you.[118]

It is difficult to judge the validity of these comments and assess their truth in the light of Komsomolsk-na-Amure's reality. Yet these remarks nevertheless represent an emic point of view on the social reality of organized crime and hint at the multivocality of the discourse on organized crime in contemporary Russia.

In her analyses of popular discourse on the mafia, Nancy Ries (2002) also found that Russians used discussions about the mafia to talk about justice and order. The statements she recorded were often contradictory; informants described the mafia as both a destroyer of justice and order and a source of the same. She found it significant that the mafia was described at times as honest and decent, and seen as an institution that was urgently needed in the predatory economic environment of post-Soviet Russia (Ries 2002: 278). Across the former Soviet Union, talk about organized crime is a popular moral discourse on chaos and order (Nazpary 2002: 88). It is not so much about an order that state power is supposed to guarantee, but rather about the chaos the state seems unable to control. Powerful organized crime groups emerge in this context as a dependable guarantor of stability and order, as an institution that fulfils the functions of discipline and control the state has apparently lost (Ries 2002: 309).

Organized Crime in Vladivostok and Primorsky Krai

'Where there is money to make, you cannot do without the mafia'.
– Vadim, age 25, customs official

The evolution of organized crime networks in Russia after the collapse of the Soviet Union offer a glimpse into the intrinsic dynamics and developments of local crime groups. In the following pages I sketch the evolution of organized crime beginning in the mid 1980s in the Russian Far East, especially in Vladivostok. Since a detailed and encompassing account of Vladivostok's criminal history would exceed the scope of this work by far, I will rather concentrate on a number of key figures who represent different phases and branches of organized crime in the Russian Far East. Connections between big business and organized crime groups are of special interest. Organized crime groups are flexible social and economic structures, able to adapt innovatively to changing economic and political environments.

---

[118] Sergey Dyupin, 'Batyu khoronyat vsem mirom', *Kommersant*, 27 October 2001.

Although informants and scholars alike often reference groups as if they are distinct, it should be clear from this account that few clear boundaries persist for long. Crime groups are in constant interaction with allies and competitors. A diachronic perspective, focusing on process as well as on structure, will illustrate the evolution of organized crime groups in Vladivostok and capture its complex dynamics.

Unlike Komsomolsk-na-Amure, Vladivostok was never a city controlled by *vory*. Vladivostok's status as a closed city and the dominant presence of military structures during the Soviet Union made it extremely difficult for *vory v zakone* to establish a hegemonic presence in Vladivostok's underworld, as they had successfully accomplished in Komsomolsk-na-Amure and Khabarovsk. Vladivostok was known as a 'red city', a city predominately under the protection of state security organs.

In the 1980s, crime groups that were not affiliated with the *vory* did establish operations and strongly protected their spheres of influence. The aforementioned 'nightshift' and its key figures Koval and Kaban were an early example of underground entrepreneurs who used Vladivostok's geographical and infrastructural particularities to their advantage. They were not the only ones. Vladivostok's harbour presented a highly attractive economic zone for all manner of illicit entrepreneurs. Growing economic freedom and the nascent private market, initiated during the mid-1980s, led to a growing numbers of entrepreneurs in the city. As private entrepreneurs in a socialist economy, these businessmen and traders, often operating at the brink of legality, were easy targets for blackmailing and racketeering schemes conducted by a variety of criminal groups. These groups were led by professional criminals often with extensive prison background, the so-called *ugolovniki* (convicts) or *sinie* (lit. blue ones) because of the blue prison tattoos on their fingers and hands.[119] In addition to Koval and Koban, Trifon, Kim, Rybak, and D'iak were among the better known authorities and leaders of those groups during the late 1980s and early 1990s.[120]

After the breakdown of the Soviet Union, Vladivostok was opened to international shipping and commerce, offering myriads of business opportunities, both legitimate and illegitimate. Similar to other regions and cities in Russia the origins of post-Soviet organized crime in Vladivostok can be traced back to the emergence of street rackets that systematically preyed on an evolving class of street traders and small-scale entrepreneurs.

---

[119] *Sinie* and *ugolovniki* are generic names for hardened criminals who have spent substantial time in prison. In contrast to the *vory*, they are not 'crowned' and not necessarily part of the thieves' brotherhood.

[120] VTsIOP, 'Khronika organizovannoy prestupnosti (obzor pressy 1997-2002)', p.7, electronic document, http://crime.vl.ru/docs/obzor/obzor_dv.htm, accessed 23 February 2006.

Neighbourhood gangs transformed rapidly into structured criminal groups who forced their dominion onto the small businesses of the city by extracting protection fees. The *sportsmeny*, using their physical skills to intimidate and enforce, soon emerged as dominant players in Vladivostok's underground.

Vadim, one of my key informants, had witnessed these developments from their early beginnings. He had been a boxer and part of a local gang. During the numerous conversations we had with each other, he always surprised me by his intimate knowledge of the city's criminal underworld. Yet his own involvement remained an unspoken taboo, and my inquiries into his criminal past were always answered with a smirk and ominous silence. At the age of 25, after several years of law school, he had turned his back to the street. When I met him, he had started work as a judicial specialist in the department of customs inspection. With convincing clarity and insight, Vadim shared with me the history of Vladivostok's criminal underground and helped me to understand its numerous factions and transformations during the 1990s. It all had begun with the rackets:

> At the beginning of the 1990s racketeering started; or *bykita* as it was called. Small groups [*gruppirovki*] appeared who were under nobody's control; they were working on their own. They might listen to an older authority figure and give him tribute [*dayut dan'*]. That means people in their early twenties paid respect to people in their late twenties. They engaged in racketeering in the markets. Most of their capital was coming out of the racket. That's how anybody started, knocking out the money from some firms.

During the early 1990s, the individual groups concentrated on racketeering as their main illegal income and strictly operated inside their territorial boundaries divided along Vladivostok's *rayony* (city districts). This time was characterized by recurring violent confrontations between opposing gangs staking their claims in the city. The individual *gruppirovki* (criminal groups) were organized in a pyramidal structure. At the top of the group was the *rukovoditel'* (leader), overseeing and planning the group's general operations. His *klichka* (criminal alias) was normally used as the group's designated name. The group was divided into several subgroups, the brigades (*brigady*), which operated independently from each other, often assigned to specific tasks or territories. A *brigadir* (brigade leader) was responsible for the day-to-day operations of his group, coordinating the brigade's operations. A *kommersant* (business manager) at the brigade leader's side was in charge of overseeing the group's economic activities. At the base of the hierarchical structure were the *soldaty* (soldiers) or *byki* (bulls). Each brigade included between 10 and 20 members, who were responsible for enforcement of contracts and intimidation of uncooperative targets.

With a rapidly progressing privatization of former state enterprises, more profitable opportunities emerged and a shift from territorial dominion to the control of economic spheres occurred. According to Vadim, economic specialization took priority over spatial control without completely overriding the territorial divisions:

> Before, during the time of the violent confrontations [*razborki*], there was a strong division into different territories. For example, Pervorechenskiy Rayon is mine and Sovetskiy Rayon is yours, and if you come into my territory you will be beaten up. That does not exist anymore. Now the fight is about economic spheres, about influence in the big business. Of course the racket still exists, and territory is still important, but it takes on a different meaning nowadays. Of course, you do not want the others to operate on your territory, after all the chicken still feeds on its own seeds, but influence in the economic sphere is now more important [...] The groups nowadays are cooperating, back then they stabbed each other. From 1995 to 1998 the large violent confrontations happened, now things have calmed down. The guys understood that it is merrier [*veselee*] to cooperate.

The rise and fall of the Larionov group is an early example of the evolution of these increasingly business-oriented new criminal groups. Sergey Larionov graduated at the end of the 1980s from the Far Eastern Polytechnic Institute and became a Komsomol leader in one of Vladivostok's main shipping companies, the refrigerator fleet Vostokrybkholodflot (VRKhF), heading the company's sport and technology club.[121] Using the club as an umbrella, Sergey Larionov and his brother Aleksandr started the criminal organization Sistema (System).[122] At the same time, the Larionovs established themselves as the business leaders of the cooperative Rumas, Vladivostok's first private company with the right to license new drivers, which had its physical address on the premises of VRKhF. They also owned a security agency.

---

[121] The position as a Komsomol leader during the late 1980s in the Soviet Union gave access to the new economic privileges implemented by Gorbachev in 1987. So-called technology clubs were one of the first entities that allowed for private entrepreneurial initiatives and currency exchange. Several of Russia's future oligarchs started their business career in these positions and clubs (Hoffmann 2002).

[122] Yevgeniy Itarov, 'V istoriy s 'chernym peredelom' ostalis' belye piatna', *Zolotoy Rog*, 28 January 2000.

The criminal operations that the brothers oversaw were small, involving only 5-10 people at a time, but the profits were astonishing. They specialized in the importation of cheap cars from Japan; they bought the cars for US$400-800 and re-sold them for US$2,000-2,500.[123] The security agency owned by the Larionov brothers presented sufficient cover for their activities and numerous armed security forces. Close cooperation with the police helped them to limit the success of competitors involved in the same business. The military-like internal structure of the brothers' criminal group included an intelligence branch headed by Vladimir Poluboyarinov, a former Pacific Fleet counterintelligence officer, systematically collecting information on the city's criminal authorities, major businessmen, and important members of the security organs.[124]

The privatization of VRKhF at the beginning of the 1990s and its subsequent transformation into the shareholding company Vostoktransflot (VTF) presented the Larionovs with yet another sphere of influence. Through threats and assassination attempts on competing shareholders, they acquired a large block of shares and staged a *chernyy peredel* (black takeover), placing Vladimir Mistiuk and Viktor Ostapenko at the top of the shipping company. Under this leadership most of the refrigerating fleet was sold (92 ships out of 135) in an asset stripping scheme from 1992-97.

But the Larionovs did not long harvest the fruits of their work. Rumours and anecdotal evidence point to an ongoing battle over the control of VTF, with fatal results.[125] Aleksandr Larionov was stabbed to death during a dispute in 1993. Retaliation killings initiated by his older brother Sergey further decimated the group's leadership. Sergey Larionov and nine members of his group were arrested in 1994. During the arrest, the police confiscated 60 grenades and more than 50 kilograms of explosives, including bomb detonators. The investigation lasted four years, the trial another one and one half years, and in the end, fifteen different criminal charges were levied against the gang, including 18 separate murder charges. Sergey Larionov did not live to the end of the trial. Still in pre-trial detention, he was killed by a fellow inmate on 24 February 1998.

Two months later, on 22 April 1998, Nadezhda Samikhova was shot dead. She was the *krestnaya mat'* (godmother) of Sergey Larionov at his Orthodox baptism in 1996, and had served as the lawyer for Vadim

---

[123] Margarita Usova, 'Zashchita Larionovykh', *Zolotoy Rog*, 21 March 2000.
[124] 'End to a bloody era: 9 gangsters sentenced', *Vladivostok News*, electronic document, http://vn.vladnews.ru/arch/2000/iss207/text/upd4.html, accessed 13 February 2005.
[125] VTsIOP, 'Khronika organizovannoy prestupnosti (obzor pressy 1997-2002)': 8; and D. Khabalov, 'Banda Larionovykh ostalas' bez brat'ev', *Vladivostok*, 27 February 1998.

Goldberg, a co-accused in the Larionov trial.[126] Samikhova's death was the first recorded contract hit on a lawyer in Vladivostok. These victims were only a part of a larger series of high-profile killings that ravaged Vladivostok's underworld during the mid to late 1990s. It is important to view those killings not just in relation to the Larionovs' fall, but within the overlapping interests of crime groups active during this period.

As mentioned above, the peculiar economic circumstances at the beginning of the 1990s nurtured a new generation of criminals in Vladivostok. The *sportsmeny* joined the underworld, dominated previously by the older and more established groups of professional criminals like the *sinie*. The *sportsmeny* soon established their own spheres of influence. In addition to territorial control, these groups occupied specific niches in Vladivostok's underground economy. At least six major groups could be identified in 1997 (see Figure 9, Appendix).[127] By 2004, the influence of several of the groups had dwindled. The most spectacular changes occurred within Baul's group, resulting in the rapid rise of Vinni-Pukh, whose story I describe later.

The six major groups, known by their leaders' nicknames, had distinct profiles, which I outline briefly below.

Petrak – In the early 1990s the group of Vladimir Petrakov, alias Petrak, attempted to control Vladivostok's mini-bus transportation system. This was a highly profitable business, and several criminal groups tried to exert their influence to establish a monopoly over it.[128] The group's main income stemmed from the import of food products into the city. Petrak retreated effectively from his illegal economic activities at the end of the 1990s. Vadim, the knowledgeable interview partner introduced above, offered the following insight, 'Petrak stepped back in 1999. He was controlling the Nadechinskii Rayon in Vladivostok and was recruiting street children for his gang. But then others scared him a little bit, and word reached him that he should lay low for a while and so he did. After all, your life is more valuable

---

[126] 'Two gunned down as mob hits continue', *Vladivostok News*, http://vn.vladnews.ru/arch/1998/iss166/text/news7.html, accessed 12 March 2005.

[127] I am excluding here crime groups organized along ethnic lines, partially for lack of available evidence and partially because of the subordinate role they played in Vladivostok's underworld; most of them concentrate on the racket of fellow nationals in the open-air markets. An exception is the Chechen Mafia, which controlled a majority of the smaller businesses in the city's Churkin district and constituted a military strong group with approximately 100 members. For a more detailed account of Vladivostok's underworld and criminal gangs see, Nomokonov 1998: 121-51, or Aleksandr Tomin, 'Sem'ya, ili Mafia po Primorskiy', *Zolotoy Rog*, 24 June 1997.

[128] See VTsIOP, 'Khronika organizovannoy', op. cit.: 15.

than your money'. During the early 2000s, Vladimir Petrakov moved into the banking sector.

Aleksey – In terms of sheer numbers, the group headed by Aleksey Gorbachev is one of Vladivostok's strongest with several hundred members at its disposal. It is composed mostly of *sportsmeny*, and controls several security companies. The group uses the blurred border between protection and racket to exert control over nightclubs and commercial structures. Vadim characterized the group as follows:

> The members of the group were called the Aleksevskiy. This is one of the biggest groups in town right now [2004]. I know that they control the protection agencies. Nowadays, these protection agencies have not only the function of guarding and protecting, but they also are involved in racketeering. A member of a protection agency can be used not only to protect, but also to collect money from entrepreneurs. This is how they legitimized the bandits by making them in to security guards. You can also call them "bandits in the law" [*bandity v zakone*]. Approximately 20 to 30 people work in every protection agency. As you see, they are able to control a large amount of these agencies and can bring in a lot of people to a *razborka*.

Mikho – Born in 1952, Mikhail Osipov had been arrested for his involvement in the underground economy first during Soviet times. His approximately 100-member-strong group was mainly involved in entrepreneurial activities and provided the protection roofs for several commercial structures (Nomokonov 1998: 134). Some evidence points to an affiliation between Mikho and Dzhem's *obshchak* and the possibility that Mikho himself acted as Dzhem's *polozhenets* (consul) in Vladivostok.[129]

Kosten – Under the leadership of Aleksandr Kostenko, this group of *sportsmeny* controlled a nightclub and several security agencies. Not significantly involved in larger enterprises, the group had lost a significant amount of influence as a vital criminal actor during the early 2000s.[130]

Trifon – Yuri Trifon is probably one of the oldest criminal authorities in Vladivostok and is considered to be part of the group of professional criminals with extensive prison backgrounds (*sinie*); he had served almost 20

---

[129] VTsIOP, 'Khronika organizovannoy', op. cit.: 7.

[130] VTsIOP, 'Organizovannaya prestupnost' na Dal'nem Vostoke (obzor pressy 2004)', http://www.crime.vl.ru/docs/obzor/obzor_2004, 18, accessed 11 March 2005.

years. Although Trifon never received his coronation as a *vor*, he has been ideological as well as personally close to *vory* of the Far Eastern Obshchak. By the late 1990s, Trifon had left the city, but his group still exerts its influence over the business and transportation hub of Vladivostok's Vtoraya Rechka Rayon.[131]

Baul – Sergey Baulo's group plays an important role in the evolution of organized crime networks in Vladivostok. It initially started as a group of *sportsmeny* and soon took control over a viable part of Vladivostok's car import business and facilitated several protection arrangements for larger commercial enterprises in the shipping and fishing industries.[132] Baulo's group and its later division was a seeding ground for a new generation of political figures who emerged from the shadow of organized crime. At the same time, Baulo's death in 1995 marked the beginning of a violent period of turf wars between competing groups that transformed Vladivostok's criminal underworld in lasting ways.

Protection rackets, the import of used cars, shipping companies, and fisheries were highly contested and ultimately limited resources of the underground economy. Violent clashes erupted between the criminal groups over these resources. A series of high-level gang related contract killings took place in Vladivostok after 1995, with a peak between 1997 and 1998. The deaths appear to begin with that of Sergey Baulo (Baul) who died during a mysterious diving accident off the coast of Vladivostok on 18 August 1995, in which his oxygen tank apparently contained the wrong mixture of gases.[133] Other deaths followed. On 3 October 1995, Andrey Zakharenko, Baul's close acquaintance and the general director of the fishing company AO Primorrybrom (AO PRP), was killed by a bomb in his private home.[134] Anatoliy Makarenko (Makar), one of the city's first *sportsmeny*, was killed on 27 September 1995. Koval was killed on 30 June 1997. Mikho was gunned down in front of the Hyundai Hotel in the centre of Vladivostok on 4 October 1997. Vrezh Babakckhian, an influential Armenian businessman and nightclub owner with alleged criminal connections, was shot in his car

---

[131] Ibid.: 19.

[132] VTsIOP, 'Khronika organizovannoy', op. cit.: 7.

[133] Baul's funeral was held at Gorki Theatre. It was a lavish affair, which attracted several thousands guests and a large array of black BMWs. The funeral led also to the temporary closure of Svetlanskaya Street. Baul's body was laid to rest in a conspicuous tomb, next to the monument of the perished submarine crew in Vladivostok's maritime graveyard (*morskoy kladbishche*). V.I. Shul'ga et al., 'Osnobvnye organizovannye prestupnye gruppirovki Primorye', VTsIOP, http://www.crime.vl.ru/docs/books/book2/g2/3.htm, accessed 13 November 2005.

[134] Oleg Logunov, 'Baula nashli s pererezannym shlangom', *AiF-Dal'inform*, March 1996.

outside the Royal Park Casino on 17 February 1998. Sergey Larionov was stabbed to death in prison on 25 February 1998. Karp was killed with a sniper rifle in front of his own restaurant Prestige on Svetlanskaya Street on 1 May 1998. Several of the deaths, including those of Koval and Mikho were supposedly the results of the same struggle for control over major enterprises in the shipping and fishery industry (Nomokonov and Shulga 1998: 679). These killings significantly reduced competitor groups, and at the beginning of 2001 only four major groups remained intact in the city; the groups of Kosten, Trifon, Aleksey, and the newly emerged group of Vinni-Pukh.

The winners took all, and the phase of legalization began. Sasha, a former policeman, explained this process to me:

> All the criminal groups moved into business and factually legalized themselves. In the 1990s we had several groups, like the Aleksey and Larionov groups. Aleksey moved into legal business. There was also Baulo, who died, and the groups of Karpov, Darkin, and Vinni-Pukh. They also legalized their business, or died, like Karp. By the way, I think Vinni-Pukh was here involved. Then there is still Trifon, who had spent 20 years in prison. He is now also a business man [...] There used to be a sports mafia [*sportivnaya mafia*], which was formed by athletes coming out of the former Komsomol. Back then, they were all proud of being racketeers and criminals, but now they all say, "What are you talking about, I am not a criminal!". Time has changed. They lived through the time of dividing up the capital and robbing the entities that were leftovers from Soviet times. Now they all say: "We are just regular businessmen". Why attract attention to yourself? They just keep silence, being no longer proud of their criminal past [...] Now, what everybody strives for is not to be in the spotlight but to stay in the shadow.

In the following section, I provide a focused analysis of this clandestine world where criminal and business networks entangle, to provide a better understanding of these recent transformations of the city's underground (see Figure 10, Appendix).

Baul's organization had been one of the first racketeering groups in Vladivostok. Sergey Baulo was born in 1958 in the town of Dal'negorsk in Primorsky Krai. Nearby, at the submarine base Rakushka, Baul received training as a navy diver. In addition to diving, he was a boxer and had earned the Soviet title of Master of Sports. Baul and his group of *sportsmeny*, divided into several brigades, expanded early from racketeering and used car schemes into larger business operations that were connected to shipping companies and fisheries. At the beginning of the 1990s, Baul took control of the newly founded shareholding fishing company Primorrybrom.[135] In addition, his organization provided the protection and security for the Vladivostok Base of the Trawler and Refrigerator Fleet, as well as for Roliz, a ship and equipment leasing company. Roliz was headed during that time by Sergey Darkin, a friend of Baul's from Rakushka and the recent governor of Primorsky Krai.[136] One of Baul's relatives, a former colonel of the Interior Ministry, headed the in-house security service of the company Roliz.[137] In addition to the involvement in the shipping and fishery industry, Baul controlled several shops and smaller enterprises (e.g. Tri-S, OOO Velikie Vorota, Darymoria), and the largest theatre in town.

Baul's death on 18 August 1995 led to the partition of his diversified business and protection empire. Two of his former *brigadiry* (brigade leaders), Karp and Vinni-Pukh, took control and divided the holdings. The actual terms of distribution were not public knowledge at the time of my research, but the process seems to have involved a high level of contestation between Karp and Vinni-Pukh.[138] The relation between the two successors remained strained until Karp died on 1 May 1998, after which Vinni-Pukh took control of parts of Baul's former criminal franchise. Sergey Darkin married Karp's widow, the actress Larisa Belobrova, and supposedly inherited part of the business Karp had signed under her name.[139]

Vinni-Pukh's biography is here of special interest, not only because his group became one of the most powerful criminal organizations in Vladivostok at the end of the 1990s, but also because his vita exemplifies the successful step of a former criminal into legal business and subsequently into the political realm. Vinni-Pukh was born Vladimir Nikolaev in 1973 in Vladivostok. A proficient boxer[140], Nikolaev quickly rose in the ranks of Baul's organization to the position of a brigade leader, specializing in rackets and car sales. A survivor of two attempts on his life, he did not restrain from violence himself. In 1999 he was sentenced to three and one half years for his involvement in death threats and assaults on the management of the Olimpiets sports complex, of which he served one year

---

[135] Ibid.

[136] Darkin himself had entered Vladivostok's business world in 1991 by taking control of the stocks in a company called Elena.

[137] Inna Luk'yanova, 'Dar'kin s morya', *Profil'*, 16 July 2001.

[138] Igor' Korol'kov, 'Gubernator i Vinni Pukh: Novyy rukovoditel' administratsiy Primorskogo kraya ne slishkom razborchiv v vybore druzey', *Moskovskie Novosti*, 3 July 2001.

[139] 'Kriminal'nye podmostki', *Arsen'evskie Vesti*, 14 June 2001.

[140] In 2000, Nikolaev became head of the Far Eastern Kick Boxing Association.

and three months.[141] Never regarded as a criminal authority himself, Vinni-Pukh nevertheless knew how to play to his strengths. Vadim explained that Vinni-Pukh 'was never an authority [*avtoritet*]. He was just a leader of one of the groups. Just a tough person, and he achieved everything not by being smart, but with his strength. For example, he acquired a large block of the shares from Turnif by taking them by force from the head of the company who was later found with two broken legs. He is just an ordinary bandit'.

After the deaths of Baul and Karp, Vinni-Pukh moved into the leadership vacuum of Baul's original organization and took control of its structure. It was estimated that Vinni-Pukh's group included up to 300 members, some with exceptionally good connections to the state security organs (i.e. OMON and SOBR).[142] This organization presented Vinni-Pukh with a substantial base for his operations, which concentrated increasingly on the control and takeover of profitable enterprises. He acquired a major block of shares from the fishery and research company OAO Turnif, and took control of the meat processing factory Vladivostokiy Myasokombinat and of the timber enterprise Terneyles.

Politics was his next step. In 2001, Vinni-Pukh, presenting himself under his legal name, acquired a seat in the regional parliament (Zakonodatel'noe sobranie Primorskogo Kraya) as a representative from Partisansk, a town 200 kilometres to the east of Vladivostok. In 2004, he was elected mayor of Vladivostok. On election night, Nikolaev's victory was celebrated boisterously by his cronies in a local Italian restaurant, expressing their *coup d'état* in explicit language: 'We fucked the whole city from behind (*postavali rakom ves' gorod*) [...] Be prepared, this is only the beginning'.[143]

Vladimir Nikolaev's rise from underworld authority to political power presents a case where the rhetoric of law and order played an important role. In his election campaign broadcast through local media, Nikolaev engaged in a visible fight against the urban disorder of Vladivostok. Criticizing the incumbent mayor on a wide range of topics, from road conditions to the dire housing situation, Nikolaev presented himself as a guarantor of order and stability in a time of chaos. After his inauguration as the city's mayor, he promptly started to encroach on several of Vladivostok's informal economic networks. On Nikolaev's orders, street prostitution was abolished almost

---

[141] Galina Sapozhnikova, 'Pochemu Vladivostok vybral krutogo mera?', *Komsomolskaia Pravda*, 16 August 2004.

[142] Dmitriy Markin, 'Medvezhniy ugol dlya Vinni-Pukha', *Moskovskiy Komsomolets*, 9 June 2004.

[143] Press release of the Mauro Dzhanvanni restaurant chain, 'Gotov'tes', eto tol'ko nachalo', 19 July 2004.

overnight, the scales of vegetable traders in the open-air markets were verified, the muddled open-air market in Lugovaya Square was dissolved, and the fraying ends of Sportivnaya Market were curtailed.

Plate 16. Graffiti on an apartment block in Vladivostok, 2004. The graffiti reads 'Vinni-Pukh – bandit' and overwrites the slogan for Nikolaev's mayoral campaign: 'Primorye – a decent life. N. Nikolaev'. The steel door was a campaign gift to the residents from Nikolaev.

Russian Organized Crime in Perspective

> 'It is nobody's fault that somebody turns out to be like this, and another to be like that'.
> – Sergey Darkin, Governor of Primorsky Krai (2001-2012)

Russian organized crime has captured public as well as academic imagination since the mid-1990s with increasing intensity. Scientific and popular discourses on organized crime rose sharply after the demise of the Soviet Union, evoking the grim picture of an inconsolable threat to the stability of the Soviet successor states and to the security of Western countries in general. To convey the image of a rising threat emanating from the former Soviet Union and spreading out to the rest of the world, authors often take recourse to animal metaphors to evoke the qualities of organized crime. Organized crime groups have been described as octopuses reaching out to every corner of society (Sterling 1991), or as creatures that tighten their tentacles to choke their host (Lintner 2003). Other authors have stressed the carrion-eating qualities of 'corrupt officials and criminals – somewhat in the manner of hyenas and vultures […] carving up the body of the old Soviet State' (Finckenauer 2004: 63). Such metaphors are widespread across languages. For example, an Italian TV series which gained popularity in Russia in the 1990s was called 'Piovra – potenza della mafia' (Octopus – Power of the Mafia) (Galeotti 1998: 416). In Russia too, these animalistic images have settled in public discourse. In particular, the image of sprut (octopus) is now widely used as a synonym for organized crime.

In a similar manner, albeit with less graphic language, various state organs have addressed Russian organized crime as an engulfing and far-reaching threat to other societies that rides the wave of globalization. A United States Department of Justice report on Russian organized crime stated that, 'in the decade since the collapse of the Soviet Union, the world has become the target of a new global crime threat from criminal organizations and criminal activities that have poured forth over the borders of Russia and other former Soviet republics such as Ukraine' (Finckenauer and Voronin 2001: 1). The West is seen as coming under the growing influence of organized crime groups that originated in the former Soviet Union, and makes these groups responsible for the rise in violent crimes in Western Europe (Handelman 1994: 95).

Beyond the metaphorical understandings of organized crime groups and mafia-like organizations, a substantial debate about the nature of organized crime exists in the sociological, criminological, and anthropological literatures.

In the 1960s, interest in organized crime was generally circumscribed by the field of sociology or appeared in the form of governmental hearings. In both cases, it was the organizational features that gained most attention. Following the institutional approach in economics, this paradigm primarily focused on the formal features of organized crime and depicted criminal structures as 'viable organizations', comparable to the organizational configuration of a large company (McIllwain 1999: 303).

In the 1970s and early 1980s, however, long-term anthropological studies conducted in Mediterranean societies, especially in Sicily, added another viable perspective to the study of organized crime (Blok 1969; Hess 1973; Schneider and Schneider 1976). These studies focused on a social network approach, stressed the cultural code underscoring the Italian mafia, and rejected the notion of a formal organization. These studies described the mafia as being composed of a loose association of personal and family networks infused by cultural codes of behaviour that regulated access to land and resources. Individuals, rather than the mafia as a whole, moved into the centre of inquiry. Social interaction became paramount to understanding the patron-client relationships that underlie the social structure of the Italian mafia. As mediators between rural areas and urban centres, Sicilian mafiosi were seen as power brokers with personal contacts as their main asset (Schneider and Schneider 1976: 11).

Beginning in the mid-1980s, the focus shifted again. This paradigm shift coincided with the first extensive anti-mafia trials in Italy, the so-called maxi-trials, where judicial proof of well- organized mafia groups finally surfaced (Paoli 2003: 15). The entrepreneurial features of organized crime structures moved to the foreground. Organized crime structures were seen as clandestine business empires that regulated and thrived on the flow of illicit goods (Arlacchi 1988). As an extension of the economic paradigm, the business of private protection, or the conversion of potential violence into a marketable commodity, became a defining feature of organized crime (Gambetta 1993). By way of illustration of the new paradigm, Diego Gambetta retold the statement of a Sicilian cattle breeder, 'When the butcher comes to me to buy an animal, he knows that I want to cheat him. But I know that he wants to cheat me. Thus we need, say, Peppe [i.e. a third party] to make us agree. And we both pay Peppe a percentage of the deal' (1993: 15).

This entrepreneurial approach to organized crime has settled in most of the recent official definitions of organized crime, now mostly seen as 'a continuing enterprise operating in a rational fashion and focused toward obtaining profits through illegal activities' (Paoli 2003: 55). Along similar lines, the 1994 definition of organized crime prepared by the United Nations Economic and Social Council stressed an economic entrepreneurial framework:

> Participants in criminal organizations are considered to be persons associated for the purpose of engaging in criminal activity on a more or less sustained basis. They usually engage in enterprise crime, namely the provision of illicit goods and services, or of licit goods that have been acquired through illicit means, such as theft or fraud. [...] The activities of organized crime groups require a significant degree of cooperation and organization to provide illicit goods and services. Like any business, the business of crime requires entrepreneurial skill, considerable specialization, and a capacity of coordination, and this in addition to using violence and corruption to facilitate the conduct of activities (cited in Paoli 2003: 64).

Other official institutions adopted a similar perspective. For instance, the United States Department of Labor defined organized crime as, 'activities carried out by groups with a formalized structure whose primary objective is to obtain money through illegal activities' (U.S. Department of Labor 2001: 48). Similarly, Interpol based its definition of a crime group with reference to corporate structure as 'any group having a corporate structure whose primary objective is to obtain money through illegal activities, often surviving on fear and corruption' (Bresler 1993: 319). These definitions illustrate that organized crime has been used synonymously for the conduct of illegal enterprise.

Russia is no exception in this respect. Studies of organized crime in Russia have been dominated mainly by the economic paradigm. Several authors have stressed the illicit economic orientation of organized crime groups in contemporary Russia by focusing on their specialization in racketeering and the takeover of private businesses. The Russian cases of racketeering groups and private protection agencies show the ambiguous character of protection in contemporary Russia. Protection is oriented towards an external threat, yet in the case of Russia's new class of 'protection entrepreneurs' the source of protection more often conflates with the origin of the threat. Charles Tilly has addressed this ambiguity, the blend of a potential threat with the protection from the very same in the context of European state formations, where governments artificially created external threats to justify the expansion of their own power and influence (Tilly 1985: 171). This perspective helps to understand the evolution of organized crime groups not only in the Russian Far East. Although violent networks of predation were a common stage in the accumulation of capital, the historic relation between extortion, protection, and state-making in Europe exemplified the fact that protection presented more than a mere commodity or economic base for criminal groups. Predation and protection services in an emerging market economy in the form of organized extortion was only one step in a more complex evolution of organized crime groups in contemporary Russia. The evolution of racketeering gangs in the Russian Far East showed a progression from street racket and territorial control to the monopolization of economic spheres and eventually to extended political control. The economic paradigm in organized crime research falls short of explaining these developments.

The sociological and anthropological traditions of mafia studies offer several models to explain the emergence of alternative powers that challenge those of the state. The political model sees the mafia as a corollary of state failure and the role of mafiosi as power brokers, while the economic model conceives the mafia as a business of private protection that concentrates on the conversion of potential violence into a marketable commodity. I do not see these differing approaches as mutually exclusive, but rather argue that they each address different aspects of organized crime groups. Recent research has challenged the economic paradigm of organized crime studies, arguing for a more pluralistic view of the mafia's functions. I follow here Letizia Paoli's approach, which considers the mafia organizations of southern Italy as 'multifunctional entities' with a plurality of goals and functions (Paoli 2003: 174).

It is important to briefly focus on a distinction between organized crime and mafia. According to Federico Varese, mafia is a subset of organized crime groups which are engaged in protection rackets. The mafia interferes with the state's monopoly on violence, and in this way 'the mafia differs from organized crime in its relation to the state. The mafia and the state are both agencies that deal in protection. While the mafia directly impinges on the state's jurisdiction, organized crime does not' (Varese 2001: 5). Such specification is necessary to adequately address the heterogeneity of Russia's criminal underworld. Economic definitions of organized crime cannot otherwise make distinctions that are locally relevant.

Organized Crime as a Multifunctional Entity

Russian crime groups are able to carry out a variety of functions. The economic functions of organized crime groups in the Russian Far East are apparent. Racketeering, protection services, and the illegal takeover of businesses present an important economic base for the involved groups. Nevertheless, the variety of their involvement in both licit and illicit activities redoubts the assertion that Russian organized crime is mostly a business of private protection. Extortion and racketeering can be only one step in a process of capital accumulation, leading to the acquisition of controlling shares in legitimate enterprises or to the creation of a monopoly in certain economic spheres.

Aside from the obvious economic occupation, criminal groups in the Russian Far East have a variety of social functions. As several biographies of gang leaders exemplify, their criminal career elevated them from the street racket to the world of big business. The rise to power presented those individuals with a ladder for social upward mobility. Although criminal leadership in Russia is a way for rapid social advancement, the rank-and-file members of criminal groups are mostly excluded from this social mobility when the leadership eventually legalizes their operations, a phenomenon Vadim Volkov addressed as 'vertical disintegration' (Volkov 2002b: 124).

In addition, criminal gangs have also an integrative function for their members and members' families. With gang membership comes prestige and street credit. Notions of masculinity find fertile grounds in youth gang culture (Koehler 2000). The longing for respect in a social environment is not only confined to the foot soldiers of organized crime gangs. High-ranking Italian 'men of honour' have repeatedly stated the enhancement of prestige that came with joining the fraternity. For instance, the Italian mafioso Marino Mannoia described his rise in personal prestige, 'Do you know why I entered Cosa Nostra? Because before in Palermo I was Mr. Nobody. Afterward, wherever I went, heads lowered. And this for me was worth any price' (cited in Paoli 2003: 152). The Russian examples are not exceptions. The unique prestige of the *vory* in Komsomolsk-na-Amure, mentioned by members of the families close to the organization, attests to a similar function. Extended friendship networks and fictive kinship relations (godparenthood) underscore the social dimension of that particular criminal organization.

Another often ignored function of organized crime groups is the exercise of political power. Recent developments of organized crime groups in Vladivostok, as sketched above, illustrate the increase of political influence of individuals with a criminal past and their extended control of economic and political spheres.

Criminal groups constitute local systems of power, and locality plays an important role in the formation of organized crime groups. The nucleus of many of Vladivostok's gangs and crime groups formed around neighbourhoods or city districts. Subsequently this territoriality was replaced by an extended influence in vital sectors of the local economy, especially in the shipping and fishery industries. In Vinni-Pukh's case, the control of local resources and the attempt to establish economic monopolies peaked in the political control of a whole city. This process shows that, although the economic function is a necessary step, it is only secondary to the ultimate goal, which is political dominion.

The goal of political control expressed by today's criminal groups is not unrelated to the behaviour of *vory* in Soviet prison camps. As mediators and ultimate judges, the *vory* of the Soviet penal system were first and foremost bearers of hegemonic power. Their strict reign inside the prisons constituted local systems of dominance, a parallel power structure with its own legal code and arbitration courts. This hegemony was not restricted to the prisons, as the example of Komsomolsk-na-Amure and its shadow ruler Dzhem illustrate. Dzhem and his fellow *vory* had established quite openly an informal system of power in the city, a zone of informal order, partially replacing the judicial authority of the state. For instance, to collect an overdue personal debt one of my informants did not approach an arbitration court, but rather sought the help of the brotherhood in retrieving his money. Although he had to pay a 50 per cent fee on the sum in question, he preferred this immediate and fast solution, rather than dealing with a dysfunctional judicial system, which he considered to offer little hope to successfully resolve his case. Criminal authorities function in this case as mediators and power brokers and carry out a function that was stressed by Jane and Peter Schneider in the context of their research in southern Italy, 'Broker capitalists control only marginal assets, their most significant resource being their networks of personal contacts' (Schneider and Schneider 1976: 11). Yet the case studies from the Russian Far East present a slightly different picture. The new broker capitalists of Vladivostok and Komsomolsk-na-Amure control much more than only marginal assets. The region and its resources offer organized crime groups valuable assets to back up their influence and power. Even more, the persistence and degree of influence of individual crime groups seems to be a result of a successful conversion of economic assets into political power. Dzhem stumbled over his role as the shadow power of Komsomolsk-na-Amure, but Vinni-Pukh ended as a victor who successfully integrated his economic power into the established political system.

These cases show clearly the multiplicity of functions that organized crime groups can fulfil, both in a historic framework and in the context of contemporary Russia. What constitutes the core of these informal social formations? Letizia Paoli defined the mafia as an organization based on status and fraternization contracts that carry out a plurality of functions (Paoli 2003: 19). This definition seems to apply to the brotherhood of the *vory v zakone* and post-Soviet criminal groups. The new criminal authorities present a slightly different case. Formal fraternization contracts, like the oath of adherence to the thieves' code, do not exist. Instead, notions of male friendship and territorial alliance seem to play an important role in the formation of racketeering and organized crime groups of the Russian Far East.

Organized Crime as an Interpenetrative Network

The case studies I have presented from the Russian Far East show the heterogeneity of organized crime in post-Soviet Russia. They also illustrate the shift from the traditional crime networks of the *vory v zakone* to a new class of violent entrepreneurs after the breakdown of the Soviet Union. In the case of Vladivostok's underworld, the influence of criminals with their roots in Soviet times was sidelined by the new gangs of *sportsmeny*. These groups subsequently entered the licit business world, and legalized their questionably-attained assets. By the early 2000s, former gang leaders had entered the political stage. Vadim Volkov argued that the change from *vory* to *sportsmeny* encompassed a switch from normative power based on moral authority to political power based on coercion (Volkov 2002b: 60). This shift can be seen as the influence of criminal groups evolved through the territorial control of a racket, to the control of businesses in various economic spheres, and subsequently into the realm of political power. The evolution of Vinni-Pukh's group in Vladivostok illustrates the transformation from street racket to political actors in an exemplary way.[144]

Yet the pattern of linear economic and political evolution of criminal groups is an oversimplification of the reality of organized crime in contemporary Russia. During the Soviet period, two branches of organized crime could be distinguished. One branch, the *vory v zakone,* exercised its control inside the penal system and established an extended network of professional criminals throughout the Soviet Union. The other branch, referred to as *mafia* during Soviet times, composed of an alliance of private entrepreneurs and party officials, concentrated on the flourishing black market. The first created a society of parallel power, the latter prospered in a symbiosis with the state. An even more complex picture emerged during the post-Soviet period, where parallel evolution led to different coexisting strands of organized crime. During these latest developments, clear borders between the different types of criminals (i.e. *vory, sinie,* or *sportsmeny*) tend to occasionally blend.

Dzhem's criminal network, the Far Eastern Obshchak, stands as an example for an organization of *vory* that continued to exist after the breakdown of the Soviet Union. Even though it adapted to the post-communist economic environment, Dzhem's group greatly relied on the thieves' traditional values. Dzhem's authority as a 'crown bearer' and his connections to a larger network of professional criminals helped him to establish a power dominion in the city of Komsomolsk-na-Amure. As he proclaimed, 'This is my region, and I want order here'.

In Vladivostok , organized crime was dominated by late Soviet and post-Soviet group types. Racketeering groups from the 1980s went into the legitimate business of protection services (Koval); *sportsmeny* controlled markets and used car businesses (Baul). Business-oriented groups concentrated on the economic potential of cars, fish, and ships (Larionov brothers). Finally, a former *sportsmen* and *brigadir* wrestled successfully for political control and rose to the ranks of city mayor (Vinni-Pukh).

At the local level, organized crime groups in contemporary Russia are alliances based on friendship, territory, and applied violence, which carry out a variety of social, economic, and political functions. As several comments and biographies of criminal authorities in Vladivostok suggest, friendship represents a powerful bond and formative feature at the heart of post-Soviet

---

[144] The transformation of the Uralmash crime group (*uralmashevskaya*) in Yekaterinburg into a political party (OPS Uralmash) at the end of the 1990s is another example (Volkov 2000: 740).

criminal groups. For instance, Baul spent his military service at the submarine base Rakushka where he met Sergey Darkin, who was born in the neighbouring village of Veseliy Yar. Darkin commented on their long friendship and Baul's career choice: 'I had been friends with Baul since I was a youngster. He served in our submarine military base. It is nobody's fault that somebody turns out to be like this and another to be like that'.[145] Relations of friendship, kinship, and patronage fuse in reciprocal protection arrangements. Baul facilitated the roof for Roliz, Sergey Darkin's enterprise, by placing one of his relatives as the head of the company's security service.[146] Marriage also enforces the social bonds. Sergey Darkin married Karp's widow, Larisa Belobrova, thus allegedly inheriting a major part of Karp's business empire. Patronage and long-term friendships constitute the core of licit and illicit networks alike and structure the foundations of political elite formations in the Russian Far East. The social intimacy within and between criminal groups, as well as between criminal groups and the state, becomes visible at the funerals. Photographs from Baul's memorial service, for example, show Governor Darkin as an intimate participant in the rite, close to the coffin.

The evolution of crime networks in Vladivostok illustrates the multiplicity of functions organized crime groups can fulfil, both in a historic perspective and in the context of contemporary Russia. Mafia-like organizations in Russia can be understood as multifunctional, violent, informal networks in a shifting alliance with the state that represent dynamic structures of state penetration and cooperation in the form of protection arrangements. Organized crime in Russia is exemplified as a changing alliance between parallel power structures and the state.

As Nancy Ries (2002) concluded, organized crime in Russia is best characterized as an interpenetrative network that is able to bridge between different social and economic spheres (e.g. criminals, the state, political power, or private business).[147] Janine Wedel follows a similar argument by recognizing the ability of these networks to 'operate in, mediate, and blur different spheres' (2003: 33) as part of their success and dominant prevalence in Eastern Europe after the breakdown of the Soviet Union. Joma Nazpary too made a similar argument for post-Soviet Kazakhstan, when he

---

[145] Luk'yanova, '*Dar'kin s Morya*', op. cit.

[146] Ibid.

[147] This is of course not a phenomenon restricted to contemporary Russia. Italy, for instance, had its unique alliances between mafia groupings and bearers of political power. The informal coalition between mafia structures and the Christian Democratic Party in Italy during the land reform in the 1950s, gave mafia groups access to new domains; e.g. administration of the land reform, the urban produce market, and new house construction (Schneider and Schneider 2005).

argued that, 'the emergence of the new private commerce underpinned the emergence and consolidation of the mafia. The mafia had a twofold relation with such commerce. First, they provided a *krysha* for protection fees. Second, they were among the shareholders and part of the new businesses' (Nazpary 2002: 44).

In the Soviet Union organized crime existed either in a secluded zone, such as the prison system, or was intrinsically intertwined with state structures, exemplified by the cooperation between party bureaucrats and black market entrepreneurs. The latter symbiotic coexistence ceased when the state collapsed. The *mafia* was part of the political structure during the Soviet Union. After the breakdown it developed into a counter-structure, challenging the state's very monopolies. During the 2000s, organized crime began to reintegrate itself into the state. A question remains: does the reintegration of criminal organizations into legitimate political structures lead to a legalization and consolidation of the former, or to a criminalization of the latter? Time will tell, but one point seems obvious: organized crime in Russia, both in its conceptual form as a discourse on a rapidly changing society and as an actual system of interlinkages between criminal networks, big business, and political elites, played and still plays a crucial role in the remaking of Russia's society after the breakdown of the Soviet Union.

Chapter 6
The Social Organization of the Shadow: A Conclusion

What are the defining and comparable features of shadow networks? In the preceding chapters, I have approached this question from different angles, illustrating and analyzing different shadow networks in the Russian Far East. In these analyses I was guided by questions such as what do shadow networks look like, of what elements are they composed, and what is their social reality? Describing the shadow raises methodological as well as theoretical problems. I have sketched several of them in the proceeding chapters, like emic and etic perspectives on organized crime and smuggling, theoretical debates on mafia structures, and various concepts of the border.

To distinguish the different shadow networks that I presented in the foregoing chapters and to explore at the same time the intrinsic relationship between commodity flows and economic actors, I employ an alternative understanding of informal economies, which rests on the specific relational ties that underlie these social and economic networks. Since the 1960s, social scientists studying complex societies have searched for ways to describe fluid social interactions, moving the topics of social networking and the quality of social relationship into the centre of attention (Mitchell 1969). In this work, I have I followed Jeffrey S. McIllwain's minimal definition that a 'social network refers to the set of actors and the ties among them' (McIllwain 1999: 305). In other words, a social network is a set of actors interconnected by social ties.

Social networking and social relationships are at the centre of shadow economics, and they link the 'shadow' with the official economy. As Alan Block explained, the social system of organized crime refers 'to the notion that organized crime is a phenomenon recognizable by reciprocal services performed by professional criminals, politicians, and clients. Organized crime is thus understood to lie in the relationships binding members of the underworld to upperworld institutions and individuals' (Block 1994: 10). Jeffrey McIllwain's social network approach to organized crime also emphasized the human relationships and networks which underlie organized criminal activities (McIllwain 1999: 319). Like McIllwain, I have attempted to describe several shadow economies in social terms – Chinese guilds at the beginning of the twentieth century in the Ussuri region, ethnic entrepreneurs in the open-air markets of Vladivostok, Russian *chelnoki* participating in the Russian-Chinese cross-border trade, the criminal brotherhood of the *vory v zakone* in the Soviet penal system, and the new organized crime structures in the Russian Far East. In the following pages I expand my analytical perspective on shadow networks to address the environment in which each of the described shadow economies was situated, the type of commodity flow involved, the character of relational ties underlying the networks, and the participating key actors (see Table 4).

Table 4: A diachronic summary of shadow networks and their underlying relational ties

Shadow Structures (shadow networks)	Environments (social, physical, economic)	Commodity Flow	Relational Tie Strategies (social networking)	Key Actors
Chinese guilds	Frontier	Furs and other bio-resources Trading monopoly	Guilds; hunting brigades	Village elders; landlord
Ethnic entrepreneurs	Transnational labour migration	Supply lines to home countries Labour migration	Kinship ties; co-ethnic networks	Close kin relatives (*rodstvenniki*); fellow countrymen (*zemlyaki*)
Informal cross-border trade	Borderland	Apparel and other imported goods Cross-border trade	Acquaintance and economic networks	Hired shuttle traders (*pomagaiki, naemniki*); independent (*svobodnye*) shuttle traders; small-scale businesses
Organized crime *vory*	Prison camps	Thievery, embezzlement, extortion, etc.	Brotherhood	Thieves (*vory*); consuls (*polozhentsy*)

| 'violent entrepreneurs' | Post-Soviet economic and political milieu | Rackets, shipping, seafood, cars, and control of other sectors of the economy | Patronage and male friendship networks | criminal authorities (*avtoritety*); brigade leaders (*brigadiry*); foot-soldiers (*byki, soldaty*) |

Chinese Guilds

The Chinese guilds in the backcountry and cities of Primorye at the end of the nineteenth and the beginning of the twentieth century operated in a frontier zone of the Russian Empire. Officially granted to Russia, the areas to the left bank of the Amur River and east of the Ussuri River were nevertheless partially under Chinese control, especially in the backcountry of the Sikhote-Alin Mountains where the influence of the Russian government was hardly felt. As mentioned in chapter 2, trading guilds in the late nineteenth century established a political and economic hegemony in the region. In a combination of kinship ties and economic bonds, the guilds created a trading monopoly on furs and other resources of the taiga, commodities which they extracted from the local indigenous population. Up to their final destination on the Chinese market, the goods moved through the multi-level edifice of a trading guild. At the lowest level was the *pao-tou* (hunting federation), subdivided into individual units that arranged the harvest of fur animals or the collection of ginseng. Statutes, a law codex, and regular court meetings underscored the guild's organizational structure. *Da-je* (elders) played a central judicial role as jurors in resolving conflicts with native groups or with members of the federation. The *zaitun* functioned as district supervisor and at the same time fulfilled the role of a broker between the resources of his district and the larger trading society with headquarters in several cities of the Russian Far East (Vladivostok, Ussuri, and Khabarovsk). In addition, the landlord controlled the inflow of Chinese commodities into his district – flour, clothes, gunpowder, tea, and alcohol – which were mainly used as trade objects with the indigenous population. The trading societies themselves were linked upwards to a trading house in mainland China, which represented the umbrella organization of the society.

Ethnic Entrepreneurs

Ethnic entrepreneurs in the open-air markets of Vladivostok are part of transnational labour migration into contemporary Russia. As the example in chapter 3 illustrates, backward links to family members constitute important supply chains from the home country. Imported commodities, like the spices in the example of the network of Uzbek traders, move through networks that are organized along kinship lines. Kinship ties are also central to the organization and conduct of everyday trading activities. The example of the Uzbek brothers who ran several sales booths in Vladivostok's open-air markets showed that clearly. Yet affiliations and networks extend beyond the nuclear family. Extended family members as well as *zemlyaki* (fellow countrymen) were included to different degrees in the transactions of ethnic traders. I have shown how these ethnic networks give traders several advantages in terms of their business conduct. In addition, in the case of the Uzbek traders, close kinship cooperation reduced the apparent risks of working illegally in the market.

Informal Cross-Border Traders

Shuttle traders and smugglers prosper on the opportunities of the Russian-Chinese borderland. The cross-border trade flows two ways and includes commodities imported from China (e.g. apparel, shoes, car parts) and contraband exported from Russia (e.g. ginseng, bear and tiger parts). Cross-border trade moves through networks of shuttle traders and smugglers incorporating individual *chelnoki* and wholesale dealers in different trade circuits. The proposed social perspective on various shadow networks that are involved in cross-border trade reveals significant differences amongst them. The characteristics of the underlying networks depend here on the specific form of cross-border trade: hired shuttle traders operate in groups assembled by wholesale dealers; independent shuttle traders rely on close family or friendship networks in their business; and smugglers are enmeshed in complex trade circuits with poachers and wholesalers. Different forms of cross-border trade can be distinguished according to the underlying social ties. In the first case, the *naemnye chelnoki* (hired shuttle traders), are temporarily assembled groups, bound together by the sole purpose of their journey, which is the transportation of goods for a wholesale dealer. *Svobodnye chelnoki* (independent shuttle traders) on the other hand, have to rely on more complex social networks for their informal import activities, incorporating family members and acquaintances in their individual businesses and establishing long-term social and economic ties to wholesale traders on both sides of the border. A special characteristic of the networks of shuttle traders is the inherent mobility for individual cross-border traders, which allows for vertical economic advances.

As shown in the preceding chapters, the specific micro-economical environment of cross-border traders in the Russian-Chinese borderland is characterized by the lack of trust in state institutions. Similar to other cases of informal cross-border networks which lack a formal regulatory regime, the informal transactions are strongly based on trust (Yükseker 2004). The repeated transactions with Chinese business partners create trust in an environment with no formal ways to enforce contracts. Mutual trust of economic actors is the social glue that connects and reassures those informal economic relations (Portes and Haller 2005: 408). Informal social sanctions enforce the economic contracts and in cases when proper social ties are ignored, trade becomes immoral and usually spells the end of a cross-border business venture (Scheele 2012: 123).

Organized Crime

The social structures of organized crime networks present an even more complex picture. Seen from a social network approach, different branches of organized crime can be distinguished through time as well as in the present. As is the case with cross-border traders, a social network approach to organized crime structures reveals fine but nevertheless significant differences between various forms of organized crime. As indicated in chapter 5, the society of the *vory v zakone* represents an organization based on status and formal fraternization contracts, a brotherhood with distinguishing insignias (i.e. tattoos), and a unifying moral codex. Internal order and hegemonic control over the prison zone's internal economy was an established goal that partially led to the rise of a parallel power inside the Soviet penal system. The brotherhoods were to a certain degree able to transfer their hegemonic influence over the underworld of the prison camps into post-Soviet times, as illustrated with the example of Dzhem, the shadow ruler of Komsomolsk-na-Amure. Particular features of *vory* social organization, like the *obshchak* (communal fund), were upheld.

The new 'violent entrepreneurs' who stepped onto the stage during the transition period after the breakdown of the Soviet Union present yet another picture from a social network perspective. Male friendships and territorial alliances, mostly based on neighbourhood districts, characterize the social networks of the new organized crime groups. While extortion and racketeering stood at the beginning of many of the groups' economic activities, key resources of the Russian Far East, especially fish, and the monopolization of certain imports (e.g. used cars from Japan) played an increasingly larger role. The territorial principle was replaced by hegemonic influence over certain economic spheres. As of the early 2000s, organized crime groups in Vladivostok controlled the flow of goods in whole sectors of the economy. To control and partially monopolize these commodities, the various crime groups are based on the principle of individually operating cells, the *brigady*, which conduct the individual businesses of an organization. The individual cells are kept together by a hierarchical organization with an *avtoritet* (criminal authority) at its top. Not vested with the moral authority of a *vor*, these criminal authorities nevertheless exert control over the individual brigades, which are led by the *brigadiry* (brigade leaders) and incorporate the bulk of the foot soldiers. In addition, political patronage plays an increasing role.

Commodities do not flow through vacuums, neither do social networks exist independent of locality. As already outlined in the preceding chapter, organized crime has its own geography, from the spatial organization of neighbourhood gangs to the transnational smuggling routes of Vladivostok's crime syndicates. The same can be said of the other illustrated shadow networks. The specific geography of Primorsky Krai has influenced the genesis and specific nature of the described economic shadow networks. The location of the region in a multinational borderland and its proximity to the ocean play a central role. Well before the end of the Soviet period, Gregory Grossman pointed out the 'geographic pattern' of the USSR's second economy (Grossman 1977: 34). Port cities like Leningrad (St. Petersburg) and Odessa were centres of illegal imports, while the borderlands of the Caucasus region and Central Asia played an equally important role in black market activities that were focused on foreign commodities.

In a general sense, shadow activities correlate with border porosity (Ayres 1996: 16). Primorsky Krai is at the same time a politically peripheral and economically significant region, thus presenting an ideal environment for the creation of shadow economies. In the historic case of Chinese traders, the lack of state control in the geographically peripheral Far Eastern frontier created the background for the parallel non-state networks of trading guilds. The porous borders between Russia and China and the Central Asian successor states created transnational informal networks of commodity flows in various forms, like labour migration of ethnic entrepreneurs, shuttle trade, and the smuggling of bio-resources. Organized crime networks in the Russian Far East heavily specialize in border commodities, goods that become profitable trading commodities after they cross international borders and value regimes (e.g. fish caught in Russian waters and exported to Japan, or the used cars imported from Japan into the ports of Primorsky Krai). Although diverse in character, these shadow networks have one feature in common: they all thrive on the porosity of the border or profit from the political vacuum of the frontier. They represent emergent social and economic structures in the border zone of a porous state.

A range of actors uses the border as a resource, from small-scale traders to well-connected individuals inside of state institutions. In the Russian-Chinese borderland informality plays a central role, not only as a means to increase profit for individual traders, but also as a strategy that allows for an easier, more predictable, and less restricted way of organizing commodity flows. In the absence of trust in state institutions, specifically the customs office, more practical and consequently more reliable solutions are developed. This is especially true for the small-scale traders of Primorsky Krai who seek informal solutions for commodity flows outside of state control by relying on their own cross-border networks. Investigating the reality of smuggling networks not only sheds light on the specific social and economic mechanisms of the trade, but also exposes a particular relationship of individuals to the state and its institutions. The crafty anti-programme of smuggling operations, which subverts the border regime on a regular basis, demonstrates not only the decidedly creative and practical solutions of cross-border traders and exposes as well the rather ambiguous relationship of borderlanders to their own state.

The relation of informal networks to the state is essential to understand this phenomenon. As Henner Hess had already observed in the early 1970s in southern Italy, 'The chronic weakness of the state resulted in the emergence of self-help institutions and the exclusive power positions of informal groups made it impossible for the state to win the loyalty of the public, while its resultant weakness gain strengthened the family, the clientele and *mafioso* positions' (Hess 1973: 25). Yet, by describing a favourable environment for informal groupings, the 'weak state theory' only partially explains the emergence of shadow networks. As mentioned above, the geography in which shadow networks flourish plays also a decisive role.

In addition, not only is the absence of state power or inaction of state institutions responsible for the creation of shadow networks. Rather actions undertaken by the state have a definitive effect on those networks too. Caroline Humphrey has hinted at the possibility that the creation of cooperatives in the late Soviet period had a formative influence on the emergence of systematic racketeering. As economic structures, the new cooperatives were easy targets for criminal predation (Humphrey 1999: 223). Analogous arguments can be made in respect to the other depicted shadow networks. The Treaty of Aigun, for instance, created a legal pretext for self-governed Chinese settlements on Russian soil. Likewise, Russian import laws created a legal loophole which could be exploited by shuttle traders. Laws on private security services allowed for the armament of informal power groups and partially legalized racketeering. Instead of following along the lines of a weak state theory, concentrating on the institutional framework in which parallel structures thrive, I rather focus here on the relationship of different shadow networks to the state (see Table 5).

Table 5: Shadow networks and their relationship to the state

Shadow Structures (shadow networks)	Relationship to the State
Chinese guilds	Parallel power
Ethnic entrepreneurs	Evasion and invisibility
Shuttle traders and smugglers	Evasion and subversion of territorial hegemony and tax monopoly
Organized crime Vory Soviet *mafia* 'Violent entrepreneurs'	Parallel power Symbiosis State penetration and entanglement

Chinese trading guilds were characterized by their complete separation from the state. In the backcountry of the Sikhote-Alin Mountains they established a political and economic system that was more or less independent from any influence of the Russian state. Only their forced and final dissolution after the Russian Revolution led to the disappearance of these shadow networks. Ethnic entrepreneurs on the other hand relate to the state in a more immediate way. Although their kin-based networks allow a certain degree of independence, they nevertheless have to confront state institutions, in the form of immigration police for instance, on an almost daily basis. Tax evasion among ethnic entrepreneurs is another widespread characteristic that defines the relation to the state. Thus the relational quality of ethnic entrepreneurs in the open-air markets to the state is avoidance and invisibility. Shuttle traders undermine, in a comparable manner, the state's monopoly on taxation. In addition, their systematic cross-border trade uses the porosity of the state border for private gain, thus penetrating the state's territorial hegemony. As shown in the preceding chapter, organized crime structures in Russia can be distinguished according to their varied relationships to the state. The *vory v zakone* existed as a parallel, but largely independent, structure to the state that established a dominion in the prison system. On the other hand, the *mafia* during Soviet times existed in close symbiosis with the state and subverted state mechanisms for personal gain. Organized crime groups after the breakdown of the Soviet Union developed first as a counter-structure that challenged the state's monopolies on taxation and violence. Yet in recent times, especially obvious in the Vladivostok example, these organizations reintegrate themselves into the state through a penetration of formal economic and political structures.

In the form of parallel structures, shadow networks imitate formal state institutions, thus undermining and subverting the hegemony of the state. Alternative forms of taxation, protection, and banking partially replaced the state sanctioned institutions. The extent of autonomy and hegemony that a shadow network can encompass hinges on its degree of independence from the state. The almost complete separation of shadow networks from the state, the phenomenon I addressed here as parallel power, led to the creation of stable institutions. In both cases, Chinese trading guilds at the turn of the last century and the *vory v zakone* inside the Soviet penal system, led to the creation of shadow institutions that replaced and also imitated state institutions. The Chinese guilds as well as the thieves' world were organizations based on a moral and judicial codex – in both written and oral form – that prescribed collective behaviour and regulated punishment for trespassing the fraternities' laws. A whole judicial system of courts, judges, and jurors enacted and enforced those codices. The resemblance between the two parallel networks extends to the social layering of their internal structure. Both the Chinese guilds as well as the brotherhood of the *vory* were based on a pyramidal hierarchical social structure.

The specific antagonistic relationship to the state that surfaced in interviews with small-scale traders in the Russian-Chinese borderland underscores the notion of subversive economic practices that exist in an economic space outside of state control. Small-scale smuggling can thus be seen as a set of practices that make use of informal channels to undermine the border monopoly of the state. These practices do not exist outside of the state per se, but rather develop in constant exchange with it as responses to centralization efforts, changing border regimes, the material dimensions of border crossings, specific techniques of border control, and the actual practices of customs agents. Furthermore, the informal does not clearly demarcate a sphere outside of the state, as zones of informality equally exist inside the state in the forms of bribes, corruption in the customs office, and the complicity of border agents in smuggling operations.

The described informal strategies to sidestep and outwit the border programme posses a paradoxical quality that has been similarly attested for the system of informal governance that significantly expanded under Vladimir Putin's strengthening of the power vertical since the early 2000s.

Alena Ledeneva has argued in this respect that the system of network-based governance in Russia is trapped in a systemic paradox: the informal strategies that arose to cope with society's problems are at the same time undermining its very foundation (Ledeneva 2013). This observation holds equally true for the described informal cross-border solutions, which are based on economically rational decisions, but at the same time subvert state institutions. Local elites and state representatives in the Russian Far East have similarly undermined formal economic structures and secured profitable deals in the shadows. In phases of regional suspension, informal strategies play a paramount role in economic survival, both for elites and non-state actors alike.

Small-scale traders in the Russian-Chinese borderland operate in a porous zone where legal and illegal practices coexist, where formal and informal domains are not clearly demarcated, and where illegality frequently shifts between formal and informal organizations (Heyman and Smart 1999: 18). These fuzzy boundaries become even more blurred when changing the focus from petty smuggling to large-scale smuggling. I have argued that commercial smuggling and petty smuggling not only differ in levels of social organization, as Bruce Wiegand (1993) has suggested, but also contrast in their elementary relation to the state itself. Small-scale cross-border traders circumvent and avoid state laws; they are literally engaged in trading against the state. But, the higher one moves up the informal economic chain, or the higher the volume of smuggled goods becomes, the more likely one finds the large-scale involvement of state actors. Again, this reflects the 'ambiguity of informal practices' (Ledeneva 2013: 11) which play both supportive and subversive roles vis-a-vis the state's authority. With the implicit involvement of state actors in smuggling, these economic practices can turn into what Carolyn Nordstrom has termed 'shadow networks', where the boundaries of legality and illegality, state and non-state power are inverted, and which 'are not marginal to the world's economies and politics, but central' (Nordstrom 2000: 37).

Despite the differences, the illustrated networks have one commonality. They each represent social strategies for ordering economic activities in the shadow of formal institutions. These social strategies are specific to the physical borderland of the Russian Far East and to the economic and political transitory stage of the post-Soviet era. Social relationships are at the centre of those networks. I have followed Carolyn Nordstrom's observation that one of the core features of shadow networks is that they represent societal systems governed by social principles that cut across national, linguistic, and ethnic collectives (Nordstrom 2004: 107-09). Small social units constitute the centres of these networks. Regardless of the seemingly chaotic outward appearance of some of the described networks, like open-air markets or shuttle trading, shadow networks are well-organized social and economic structures. Ethnic traders organize their business around the members of an extended family, and several of the described networks are based on a brigade or cell structure. As shown above, different social ties – fraternal contracts and kinship relationships, as well as simple temporary economic bonds – underscore the basic social units.

I see the described shadow structures as dynamic social strategies that create their own regimes of order and stability in a social, political, and economic vacuum. Order and stability are achieved by both informal and formal means. The inherent trust and simplicity of kinship relations among ethnic traders represent immediate forms of reliability, thus creating zones of order in the market. Formal ways of creating and maintaining stability are encountered among those networks which I characterized as parallel power structures in relationship to the state (i.e. Chinese trading guilds and the *vory*). These networks relied on a law codex or behavioural code to maintain order among their members and to create stability in their respective zones of influence.

This example not only illustrates the interplay between different shadow networks, but also exemplifies the intrinsic dynamics of these structures. In the cases of open-air markets, shuttle trade, and organized crime, a general tendency of consolidation and legalization of informal structures can be observed. Open-air markets in Vladivostok slowly but inevitably turn into shopping centres, shuttle trade is channelled into formal cross-border trading in the form of joint-ventures or the creation of free-trading zones, and organized crime structures step into legal business and political co-determination. Underlying these processes is the change from an informal economic sphere to the formal economy.

The political and economic vacuum after the breakdown of the Soviet Union led to the emergence of alternative networks. New forms of networking emerged as a response to the perceived chaos of the post-Soviet transition period. The core units of the shadow networks, consisting of strong social ties, made them resistant and adaptive at the same time. Small social units, like close-kin networks, *chelnoki* groups, or criminal brigades undergirded those structures. In times of social and economic change, such small-scale units represent social reserves for creating order in the absence of a strong regulating state power.

Moreover, shadow networks in the Russian Far East thrive on the specific characteristics of a borderland and are able to react with flexible strategies to newly emerging flows of commodities and people. Functionally adjusted to a porous economic environment, the resilience of the described networks stems from their ability to penetrate and to some extent replace the functions of state institutions. Russia's shadow networks are adaptive social and economic strategies that ascend in environments of state erosion and border porosity and thus represent successful social blueprints in a situation of rapid social and economic change.

Appendix

Figures

Figure 2. Balyaeva Market

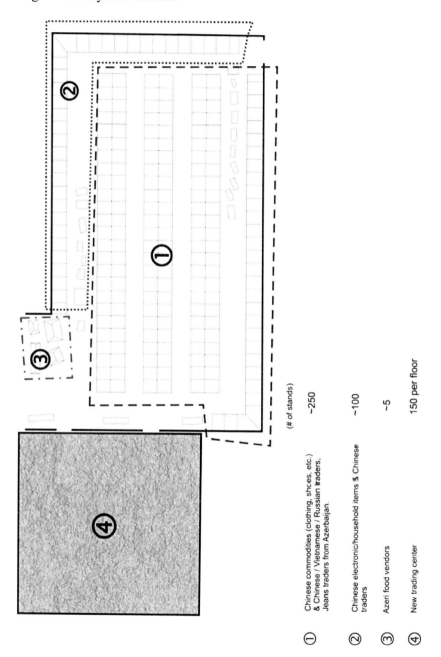

Figure 3. Sportivnaya Market

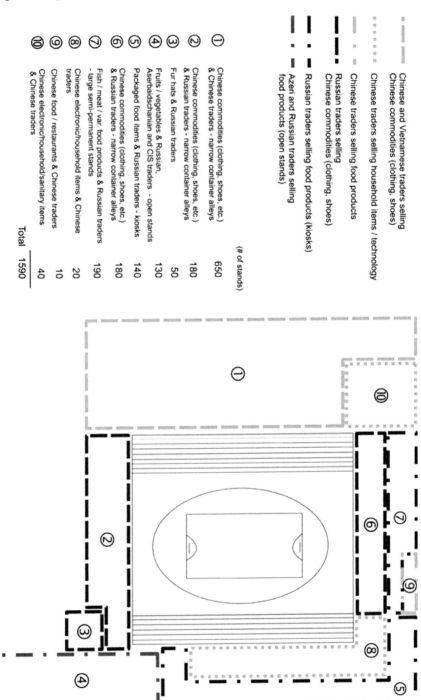

Figure 4. Vtoraya Rechka Market

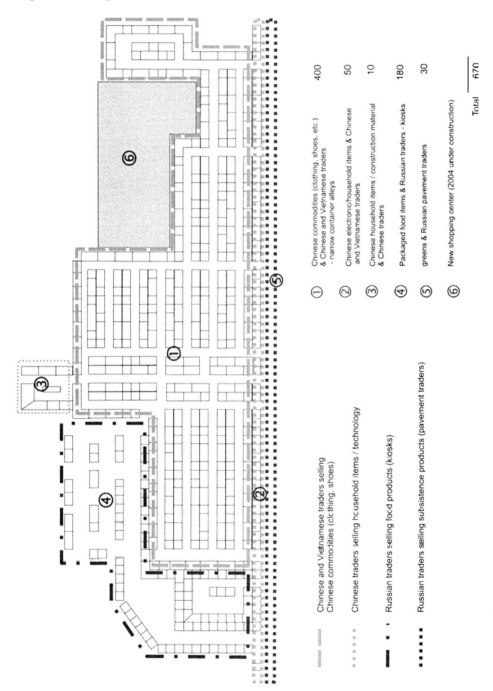

Figure 5. Spatial transformation of the Lugovaya Market (before 2003; 2003; August 2004; November 2004)

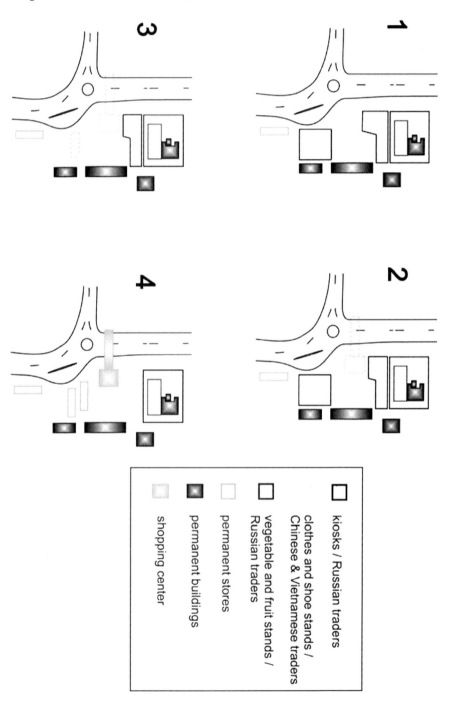

APPENDIX 195

Figure 9. Evolution of criminal organizations in Vladivostok

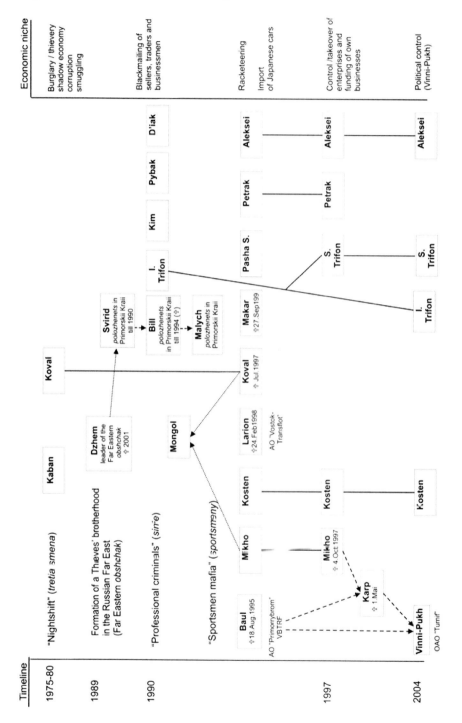

Figure 10. Baul's shadow franchise (1990-2003)

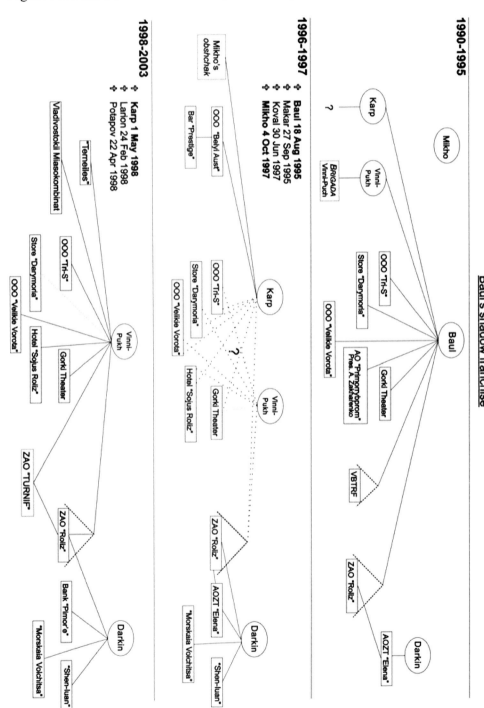

Table

Table 2. Main bio resource exports of the Russian Far East

Latin name	Russian name	English name	Part used	Region of origin	Region of destination
Panthera tigris altaica	*Amurskiy tigr*	Amur tiger	All parts: meat, skin, bones, bile, etc.	Primorsky Krai	China, Asian-Pacific Countries
Panthera pardus orientalis	*Dal'nevostochnyy leopard*	Far eastern leopard	All parts: meat, skin, bones, bile, etc.	Primorsky Krai	China, Asian-Pacific Countries
Ursus arctos horribilis	*Buryy medved'*	Brown bear	Gall, paws, skins	Russian Far East, Siberia	China, South Korea, North Korea
Ursus tibetanus	*Gimalaiskiy medved'*	Asiatic black bear	Gall, paws, skins	Russian Far East	China, South Korea, North Korea
Cervus elaphus xanthopygus/ sibiricus	*Izybr/ maral*	Manchurian wapiti/ Siberian red deer	Panty (unossified antler/ velvet antler), tail, penis	Russian Far East	China, South Korea
Moschus moschiferus	*Kabarga*	Siberian musk deer	Musk gland		China, South Korea, North Korea

Rana semiplicata	*Dal'nevosto chnaya lyagushka*	Asiatic grass frog	Meat, glands, eggs	Primorsky Krai	China
Pelodiscus sinensis	*Dal'nevosto chnaya cherpakha*	Chinese softshell turtle	Live animal	Primorsky Krai	China
Falco rusticolus	*Krechet*	Gyrfalcon	Live animal	Chukotka	Middle East
Apostichopus japonicus	*Dal'nevosto chnyy trepang*	Sea cucumber	Dried - salted/ pickled in honey	Primorsky Krai	China
Panax ginseng	*Zhen'shen'*	Ginseng	Whole roots	Primorsky Krai	China, Japan
Tricholoma matsutake	*Matsutake*	Matsutake mushroom	Dried mushrooms	Primorsky Krai	China, Japan
Pinus (sibirica/ koraiensis)	*Orechi sosny sibirskoy/ koreyskoy*	Pine nuts (Siberian/ Korean)	Processed nuts, oil	Primorsky Krai	China
Osmunda spectabilis	*Paparotnik osmund*	Osmunda (royal fern)	Young sprouts	Primorsky Krai	China

Bibliography

Abraham, I., and W. van Schendel. 2005. Introduction: The Making of Illicitness. In W. van Schendel, and I. Abraham (eds.), *Illicit Flows and Criminal Things: States, Borders, and the Other Side of Globalization*, pp. 1-37. Bloomington: Indiana University Press.

Akhmedov, M. A. 2000. Migratsiya Azerbaidzhantsev na Dal'niy Vostok Rossii i problemy ikh adaptatsii. In A. S. Vashchuk, and E. N. Chernolutskaya (eds.), *Adaptatsiya etnicheskikh migrantov v Primor'e v XX v.*, pp. 189-202. Vladivostok: DVO RAN.

Aldrich, H. E. 1990. Ethnicity and Entrepreneurship. *Annual Review of Sociology* 16: 111-35.

Alekseev, M. A. 1999a. Chinese Migration in Primorskii Krai: An Assessment of Its Scale, Socioeconomic Impact and Opportunities for Corruption. *Working Paper*, November.

———. 1999b. *The 'Yellow Peril' Revisited: The Impact of Chinese Migration in Primorskii Krai*. PONARS (Program on New Approaches to Russian Security Policy Memo Series) Memo No. 94.

———. 2000. *Are Chinese Migrants at Risk in Primorskii Krai? Monitoring Interethnic Relations with Opinion and Event Data*. Paper presented at the 5th Annual Meeting of the Association for the Study of Nationalities, Colombia University, New York (13 April).

———. 2001. *The Chinese are Coming: Public Opinion and Threat Perception in the Russian Far East*. PONARS (Program on New Approaches to Russian Security Policy Memo Series) Memo No. 184.

Alvarez, R. R., and G. A. Collier. 1994. The Long Haul in Mexican Trucking: Traversing the Borderlands of the North and the South. *American Ethnologist* 21 (3): 606-627.

Anderson, A. 1995. The Red Mafia: A Legacy of Communism. In E. P. Lazear (ed.), *Economic Transition in Eastern Europe and Russia: Realities of Reform*, pp. 340-367. Stanford: The Hoover Institution Press.

Anderson, M. 1996. *Frontiers: Territory and State Formation in the Modern World*. Oxford: Polity.

Andree, R. 1867. *Das Amurgebiet und seine Bedeutung: Reisen in Theilen der Mongolei, den angrenzenden Gegenden Ostsibiriens*, nach neuesten Berichten, vornehmlich nach Aufzeichnungen von A. Michie, G. Radde, R. Maak u.a. Leipzig: O. Spamer.

Appadurai, A. 1986. Introduction: Commodities and the Politics of Value. In A. Appadurai (ed.), *The Social Life of Things: Commodities in*

Cultural Perspective, pp. 3-63. Cambridge: Cambridge University Press.

———. 1996. *Modernity at Large: Cultural Dimensions of Globalization.* Minneapolis: University of Minnesota Press.

Applebaum, A. 2003. *GULAG: A History.* New York: Double Day.

Arlacchi, P. 1988. *Mafia Business: The Mafia Ethic and the Spirit of Capitalism.* Oxford: Oxford University Press.

———. 1995. *Mafia von Innen: Das Leben des Don Antonio Calderone.* Frankfurt am Main: Fischer Taschenbuch.

Arsenyev, V. K. 1914. *Kitaytsy v Ussuriyskom Krae.* Khabarovsk: Tipografiya Kantseliarii Priamurskogo General'-Gubernatora.

———. 1921. *Po Ussuriskomy kraiyu: Puteshestvie v gornuyu oblast' Sikhote-Alin.* Vladivostok: Knizhnoe Delo.

———. 1923. *Dersu Uzala: Iz vospominanii o puteshestvii po Ussuriskomu Kraiyu i 1907 g.* Vladivostok: Izdatelstvo Svobodnaia Rossiia.

———. 1924. *In der Wildnis Ostsibiriens: Forschungsreisen im Ussurigebiet.* Berlin: August Scherl.

———. 1926. *Russen und Chinesen in Ostsibirien.* Berlin: August Scherl.

Ayres, E. 1996. Expanding Shadow Economy. *World Watch* 9 (4): 11-23.

Bannikov, K. L. 2002. *Antropologiya ekstremal'nykh grupp: Dominantnye otnosheniya sredi voennosluzhashchikh srochnoy sluzhby Rossiiskoy Armi.* Moscow: Nauka.

Barannik, M. I. 2002. *Kriminologicheskie i pravovye problemy borby s nezakonnoy migratsiey.* Vladivostok: VTsIOP.

Barineva, N. 1997. Trudovaya migratsiya na Dal'nem Vostoke. *Ekonomist* 3: 13-20.

Bassin, M. 1999. *Imperial Visions: Nationalist Imagination and Geographic Expansion in the Russian Far East, 1840-1865.* Cambridge: Cambridge University Press.

Bauman, Z. 1997. *Postmodernity and its Discontents.* New York: New York University Press.

Beisinger, M. R., and C. Young (eds.). 2002. *Beyond State Crisis? Postcolonial Africa and Post-Soviet Eurasia in Perspective.* Washington: Woodrow Wilson Center Press.

Benjamin, W. 1979. *One Way Street and Other Writings.* (trans. Edmund Japhcott and Kingsley Shorter). London: NBL/ Verso.

———. 1996. *Selected Writings, Volume 1: 1913-1926.* (eds. Marcus Bullock and Michael W. Jennings). Cambridge: Harvard University Press.

Berglund, E. 2000. From Iron Curtain to Timber-Belt: Territory and Materiality at the Finnish –Russian Border. *Ethnologia Europaea* 30 (2): 23-34.

Blalock, H. M. 1967. *Toward a Theory of Minority Group Relations*. New York: John Wiley.
Bliakher, L. E., and L. A. Vasileva. 2010. The Russian Far East in a State of Suspension: Between the "Global Economy" and "State Tutelage". *Russian Politics and Law* 48 (1): 80-95.
Block, A. A. 1994. *East Side – West Side: Organizing Crime in New York City, 1930-1950*. New Brunswick: Transaction.
Blok, A. 1969. Peasants, Patrons, and Brokers in Western Sicily. *Anthropological Quarterly* 42: 155-170.
——. 1974. *The Mafia of a Sicilian Village, 1860-1960*. Oxford: Basil Blackwell.
Bogaevskaya, A. N. 2002. *Kitayskaya Migratsiya na Dal'nii Vostok Rossii*. Vladivostok: Vladivostokskiy Tsentr Issledovaniya Organizovannoy Prestupnosti. http://www.crime.vl.ru/docs/books/book_4.htm, accessed 19 May 2006.
Brednikova, O., and O. Pachenkov. 2002. Etnichnost', 'etnicheskie ekonomiki' i sotsial'nye seti migrantov. *Ekonomicheskaya Sotsiologiya* 3 (2): 74-81
Bresler, F. 1993. *Interpol: Der Kampf gegen das internationale Verbrechen*. München: Goldmann Verlag.
Brooks, J. 1992. Official Xenophobia and Popular Cosmopolitanism in Early Soviet Russia. *The American Historical Review* 97 (5): 1431-1448.
Bruns, B., and J. Miggelbrink. 2011. Introduction. In B. Bruns, and J. Miggelbrink (eds.), *Subverting Borders: Doing Research on Smuggling and Small-Scale Trade*, pp. 11-20. Wiesbaden: VS Verlag.
Bruns, B., J. Miggelbrink, and K. Mueller. 2011. Smuggling and Small-Scale Trade as Part of Informal Economic Practices: Empirical Findings from the Eastern External EU Border. *International Journal of Sociology and Social Policy* 31 (11/12): 664-680.
Caldwell, M. 2002. The Taste of Nationalism: Food Politics in Post-Socialist Moscow. *Ethnos* 67 (3): 295-319.
Caygill, H. 1998. *Walter Benjamin: The Colour of Experience*. London: Routledge.
Chalidze, V. 1977. *Criminal Russia: Essays on Crime in the Soviet Union*. New York: Random House.
Chin, K. 1990. *Chinese Subculture and Criminality*. New York: Greenwood Press.
Clifford, J. 1988. *The Predicament of Culture: Twentieth-Century Ethnography, Literature, and Art*. Cambridge: Harvard University Press.

Crissman, L. W. 1975. The Segmentary Structure of Urban Overseas Chinese Communities. In J. Friedl, and N. J. Chrisman (eds.), *City Ways: A Selective Reader in Urban Anthropology*, pp. 274-297. New York: Thomas Y. Crowell Company.

Dawe, A. 1973. The Underworld-View of Erving Goffmann. *British Journal of Sociology* 24: 246-253.

Deeg, L. 1996. *Kunst & Albers Wladiwostok: Die Geschichte eines deutschen Handelshauses im russischen Fernen Osten (1864-1924)*. Essen: Klartext-Verlag.

Deflem, M., and K. Henry-Turrer. 2000. Smuggling. In C. D. Bryant (ed.), *Encyclopedia of Criminology and Deviant Behavior*, pp. 473-475. London: Routledge.

Delaplace, G. 2012. A Slightly Complicated Door: The Ethnography and Conceptualisation of North Asian Borders. In F. Billé, G. Delaplace, and C. Humphrey (eds.), *Frontier Encounters: Knowledge and Practice at the Russian, Chinese and Mongolian Border*, pp. 1-17. Cambridge: Open Book Publishers.

Deleuze, G., and F. Guattari. 1987. *A Thousand Plateaus: Capitalism and Schizophrenia*. Minneapolis: University of Minnesota Press.

Donnan, H., and D. Haller. 2000. Liminal no More: The Relevance of Borderland Studies. *Ethnologica Europaea* 30 (2): 7-22.

Donnan, H., and T. M. Wilson. 1999. *Borders: Frontiers of Identity, Nation and State*. Oxford: Berg.

Douglas, M. 1966. *Purity and Danger: An Analysis of Concepts of Pollution and Taboo*. New York: Frederick A. Praeger.

Egbert, H. 2006. Cross-Border Small-Scale Trading in South-Eastern Europe: Do Embeddedness and Social Capital Explain Enough? *International Journal of Urban and Regional Research* 30 (2): 346-361.

Encyclopaedia of the Russian Interior Ministry (*MVD Rossii: Entsiklopedia*). 2002. V. F. Nekrasov (ed.). Moscow: Olma Media Grupp.

Fanselow, F. S. 1990. The Bazaar Economy: How Bizarre Is the Bazaar Really? *Man* 25 (2): 250-265.

Feldbrugge, F. J. 1984. Government and Shadow Economy in the Soviet Union. *Soviet Studies* 36 (4): 528–543.

Finckenauer, J. O. 2004. The Russian Mafia. *Society Abroad* 41 (5): 61-64.

Finckenauer, J. O., and Y. A. Voronin. 2001. *The Threat of Russian Organized Crime*. Washington: U.S. Department of Justice.

Flynn, D. K. 1997. We Are the Border: Identity, Exchange, and the State along the Benin-Nigeria Border. *American Ethnologist* 24 (2): 311-330.

Fong, M. L. 1981. *The Sociology of Secret Societies: A Study of Chinese Secret Societies in Singapore and Peninsular Malaysia*. Oxford: Oxford University Press.

Forsyth, J. 1992. *History of the Peoples of Siberia: Russia's North Asian Colony 1581-1990*. Cambridge: Cambridge University Press.

Frisby, T. 1998. The Rise of Organized Crime in Russia: Its Roots and Social Significance. *Europe-Asia Studies* 50 (1): 27-49.

Galeotti, M. 1998. The Mafiya and the New Russia. *Australian Journal of Politics and History* 44: 415-429.

Galler, M., and H. E. Marquess. 1972. *Soviet Prison Camp Speech: A Survivor's Glossary*. Madison: University of Wisconsin Press.

Gambetta, D. 1993. *The Sicilian Mafia: The Business of Private Protection*. Cambridge: Harvard University Press.

Gaunt, M. E. 1919. *Broken Journey: Wandering from the Hoang-Ho to the Island of Saghalien and the Upper Reaches of the Amur River*. Philadelphia: J. B. Lippincott.

Geertz, C. 1963. *Peddlers and Princes: Social Change and Economic Modernization in Two Indonesian Towns*. Chicago: University of Chicago Press.

Gerber, T. 1999. *Russia's Population Crisis. The Migration Dimension*. PONARS (Program on New Approaches to Russian Security Policy Memo Series) Memo No. 118.

Gilloch, G. 1996. *Myth and Metropolis: Walter Benjamin and the City*. Cambridge: Polity Press.

Goffman, E. 1959. *The Presentation of Self in Everyday Life*. Garden City: Doubleday.

Gorenburg, D. 2010. Center-Periphery Relations after Ten Years of Centralization. *Russian Politics and Law* 48 (1): 3-7.

Granovetter, M. 1985. Economic Action and Social Structure: The Problem of Embeddedness. *American Journal of Sociology* 91 (3): 481-510.

Grant, B. 1999. The Return of the Repressed: Conversations with Three Russian Entrepreneurs. In G. E. Marcus (ed.), *Paranoia within Reason: A Casebook on Conspiracy as Explanation*, pp. 241-267. Chicago: The University of Chicago Press.

Grave, V. V. 1912. *Kitaytsy, Koreitsy, i Yapontsy v Priamure*. St. Petersburg: Tipografiya V. O. Kirshbauma.

Grossman, G. 1977. The 'Second Economy' of the USSR. *Problems of Communism* 26 (5): 25-40.

Gudkov, L. 1999. Antisemitizm v Postsovetskom Rossii. In G. Vitkovskaya, and A. Malashenko (eds.), *Neterpimost' v Rossii: starye i novye fobii*, pp. 44-98. Moscow: Carnegie Moscow Center.

Handelman, S. 1994. The Russian Mafiya. *Foreign Affairs* 73: 83-96.
Hann, C., and I. Beller-Hann. 1998. Markets, Morality and Modernity in North-East Turkey. In T. M. Wilson, and H. Donnan (eds.), *Border Identities: Nation and State at International Frontiers*, pp. 237-262. Cambridge: Cambridge University Press.
Hann, C., and I. Hann. 1992. Samovars and Sex on Turkey's Russian Markets. *Anthropology Today* 8 (4): 3-6.
Hannerz, U. 1996. *Transnational Connections: Culture, People, Places.* London: Routledge.
Hart, K. 1973. Informal Income Opportunities and Urban Employment in Ghana. *The Journal of Modern African Studies* 11 (1): 61-89.
——. 2005. Formal Bureaucracy and the Emergent Forms of the Informal Economy. *Research Paper* No. 2005/11. Helsinki: UNU World Institute for Development Economics Research.
Hauschild, T. 2006. *Volksfreunde bei der Mafia?* Unpublished manuscript, Tübingen.
Haviland, J. 1977. *Gossip, Reputation and Knowledge in Zinacantan.* Chicago: University of Chicago Press.
Heilman, S. 1978. *Synagogue Life.* Chicago: University of Chicago Press.
Hess, H. 1973. *Mafia and Mafiosi: The Structure of Power.* Farnborough: Saxon House.
——. 1998. *Mafia & Mafiosi: Origin, Power, and Myth.* Belair: Crawford House Publishing.
Heyman J. McC., and A. Smart. 1999. States and Illegal Practices: An Overview. In J. McC. Heyman (ed.), *States and Illegal Practices*, pp. 1-24. Oxford: Berg.
Hill, S. 2006. Purity and Danger on the U.S.-Mexico Border, 1990-1994. *South Atlantic Quarterly* 105 (4): 777-800.
Ho, C. 1993. The Internationalization of Kinship and the Feminization of Caribbean Migration: The Case of Afro-Trinidadian Immigrants in Los Angeles. *Human Organization* 52 (1): 32-40.
Hoffmann, D. E. 2002. *The Oligarchs: Wealth and Power in the New Russia.* New York: Public Affairs.
Holmes, L. 2008. Corruption and Organised Crime in Putin's Russia. *Europe-Asia Studies* 60 (6): 1011-1031.
Humphrey, C. 1995. Creating a Culture of Disillusionment: Consumption in Moscow, a Chronicle of Changing Times. In D. Miller (ed.), *Worlds Apart: Modernity through the Prism of the Local*, pp. 43-68. London: Routledge.

―――. 1999. Russian Protection Racket and the Appropriation of Law and Order. In J. McC. Heyman (ed.), *States and Illegal Practices*, pp. 199-232. Oxford: Berg.

―――. 2002. Traders, 'Disorder', and Citizenship Regimes in Provincial Russia. In C. Humphrey (ed.), *The Unmaking of Soviet Life: Everyday Economies after Socialism*, pp. 69-98. Ithaca: Cornell University Press.

Ivashenko, L. et al. 1997. *Primorskiy Kray: Kratkiy entsiklopedicheskiy spravochnik*. Vladivostok: Izdadesl'stvo Dal'nevostochnogo Universiteta.

Johnson, J. C. et al. 1999. *The 1999 Index of Economic Freedom*. Washington: The Heritage Foundation.

Kabo, V. R. 1990. Struktura lagerya i arkhetipy soznaniya. *Sovetskaya Etnografiya* 1: 108-13.

Kaiser, M. 1997. *Informal Sector Trade in Uzbekistan*. University of Bielefeld, Faculty of Sociology, Working Paper No. 281.

Karlusov, V., and A. Kudin. 2002. Kitayskoe prisutstvie na rossiyskom Dal'nem Vostoke: istoriko-ekonomicheskiy analiz. *Problemy Dal'nego Vostoka* 5: 76-87.

Karras, A. L. 2009. *Smuggling: Contraband and Corruption in World History*. Lanham: Rowman & Littlefield.

Katsenelinboigen, A. 1977. Colored Markets in the Soviet Union. *Soviet Studies* 29 (1): 62-85.

Kattoulas, V. 2002. Crime Central. *Far Eastern Economic Review* 165: 48-51.

Khisamutdinov, A. A. 1993. *The Russian Far East: Historical Essays*. Honolulu: A. A. Khisamutdinov.

Knight, A. 1996. *Spies without Cloaks: The KGB's Successors*. Princeton: Princeton University Press.

Koehler, J. 2000. *Die Zeit der Jungs*. Münster: LIT Verlag.

Konstantinov, Yu. 1996. Patterns of Reinterpretation: Trader-Tourism in the Balkans (Bulgaria) as a Picaresque Metaphorical Enactment of Post-Totalitarianism. *American Ethnologist* 23 (4): 762-782.

Konstantinov, Yu., G. M. Kressel, and T. Thuen. 1998. Outclassed by Former Outcasts: Petty Trading in Varna. *American Ethnologist* 25 (4): 729-745.

Kraus, K. 1986. *Half-Truths and One & One-and-a-Half Truths: Selected Aphorisms*. (ed. and trans. Harry Zohn). Manchester: Carcanet Press.

Kropotkin, P. A. 1971. *Memoirs of a Revolutionist*. New York: Dover.

Kryshtanovskaya, O. 1995. Nelegal'nye struktury v Rossii. *Sotsiologicheskie issledovaniya* 8: 92-105.

Landgraf, D. 1989. *Amur, Ussuri, Sachalin (1847-1917)*. Neuried: Hieronymus Verlag.
Larin, V. 1995. Yellow Peril Again? The Chinese and the Russian Far East. In S. Kotkin, and D. Wolff (eds.), *Rediscovering Russia in Asia: Siberia and the Russian Far East*, pp. 290-301. London: M.E. Sharpe.
──. 1998. *Kitay i Dal'nii Vostok Rossii v pervoi polovine 90-kh: Problemy regional'nogo vzaimodeistviya*. Vladivostok: Dal'nauka.
──. 2012. Perceptions of Chinese Migrants in the Russian Far East. In F. B. Chang, and S. T. Rucker-Chang (eds.), *Chinese Migrants in Russia*, pp. 69-82. London: Routledge.
Ledeneva, A. V. 1998. *Russia's Economy of Favours: Blat, Networking and Informal Exchange*. Cambridge: Cambridge University Press.
──. 2006. *How Russia Really Works: The Informal Practices That Shaped Post-Soviet Politics and Business*. Ithaca: Cornell University Press.
──. 2013. *Can Russia Modernise? Sistema, Power and Informal Governance*. Cambridge: Cambridge University Press.
Lee, R. H. G. 1970. *The Manchurian Frontier in Ch'ing History*. Cambridge: Harvard University Press.
Lenin 1964 [1922]. Wks. XXVII, R. 362. *Pravda* 21 November 1922.
Levin, M. G., and L. P. Potapov. 1964. *The Peoples of Siberia*. Chicago: University of Chicago Press.
Libmann, A. 2010. Cycles of Decentralization in the Post-Soviet Space. *Russian Politics and Law* 48 (1): 8-12.
Light, I. 1972. *Ethnic Enterprise in America*. Berkeley: University of California Press.
Lin, G., and P. Tse. 2005. Flexible Sojourning in the Era of Globalization: Cross-Border Population Mobility in the Hong Kong-Guangdong Border Region. *International Journal of Urban and Regional Research* 29 (4): 867-894.
Lintner, B. 2003. Spreading Tentacles. *Far Eastern Economic Review* 166: 54-56.
──. *Triads Tighten Grip on Russia's Far East*. Asia Pacific Media Service, http://www.asiapacificms.com/articles/russia_triads/, accessed 12 December 2005.
Los, M. 1990. Introduction. In M. Los (ed.), *The Second Economy in Marxist States*, pp. 1-10. Houndmills: Macmillan.
Lukin, A. 1998. The Image of China in Russian Border Regions. *Asian Survey* 38 (9): 821-830.
MacGaffey, J., and R. Bazenguissa-Ganga. 2000. *Congo-Paris: Transnational Traders on the Margins of the Law*. Oxford: James Currey.

Malashenko, A. 1999. Ksenofobii v postsovetskom obshchestve (vmesto vvedeniya). In G. Vitkovskaya, and A. Malashenko (eds.), *Neterpimost' v Rossii: starye i novye fobii*, pp. 136-150. Moscow: Carnegie Moscow Center.

March, G. P. 1996. *Eastern Destiny: Russia in Asia and the North Pacific*. Westport: Praeger.

Marcus, G. 1995. Ethnography in/of the World System: The Emergence of Multi-Sited Ethnography. *Annual Review of Anthropology* 24: 95-117.

Martin, B. G. 1996. *The Shanghai Green Gang: Politics and Organized Crime, 1919-1937*. Berkeley: University of California Press.

Martinez, O. 1994. The Dynamics of Border Interaction. In C. H. Schoefield (ed.), *Global Boundaries: World Boundaries*, Vol. 1, pp. 8-14. London: Routledge.

McIllwain, J. S. 1999. Organized Crime: A Social Network Approach. *Crime, Law & Social Change* 32: 301-323.

Mills, J. A., S. Chan, and A. Ishihara. 2005. *The Bear Facts: The East Asian Market for Bear Gall Bladder*. TRAFFIC network report (July). http://www.traffic.org/publications/summaries/summary-bear.html, accessed 12 June 2006.

Min, P. G. 1988. *Ethnic Business Enterprise: Korean Small Business in Atlanta*. New York: CMS.

Mitchell, J. C. 1969. The Concept and Use of Social Networks. In J. C. Mitchell (ed.), *Social Networks in Urban Situations: Analyses of Personal Relationships in Central African Towns*, pp. 1-50. Manchester: Manchester University Press.

——. 1983. Case and Situational Analysis. *Sociological Review* 31: 187-211.

Morocvasic, M. et al. 1990. Business on the Ragged Edge: Immigrant and Minority Business in the Garment Industries of Paris, London, and New York. In R. Waldinger et al. (eds.), *Immigrant Entrepreneurs: Immigrant and Ethnic Businesses in Western Industrial Societies*, pp. 157-177. Beverly Hills: Sage.

Mukomel, V. I. 1999. Demograficheskaya posledstviya etnicheskikh i regional'nikh konfliktov v SNG. *Sotsiologicheskie Issledovaniya* 6: 63-70.

Naylor, R. T. 2002. *Wages of Crime: Black Markets, Illegal Finance, and the Underworld Economy*. Ithaca: Cornell University Press.

Nazpary, J. 2002. *Post-Soviet Chaos: Violence and Dispossession in Kazakhstan*. London: Pluto Press.

Nesterenko, A. D., and M. M. Kulesh. 2002. *Ekonomika Rossiyskogo Dal'nego Vosotka v XX stoletii*. Vladivostok: Izd-vo DVGAEU.
Nomokonov, V. A. 1998. *Organizovannaya prestupnost' Dal'nego Vostoka: Obshchie i regional'nye cherty*. Vladivostok: Izd-vo Dal'nevost. uni-ta.
——. 2003. Contract Killings. *Russian Regional Report* 8 (7): 1-4.
Nomokonov, V. A., and V. I. Shulga. 1998. Murder for Hire as a Manifestation of Organized Crime. *Demokratizatsiya* 6 (11): 676-680.
Nordstrom, C. 2000. Shadows and Sovereigns. *Theory, Culture & Society* 17 (4): 35-54.
——. 2004. *Shadows of War: Violence, Power, and International Profiteering in the Twenty-First Century*. Berkeley: University of California Press.
Nyiri, P. 1999. Chinese Organizations in Hungary 1989-1996: A Case Study in PRC-Oriented Community Politics Overseas. In F. N. Pieke, and H. Mallee (eds.), *Internal and International Migration: Chinese Perspectives*, pp. 251-279. Richmond: Curzon Press.
——. 2006. Chinese Entrepreneurs in Hungary. In L. Dana (ed.), *Handbook of Research on Ethnic Minority Entrepreneurship*, pp. 534-554. Cheltenham: Edward Elgar.
Paoli, L. 2003. *Mafia Brotherhoods: Organized Crime, Italian Style*. Oxford: Oxford University Press.
Pedersen, M. A. 2007. From 'Public' to 'Private' Markets in Postsocialist Mongolia. *Anthropology of East Europe Review* 25 (1): 64-71.
Pelkmans, M. 2006. *Defending the Border: Identity, Religion, and Modernity in the Republic of Georgia*. Ithaca: Cornell University Press.
Plutser-Sarno, A. 2003. The Language of the Body Politics: The Symbolism of the Thieves' Tattoos. In D. Murray, and S. Sorell (eds.), *Russian Criminal Tatoo Encyclopedia*, Vol. 1, pp. 27-53. Göttingen: Steidl.
Polanyi, K. 1944. *The Great Transformation*. New York: Holt Rinehart.
Portes, A., and W. Haller. 2005. The Informal Economy. In S. J. Neil, and R. Swedberg (eds.), *The Handbook of Economic Sociology*, pp. 403-428. Princeton: Princeton University Press.
Portes, A., and J. Sensenbrenner. 1993. Embeddedness and Immigration: Notes on the Social Determinants of Economic Action. *American Journal of Sociology* 98 (6): 1320-1350.
Pozniak, T. Z. 2004. *Inostrannye poddannye v gorodakh Dal'nego Vostoka Rossii: Vtoraya polovina XIX – nachalo XX veka*. Vladivostok: Dal'nauka.

Price, J. A. 1974. Tecate: An Industrial City on the Mexican Border. *Urban Anthropology* 2 (1): 35-47.

Rabinovich, V. 1999. Evrei i Irkutskoe obshchestvo (konets XIX – nachalo XX. v.). In G. Vitkovskaya, and A. Malashenko (eds.), *Neterpimost' v Rossii: starye i novye fobii*, pp. 19-43. Moscow: Carnegie Moscow Center.

Radaev, V. 1999. *The Spread of Violence in Russian Business in the Late 1990s*. PONARS (Program on New Approaches to Russian Security Policy Memo Series) Memo No. 66.

Rancour-Lafferriere, D. 2001. *Russian Nationalism from an Interdisciplinary Perspective: Imagining Russia*. Lewiston: Edwin Mellen Press.

Rawlinson, P. 1997. Russian Organized Crime: A Brief History. In P. Williams (ed.), *Russian Organized Crime: The New Threat?*, pp. 28-51. London: Frank Cass.

Razgon, L. 1997. *True Stories: The Memoirs of Lev Razgon*. Dana Point: Ardis.

Razinkin, V. 1998. *Tsvetnaya Mast': Elita prestupnogo mira*. Moscow: Veche.

Reeves, M. 2007. Unstable Objects: Corpses, Checkpoints and 'Chessboard Border' in the Ferghana Valley. *Anthropology of East Europe Review* 25 (1): 72-84.

―――. 2014. *Border Work: Spatial Lives of the State in Rural Central Asia*. Ithaca: Cornell University Press.

Repnikova, M., and H. Balzer. 2009. *Chinese Migration to Russia: Missed Opportunities*. Washington D. C.: Woodrow Wilson International Center for Scholars.

Richardson, W. 1995. Vladivostok: City of Three Eras. *Planning Perspectives* 10: 43-65.

Ries, N. 2002. Honest Bandits and Warped People: Russian Narratives about Money, Corruption, and Moral Decay. In C. J. Greenhouse, E. Mertz, and K. B. Warren (eds.), *Ethnography in Unstable Places: Everyday Lives in the Context of Dramatic Political Change*, pp. 276-315. Durham: Duke University Press.

Rogers, A., and S. Vertovec. 1995. *The Urban Context: Ethnicity, Social Networks and Situational Analysis*. Oxford: Berg.

Roitman, J. 2005. *Fiscal Disobedience: An Anthropology of Economic Regulation in Central Africa*. Princeton: Princeton University Press.

Round, J., C. C. Williams, and P. Rodgers. 2008. Everyday Tactics and Spaces of Power: The Role of Informal Economies in Post-Soviet Ukraine. *Social & Cultural Geography* 9 (2): 171-185.

Ryzhova, N. 2008. Informal Economy of Translocations: The Case of the Twin City of Blagoveshensk-Heihe. *Inner Asia* 10: 323-351.
Sahlins, M. 1965. On the Sociology of Primitive Exchange. In M. Banton (ed.), *The Relevance of Models for Social Anthropology*, pp. 148-158. London: Tavistock.
Samoilov, L. 1989. Puteshestvie v perevernutyi mir. *Neva* 4: 15-64.
-----. 1990. Etnografiya Lagerya. *Sovetskaya Etnografiya* 1: 96-108.
Sahedo, J. 2012. The Accidental Traders: Marginalization and Opportunity from the Southern Republics of Late Soviet Moscow. In M. Reeves (ed.), *Movement, Power and Place in Central Asia and Beyond: Contested Trajectories*, pp. 145-164. London: Routledge.
Sanders, J. M., and V. Lee. 1996. Immigrant Self-Employment: The Family as Social Capital and the Value of Human Capital. *American Sociological Review* 61 (2): 231-249.
Serio, J. D., and V. Razinkin. 1995. Thieves Professing the Code: The Traditional Role of *Vory v Zakone* in Russia's Criminal World and Adaptations to a New Social Reality. *Low Intensity Conflict & Law Enforcement* 4: 72-88.
Scheele, J. 2012. *Smugglers and Saints of the Sahara: Regional Connectivity in the Twentieth Century*. Cambridge: Cambridge University Press.
Schendel, W. van. 2005. Spaces of Engagement: How Borderlands, Illegal Flows, and Territorial States Interlock. In W. van Schendel, and I. Abraham (eds.), *Illicit Flows and Criminal Things: States, Borders, and the Other Side of Globalization*, pp. 38-68. Bloomington: Indiana University Press.
Schneider, F., and D. H. Enste. 2000. Shadow Economies: Size, Causes, Consequences. *Journal of Economic Literature* 38 (1): 77-114.
Schneider, J. C., and P. T. Schneider. 1976. *Culture and Political Economy in Western Sicily*. New York: Academic Press.
-----. 2003. *Reversible Destiny: Mafia, Antimafia, and the Struggle for Palermo*. Berkeley: University of California Press.
-----. 2005. Mafia, Antimafia, and the Plural Cultures of Sicily. *Cultural Anthropologist* 46 (4): 501-520.
Shalamov, V. 1982. *Kolyma Tales*. New York: W. W. Norton & Company.
Shelley, L. I. 1990. The Second Economy in the Soviet Union. In M. Los (ed.), *The Second Economy in Marxist States*, pp. 11-26. Houndmills: Macmillan.
Shlapentokh, V. 1996. Early Feudalism: The Best Parallel for Contemporary Russia. *Europe-Asia Studies* 48 (3): 393-411.

Siegelbaum, L. H. 1978. Another 'Yellow Peril': Chinese migrants in the Russian Far East and the Russian reaction before 1917. *Modern Asian Studies* 12 (2): 307-330.

Sik, E., and C. Wallace. 1999. The Develpoment of Open-Air Markets in East-Central Europe. *International Journal of Urban and Regional Research* 23 (4): 751-770.

Simmel, G. 1971. The Stranger. In D. N. Levine (ed.), *Georg Simmel: On Individuality and Social Forms*, pp. 143-150. Chicago: University of Chicago Press.

——. 1997. Bridge and Door. In N. Leach (ed.), *Rethinking Architecture: A Reader in Cultural Theory*. London: Routledge.

Smith, A. 2001. *Wealth of Nations*. Raleigh: Hayes Barton Press.

Solan, L. M., and P. M. Tiersma. 2005. *Speaking of Crime: The Language of Criminal Justice*. Chicago: University of Chicago Press.

Spector, R. 2008. Bazaar Politics: The Fate of Marketplaces in Kazakhstan. *Problems of Post-Communism* 55 (6): 42-53.

Stammler-Gossman, A. 2011. 'Winter-Tyres-for-a-Flower-Bed': Shuttle Trade on the Finish-Russian Border. In B. Bruns, and J. Miggelbrink (eds.), *Subverting Borders: Doing Research on Smuggling and Small-Scale Trade*, pp. 233-256. Wiesbaden: VS Verlag.

Stephan, J. J. 1994. *The Russian Far East: A History*. Stanford: Stanford University Press.

Sterling, C. 1991. *Octopus: The Long Reach of the International Sicilian Mafia*. New York: Simon & Schuster.

Sushkov, B. A. 1958. *Post Vladivostok: 1860-1862 gody*. Vladivostok: Primorskoe Knizhnoe Izdatel'stvo.

Tilly, C. 1985. War Making and State Making as Organized Crime. In P. B. Evans, D. Rueschemeyer, and T. Skocpol (eds.), *Bringing the State Back In*, pp. 169-191. Cambridge: Cambridge University Press.

Trovimov, V. 1992. *Staryi Vladivostok*. Vladivostok: Utro Rossii.

U.S. Department of Labor. 2001. Semiannual Report to Congress (April 1 - September 30). Office of the Inspector General.

Vaisman, A. 2001. *Trawling In the Mist: Industrial Fisheries in the Russian Part of the Bering Sea*. TRAFFIC species in danger report (November).

Vaksberg, A. 1991. *The Soviet Mafia*. New York: St. Martin's Press.

Varese, F. 1998. The Society of the Vory-V-Zakone, 1930s-1950s. *Cahier du Monde Russe* 39: 515-538.

——. 2001. *The Russian Mafia: Private Protection in a New Market Economy*. Oxford: Oxford University Press.

Vashchuk, A. S. 2000. Adaptatsia etnicheskikh migrantov iz Rossii i SNG v Primor'e (90-e gody XX v.). In A. S. Vashchuk, and E. N. Chernolutskaia (eds.), *Adaptatsia etnicheskikh migrantov v Primor'e v XX v.*, pp. 158-176. Vladivostok: DVO RAN.

Vashchuk, A. S. et al. 2002. *Etnomigratsionnye protsessy v Primor'e v XX veke.* Vladivostok: DVO RAN.

Verdery, K. 1996. *What Was Socialism and What Comes Next?* Princeton: Princeton University Press.

Vitkovskaya, G. 1999a. Vynuzhdennaia Migratsiia i Migrantofobiia v Rossii. In G. Vitkovskaya, and A. Malashenko (eds.), *Neterpimost' v Rossii: starye i novye fobii*, pp. 151-191. Moscow: Carnegie Moscow Center.

——. 1999b. Does Chinese Migration Endanger Russian Security? *Carnegie Moscow Center Briefing Papers*, Issue 8 (August).

Vitkovskaya, G., and Z. Zaionchkovskaya. 1999. Novaia stolypinskaia politika na Dal'nem Vostoke Rossii: nadezhdy i realii. In G. Vitkovskaya, and A. Malashenko (eds.), *Neterpimost' v Rossii: starye i novye fobii*, pp. 80-120. Moscow: Carnegie Moscow Center.

Volkov, V. 1999. Violent Entrepreneurship in Post-Communist Russia. *Europe-Asia Studies* 51 (5): 741-754.

——. 2000. The Political Economy of Protection Rackets in the Past and in the Present. *Social Research* 67 (3): 709-744.

——. 2002a. Security and Enforcement as Private Business: The Conversion of Russia's Power Ministries and Its Institutional Consequences. In V. Bonnell, and T. Gold (eds.), *The New Entrepreneurs of Europe and Asia*, pp. 83-103. New York: M. E. Sharpe.

——. 2002b. *Violent Entrepreneurs: The Use of Force in the Making of Russian Capitalism.* Ithaca: Cornell University Press.

——. 2002c. Who is Strong When the State Is Weak? Violent Entrepreneurship in Russia's Emerging Markets. In M. Beisinger, and C. Young (eds.), *Beyond State Crisis? Postcolonial Africa and Post-Soviet Eurasia in Perspective*, pp. 81-104. Washington: Woodrow Wilson Center Press.

Wallace, C. et al. 1999. Investing in Social Capital: The Case of Small-Scale, Cross-Border Traders in Post-Communist Central Europe. *International Journal of Urban and Regional Planning* 23: 751-770.

Wedel, J. 2001. Corruption and Organized Crime in Post-Communist States: New Ways of Manifesting Old Patterns. *Trends in Organized Crime* 7: 3-60.

——. 2003. Mafia without Malfeasance, Clans without Crime: The Criminality Conundrum in Post-Communist Europe. In P. C.

Parnell, and S. C. Kane (eds.), *Crime's Power: Anthropologists and the Ethnography of Crime*, pp. 221-224. New York: Palgrave.

Wheeler, A. 2004. Moralities of the Mongolian 'Market': A Genealogy of Trade Relations and the Zah Zeel. *Inner Asia* 6 (2): 215-238.

Wiegand, B. 1993. Petty Smuggling as 'Social Justice': Research Findings from the Belize-Mexico Border. *Social and Economic Studies* 42 (1): 171-193.

Williams, A. M., and V. Balaz. 2005. Winning, then Losing, the Battle with Globalization: Vietnamese Petty Traders in Slovakia. *International Journal of Urban and Regional Research* 29 (3): 533-549.

Williams, B. 2003. The Criminalization of Russo-Japanese Border Trade: Causes and Consequences. *Europe-Asia Studies* 55 (5): 711-728.

Wilson, A. 2004. *The Intimate Economies of Bangkok: Tomboys, Tycoons, and Avon Ladies in the Global City*. Berkeley: University of California Press.

Wishnik, E. 2005. Chinese Labour Migrants in the RFE. In T. Akaha, and A. Vassilieva (eds.), *Crossing National Borders: Human Migration Issues in Northeast Asia*, pp. 68-92. Tokyo: United Nations University Press.

Yalçın-Heckmann, L. 2014. Informal Economy Writ Large and Small: From Azerbaijani Herb Trader to Moscow Shop Owners. In J. Morris, and A. Polese (eds.), *The Informal Post-Socialist Economy*, pp. 165-186. London: Routledge.

Yükseker, D. 2004. Trust and Gender in a Transnational Market: The Public Culture of Laleli, Istanbul. *Public Culture* 16 (1): 47-65.

Yurchak, A. 2006. *Everything Was Forever, Until It Was No More: The Last Soviet Generation*. Princeton: Princeton University Press.

Zabel, E. 1904. *Auf der Sibirischen Eisenbahn nach China*. Berlin: Allgemeiner Verein für Deutsche Literatur.

Zepelin, C. von. 1911. *Das Küstengebiet Primorskaja Oblastj mit dem Kriegshafen Wladiwostok unter besonderer Berücksichtigung der militärischen Stellung Russlands am Stillen Ozean, seine Besiedlung und wirtschaftliche Entwicklung*. Berlin: Ernst Siegfried Mitt.

Index

Afghanistan 108, 143, 145n
Aigun (Heihe) 24, 25, 37, 185; treaty of 37, 185
Aleksey (Gorbachev, Aleksey) 164
Amur River 20, 22-5, 28, 29, 38, 73, 129, 134, 155, 181
Amurskaya Oblast' 24, 70, 132, 134
Andijon, Uzbekistan 74, 80
architecture; container 52, 54, 56, 58-60, 63, 90, 91, 121; shopping 45-8, 51-2, 54-9, 80, 82, 111, *see also* market architecture
Armenia (and Armenians) 56, 66, 67, 133, 142, 165
Arsenyev, V. K. 19, 21-3, 26-31, 34-7, 41, 42, 88
avtoritet 133n, 134n, 168, 181, 184
Azerbaijan (and Azeri) 48, 53, 55, 56, 60

Bakhshetsyan, E. 121
Balyaeva (market) 51-4, 56, 58, 61
bandit 31, 147, 154, 157, 164, 168-9
Baul (Baulo, Sergey) 163, 165-8, 176, 177
bazaar ecology 6, 50, 51
Beijing 25, 29, 41, 96; treaty of 25, 29
Belobrova, L. 167, 177
Benjamin, W.; cityscapes 5, 11, 12; *Denkbilder* (thought images) 5; on porosity 5
bio-resources; bear paws 16, 108, 110, 111; deer antlers 16, 20, 111; frogs 16, 64, 110, 111; ginseng 16, 20, 22, 31-5, 102n, 108, 110-4, 180-2; sea cucumbers 16, 21, 38, 108, 109; tiger products 16; timber 16, 69, 88, 107, 110, 124, 126, 168, *see also* poaching of bio-resources
Blagoveshchensk 24, 31, 99
Bolshoy Kamen 109

border (and borders); as a multi-layered cultural zone 103; as a 'programme' 101, 102, 123, 127, 187; as a resource 122, 185; as 'chessboards' 104; borderland 6, 8, 13, 30, 89, 90, 100, 101, 103-4, 120, 122-4, 131, 180, 182, 184-9; crossings 4,5, 14, 15, 68, 92, 93, 98-100, 103; entrepreneurs 4, 8, 11, 16-7, 38, 45, 49-51, 58, 68, 69, 73, 75, 82, 85-6, 101, 109, 113, 121, 123-4, 127, 143, 144, 146-8, 155n, 159, 164, 172, 175-8, 180-1, 183, 184, 186; porosity/permeability 4-6, 12-3, 16-7, 86-9, 91, 93, 95, 97, 99, 101, 103, 105, 107, 109, 111, 113, 115, 117, 119, 121, 123, 125, 127, 184, 186, 190; Russian-Chinese border 6, 16, 29, 89, 100, 101, 118, 120, 122, 124-5; Russian-Finish border 100, *see also* cross-border trade
bratva 154
bribes (and bribery) 78, 79, 120, 142, 143, 187, *see also* corruption
brigadir 160, 167, 176, 181, 184
broker 53, 105, 115, 116, 124, 125, 127, 171, 172, 175, 181, *see also* middlemen
brotherhood 15, 33, 35, 36n, 135, 141, 154, 159n, 174-5, 180, 183, 187, *see also bratva*
byki 181

Camorra 12
cars; car parts 116, 118, 124, 182; used-cars 96, 97n, 105, 114-6, 165, 183, 184, *see also* smuggling of car parts
cedar nuts 111, 113
Central Asia 6, 16, 17, 43, 47, 50, 63, 68, 74n, 77, 81, 82, 104, 108, 184
chaos 1, 11, 63, 157, 158, 168, 189

chelnoki 17, 87, 89-91, 103, 117-9; as social reserves 189; different types of 94-7; *naemnye* 92, 182; *svobodnye* 92, 180, 182, see also shuttle trade

China (and Chinese); Chinese markets 16, 20, 45, 49-53, 55, 85, 91; Chinese migration 50, 68, 69, 148; Chinese poachers 34, 64; Chinese settlements 20, 28, 70, 185; Chinese tourists 69, 100n, 103; trading networks/ guilds 6, 15, 36, 37, 181, 184, 186-9

chushki 140

commodities; commodified space 12; commodity flows 8, 11, 16, 36, 50, 65, 81, 100, 103, 123, 124, 179, 184, 185

consumption 4, 14, 40, 59, 63, 66, 101, 122

contract killings 148, 165

corruption 9, 42, 103, 108n, 119, 121, 142-4, 150, 171, 172, 187, *see also* bribes

Cossacks 19, 26, 28-9, 31, 33

counterfeit 62, 116-8, *see also kontrafakty*

cross-border trade 11, 71-2, 87-9, 92, 97-101, 103, 114, 118-9, 121-4, 126-7, 180, 182, 183, 186, 188

customs; custom control zone 104; officials 33, 72, 90, 106-7, 119-22, 142, 143, 145, 150, 154, 170, 176

da-je 35

Dal'nevostochnyy Obshchak (Far Eastern Obshchak) 132

Dalzavod 1

Darkin, S. 73, 166-7, 169, 177

Dersu Uzala 22, 88

Dzhem (Vasin, Yevgeniy Petrovich) 129-35, 154, 156-7, 174-6, 183

economy; economic change 18, 149, 189, 190; economic consolidation 17; official and unofficial 9, 10, 19, 24, 28, 30n, 40, 69, 70n, 71-3, 106, 108, 118, 119, 120-2, 131-2, 137, 142-3, 145-6, 150, 154, 158, 170-1, 176, 179; second economy 8-10, 184; Soviet economy 4, 9, 61, 148, *see also* informal economy

embeddedness 14, 73, 79, 80, 85

ethnic; economies 79; enterprises/ businesses 81; entrepreneurs/ traders 11, 73, 75, 82, 85-6, 180-1, 186; groups 50, 53, 55-6, 67, 105; interaction 123-4; networks 81, 83; ties 16, 74

extortion 131, 136, 143, 149, 172-3, 180, 183

family; ties 6, 7, 16, 18, 50, 73-5, 80-2, 84, 102n, 127, 136, 179-83, 189, *see also* kinship networks

fansa 28, 20

Far Eastern State University 150

farmers; Chinese 22, 29-35; Korean 28, 32

firmy-posredniki 53

fishing (and fisheries) 17, 21, 33, 42, 67, 98, 105, 106n, 108, 132, 142, 165-7, *see also* poaching of marine products

flow 11, 14, 34, 39, 46, 61, 68-9, 81, 88, 100, 110, 124-5, 171, 180, 183-4, *see also* commodity flow

fraer 140

friendship 25, 48, 124, 154, 174, 175-7, 181-3

FSB (Federal Security Bureau) 121, 122

funeral 133, 157, 165n, 177

furs 27, 33, 91, 109-11, 180, 181, *see also* trapping

Georgia (and Georgians) 133, 142
ginseng 16, 20, 22, 31-5, 102, 108, 110, 111-3, 181, 182, *see also* poaching of ginseng
gold 1, 29, 31, 33, 38, 135
Golden Horn Bay 1, 38, 108, 114
Gorbachev, M. 161n
Grave, V. V. 30n, 40-2, 129
graves/ gravestones 3, 129, 133, 135
'Green Corner' (market) 114-6

Harbin 39, 92, 95, 96
harbour 1, 6, 19, 20, 38, 39, 41, 79, 104, 105, 108, 159, *see also* Vladivostok harbour
Heilongjiang Province, China 15, 16, 70, 87, 88, 92, 112
hunting 30, 33, 35, 108-10, 113, 180, 181

illegal; commodities 8, 9; drugs 79; immigrants 70, 79; market 9, 106; migrant workers 78, 79, *see also* legality
illicit; economies 105; illicit vs. illegal 7, 11, 118, *see also* legality
Iman River 19, 27n, 28
import taxes 10, 92n, 93, 102, 105, 117, *see also* taxes
informal; cross-border trade 100, 101, 114, 122, 123, 127, 180; economic practices 4, 7, 8, 101, 102, 118; economy 7, 8, 86, 101; income opportunities 86; networks 5-7, 13, 74, 83, 114, 177, 184, 185; space 1; strategies 50, 99, 187, 188
informality 4, 5, 7, 11, 16, 45-85 *passim*, 122, 185, 187; social organization of 11

Japan (and Japanese) 6, 25, 33; counterfeits 118; illegal trade with 105-8; in Manchuria 40; in Russia 23, 28, 39; informal trade with 94-7, 114-6, 183-4; Japanese cars 1, 95, 105, 114-6, 162; Japanese espionage 40n, 43; Sea of 20
joint-ventures 189
journalist(s) 61, 63, 64, 113n, 138, 150, 156, 157

Kaban (Ivlev, Leonid) 151, 159
kachki 146
Kamchatka 24, 106
Karimov, I. 74
Karp (Karpov, Igor) 166-8, 177
kasty 139
KGB 145-6
Khabarovsk 22, 24, 27, 30, 31, 36, 70, 120, 130, 132-4, 159, 181
Khabarovsky Krai 24, 70, 132
khosyain 76-7
Khrushchev, N. 26
khunkhusy 29, 31
kinship; network 50, 73, 81, 84; ties 75, 80, 136, 180-2, *see also* family
kiosk 48, 59
kitayskie rynki 49, *see also* Chinese markets
klichka 137, 160
Komsomolsk-na-Amure 15, 129, 130, 131-4, 155, 157-9, 174-6, 183
komsomoltsy 141
kontrafakty 118, *see also* counterfeit
Korea (and Koreans) 6, 32, 96, 110, 111; in Russia 28, 32-3, 39; Korean displacement 42-3; Korean migration 32; Korean settlements 22, 32, 43; North Korea 3, 68; Russian Koreans 53, 57, 67-8; South Korea 2, 110
koronatsiya 137
Kosten (Aleksandr Kostenko) 152, 164, 166
Koval (Anatoliy Filippovich Kovalev) 151-4, 159, 165, 166, 176

kreshchenie 131, 137
krestnaya mat' 162
krestniy otets 129
krysha 54, 78, 146, 178; *banditskaya* 147; *krasnaya* 147n
Kunst & Albers 38
Kyrgyzstan (and Kyrgyz) 68, 74, 76-7, 80

Larionov brothers 162, 176; Larionov, Aleksandr 162; Larionov, Sergey 161-2
legality 5, 8-11, 14, 16, 50, 114, 159, 188; legal vs. illegal 8-10, 14, 97, 100, 103, 104n, 122, 126, 146, 188, *see also* illicit/ illegal
Lepeshka (Lepeshkin, Sergey Aleksandrovich) 130
lotki 52
Lugovaya (market) 51, 58, 60, 61, 63, 75-6, 80

mafia; as a symbol 147-9; as 'multifunctional entities' 173, 175-7; Chechen 163n; discourse on 158, 166; Italian 12-3, 141, 150, 155, 170-1; relationship to the state 178, 186; rituals 141; Soviet 142-3, 176, 186; studies 170-3; testimonies 153, 155; Uzbek 78
Magadan 73, 82
maloletki 141
Manchuria 22, 27n, 29, 30n
mansy 30
Maritime Province 15, 20, 24, 61
market(s); administration 53, 78, 79; architecture 12, 13, 90; black market 10, 75, 78, 111, 142-3, 176, 178, 184; Chinese 16, 20, 45, 49-52, 55, 56, 85, 91, 109, 181; 'colored markets' 9; grey 10; open-air 4, 6, 8, 10, 11, 13-6, 45, 49, 50, 52-4, 56-69 *passim*, 74, 79, 80, 83, 85, 88, 91, 94-7, 111, 114, 122, 124, 146, 149, 163, 169, 180, 181, 186, 189; transformation 60, *see also* open-air markets
merchandise 45-6, 52, 53, 59, 62, 64, 69, 75, 77, 79, 81, 84, 87-8, 90, 91-7, 108, 117, 124, 125
middlemen 16, 31, 33, 81, 105, 109-11, 113, 122, 124, 127; middleman minority 60, *see also* broker
migration; anti-migrant feelings 72; Chinese migration 50, 68-9, 148; into the Russian Far East 28-9, 71, 100, 148; labour migration 4, 6, 16, 50, 67-9, 74, 100, 180-1, 184; migrants 13, 28, 30, 42, 63, 65, 67-72, 74, 79, 80; out-migration 70
Mikho (Osipov, Mikhail) 164-6
Millionka 41, 42
money transfer 74, 84, 124-5; *fei chien* (flying money) 125
Mongolia 29, 74
monopoly 4, 17, 35, 37, 109, 120, 122, 127, 144, 163, 173, 180, 181, 186-7; monopolization 4, 37n, 120, 172, 183; state 4
Moscow 4, 12, 13, 39, 60, 70, 71, 74, 81n, 86, 119-21, 133, 145n, 146, 148, 154; Soviet 12
Muravyov-Amursky, N. 23-6, 39
muzhiki (men) 140

Nakhodka 22, 61, 67, 80, 105, 109, 114, 121
Nanais 33
Naples 12, 13
Nazdratenko, Y. 68, 73
neighborhood 155
networks; criminal 178; cross-border 123, 183, 185; economic 5, 8, 9, 11, 14, 15, 34, 168, 179, 180; ethnic 81, 83, 180, 182; kinship 81; shadow 4, 6, 7-9, 11, 13, 18,

179, 180, 182, 184-9; smuggling 123, 185; social 5, 8, 11, 13, 62, 74, 80, 81n, 85, 94, 103, 182-4, *see also* informal networks
nightclub 164-5
Nikolaevsk 25, 26, 30, 38
Novosibirsk 75, 77

obshchak 132, 142, 164-5, 176, 183
Olga Bay (St. Olga) 19, 21, 28
OMON (Special Forces of the Interior Ministry) 54, 79, 168
open-air markets; and illegal trade 97, 111; and shuttle trade 91, 94-5, 122; as economic space 11, 49-50, 85-6, 91; as spatial nodes 4, 6, 13-6, 149; ethnic entrepreneurs in 8, 10, 83, 124, 169, 180-2, 186; in the former Soviet Union 49, 61-3, 68-9, 146; in Vladivostok 52-61, 74, 79-80, 114, *see also* market(s)
optovaya baza 52, 76; *optovik* 93
order 7, 14, 18, 48, 50, 56, 59, 63, 78, 96, 132-4, 136, 137, 145, 156-8, 164, 168, 174, 176, 183, 189
organized crime; as a discourse 178; as a multifunctional entity 173; as an interpenetrative network 175, 177; definitions of 171, 173; during the Soviet Union 67, 143, 144, 159; evolution of 17, 151, 158, 159, 165, 172; metaphors of 64; parasitic relationship of 10; social structure of 139, 171; symbiotic relationship of 18, 143
Orochi 33

panty 32, 110
pao-tou 35, 181
passport 41, 54, 71, 82, 86, 89, 90
patronage 4, 143, 147n, 177, 181, 184
periphery 52, 56-7, 101
Petrak (Petrakov, Vladimir) 133, 163-4

poaching; economies 105-6; of Amur tiger 102n, 110; of bears 102n, 105, 108, 110, 111, 182; of bio-resources 10, 16, 31, 111, 114, 124, 184; of ginseng 102n, 108, 110-2, 112n, 182; of (Manchurian) deer 108, 110, 111; of marine products 106, 108; of timber 16, 107, 126, 126n; poachers 16, 34, 64, 104, 106, 108-10, 113, 182
Pogranichnyy 68, 88, 89-92, 108n
Pokrovka 92, 163
police 13, 30, 41-2, 78-9, 82, 84, 86, 105, 111, 134, 142, 145n, 147, 151, 154, 162
polozhentsy 132, 180
pomogaika 90
porosity 4-6, 12, 13, 16-7, 86-127 *passim*, 184, 186, 190, *see also* border porosity/ permeability
Poset Bay 32
post-Soviet; change 4-6, 17, 49, 138, 149, 189; economy 4, 17, 62-3, 147n, 181
Priamur 19, 24, 26, 30-2, 37
prilavki (counters) 52
Primorsky Krai; administrative unit 15, 24, 132; bio-resources of 111-4, 126n; Chinese in 100, 148; Chinese markets in 49-50, 55, 76; labour migrants in 67-71, 124; media coverage in 73; organized crime in 148, 151, 158, 166-7, 184-5; poaching in 102n, 107-9; traders in 85, 96, 98, 120-1, 123; transportation hubs in 87-8, 92-3
Primorye 15, 22, 24-6, 28-30, 33, 36-7, 41, 72, 106, 165, 169, 181
prison camps (and Gulag); subculture in 131, 136, 139, 141, 174, 180, 183
private protection 145-6, 171-3
private security agencies 145
privatization 4, 17, 144-5, 161-2
produce 4, 7, 22, 31, 49, 52, 54-5, 60, 62, 65-6, 70, 73, 76-7, 81, 111,

117, 124, 131, 163, 177, see also vegetables
propusk 78, 86
Przhevalsky, N. 22
Putin, V. 101, 187

racketeering 53, 78, 146, 148, 151, 159-60, 164, 166, 172-3, 175-6, 183, 185, see also *krysha*
Rakushka 166-7, 177
razborka 164
relational ties 179-80
Russian; Empire 15, 20, 22-3, 38, 181; Federation 4, 15-6, 69-71, 91-2, 114, 132, 142; Interior Ministry 136, 142; Revolution 37, 42, 186

Sakhalin 86, 93, 109, 132, 134, 156
scrap metal 105, 110, 134
secret societies 35-7
semichki 56-7
shadow; economy 7-8, 50, 85, 108, 143, 152; networks 4, 6-9, 11, 13, 18, 179-80, 182, 184-9
Shanghai 35, 37, 39
shipping; containers 45, 48-9, 52, 54-5, 78
shopping centres (and malls) 17, 53, 56, 58-60, 90-1, 94, 189, see also *torgovyy tsentr*
shuttle trade (and shuttle traders) 10-1, 16, 71, 89-100, 103, 113-4, 117, 122-3, 125, 127, 180, 182, 184-6, 189, see also *chelnoki*
Siberia 15, 19-20, 23-4, 28-9, 38-9, 42, 61, 102, 105, 109, 111, 115, 131, 138
Sikhote-Alin (mountain range) 15, 19-23, 26, 33-4, 36-7, 104, 109-11, 181, 186
Silvester (Sergey Timove'ev) 129
Simmel, G. 67, 100
sinie 159, 163-4, 176

skhody 136
Smith, A. 102
smuggling; as an anti-programme 122-4, 127, 185; commercial 188; of alcohol 10, 97; of bio-resources 184; of car-parts 106; of drugs 79; networks 123, 185; small-scale/ petty 121-2, 187-8
social networks 5-6, 8, 11, 13, 62, 73-4, 80-1, 85, 94-5, 103-4, 156, 170, 179-80, 182-4, see also networks
Soviet Union; New Economic Policy (NEP) 12-3
spices 75-6, 79-80, 86, 182
Sportivnaya (market) 45-7, 51, 54-5, 58, 63, 66, 76-7, 81, 85, 166, 169
sportsmeny 78, 146, 160, 163-6, 175-6
Stalin, J. 136, 138, 141-2
state; actors 18, 120-2, 188; erosion 4, 190; hegemony of the 122, 186-7; monopoly of the 4, 17, 109, 122, 127, 144, 173, 186-7; relationship to the 9, 18, 86, 101, 118, 123, 143, 185-9
Suifenhe 53, 87, 89-96, 98-9, 117, 119
Suifun River 29, 32
suki 137
Svetlanskaya Street 1-3, 51, 59, 68, 165n, 166

tabor 134, 155
Tadzhikistan (and Tadzhiks) 76
taiga 15, 20, 26, 34, 113, 181
Taivanchik (Alimzhan Takhtakhunov) 129
Taiwan 110, 117
taxes/ taxation; monopoly on taxation 4, 17, 122, 184-7; tax evasion 186, see also import taxes
torgovyy tsentr 53, see also shopping centres
tourist traders 16-7, 68n, 87